Policymaking for Indian Planning

Policymaking for Indian Planning

Essays on Contemporary Issues in Honour of Montek S. Ahluwalia

Editor

SAMEER KOCHHAR

ACADEMIC FOUNDATION

NEW DELHI

First published in 2012
by

ACADEMIC FOUNDATION
4772-73 / 23 Bharat Ram Road, (23 Ansari Road),
Darya Ganj, New Delhi - 110 002 (India).
Phones : 23245001 / 02 / 03 / 04.
Fax : +91-11-23245005.
E-mail : books@academicfoundation.com
www.academicfoundation.com

in association with

SKOCH

Skoch Consultancy Services
www.skoch.in

SKOCH
DEVELOPMENT FOUNDATION

Skoch Development Foundation
www.skoch.org

Cataloging in Publication Data--DK
Courtesy: D.K. Agencies (P) Ltd. <docinfo@dkagencies.com>

Policymaking for Indian Planning : Essays on Contemporary Issues in Honour of Montek S. Ahluwalia/
editor, Sameer Kochhar.
p. Cm.
Contributed articles.
Includes bibliographical references.
ISBN 9788171889228

1. India--Economic policy--1991- 2. India. Planning Commission. I. Kochhar, Sameer.

DDC 338.954 23

Typeset and cover design: Italics India, New Delhi.
Printed and bound in India.

Contents

About the Editor/ Contributors

Editor

Sameer Kochhar is Chairman, Skoch Group. He is President of Skoch Development Foundation, which is a leading think tank on digital, social and financial inclusion issues in India. He has been passionately working towards promoting participatory democracy, empowerment, and bringing improvements in delivery systems. He is CEO, Skoch Consultancy Services, and is an industry veteran with a multifaceted career spanning over two and a half decades. He is India strategy and management consultant to several Fortune 500 as well as large Indian companies for over a decade. He is also Chief Editor of *Inclusion*—a quarterly publication focussed on development economics issues. He is considered to be one of the most respected independent voices on inclusive development and citizenship issues in India. He is a member of several expert groups and committees and his research opinion and writings have shaped many a public policy dialogue. He is a Member of the Expert Group constituted by the Ministry of Panchayati Raj, Government of India advocating a case for strengthening of Panchayati Raj Institutions (village councils) through use of technology. He is also a Planning Commission nominee on Committee formulating the national ICT plan for the Twelfth Five Year Plan. This is in addition of an e-Inclusion Committee constituted by the Department of Information Technology, Ministry of Communications and IT. He has written extensively on areas of emerging management practices, infrastructure, governance, technology, finance, economics, e-governance, *panchayati raj* and ICT for development. He has published several widely acclaimed books, namely *Infrastructure and Governance* (2008); *Financial Inclusion* (2009); *Urban Renewal: Policy and*

Response (2009); *Speeding Financial Inclusion* (2009); *India on the Growth Turnpike: Essays in Honour of Vijay L. Kelkar* (2010); *Building from the Bottom: Infrastructure and Poverty Alleviation* (2010); *Growth and Finance: Essays in Honour of C. Rangarajan* (2011).

Contributors

Kaushik Basu is Chief Economic Advisor, Ministry of Finance, India, and C. Marks Professor, Department of Economics, Cornell University. He was earlier Director, Center for Analytic Economics at Cornell. He is a member of the Board of Directors of the Exim Bank of India; and is president of the international Human Development and Capabilities Association. He has earlier been Professor of Economics at the Delhi School of Economics. In 1992, he founded the Centre for Development Economics in Delhi and was its first Executive Director. Educated in Kolkata, Delhi and London, Basu received his PhD from the London School of Economics in 1976. In November 2010, he was conferred D.Litt (Honoris Causa) by Lucknow University. He has been Visiting Professor at Harvard University, MIT and Princeton University, and Distinguished Visitor at the London School of Economics. He is Editor of *Social Choice and Welfare*, and served on the Editorial Boards of the *Journal of Economic Perspectives, Journal of Development Economics and World Bank Economic Review*. A Fellow of the Econometric Society, he has published scientific papers in the areas of development economics, industrial organisation, game theory and welfare economics. His books include: *Prelude to Political Economy: A Study of the Social and Political Foundations of Economics* (2000) and *Beyond the Invisible Hand: Groundwork for a New Economics* (2011). The latter is being translated into Chinese, Spanish and Italian. In May 2008, he was awarded one of India's highest civilian awards, the Padma Bhushan, by the President of India.

Surjit S. Bhalla obtained his PhD in Economics from Princeton University. He has worked as a research economist at Rand Corporation, Brookings Institution, the World Bank and The Policy Group; as a proprietary trader/strategist/portfolio manager at the World Bank, Goldman Sachs, Deutsche Bank and Oxus Investments. Presently, he is Chairman of Oxus Investments, a New Delhi based 'hedge fund' and emerging markets advisory firm. Dr Bhalla has served on several committees of the Government of India. He is author of several academic articles as well as three books on globalisation and its effects on the world economy: *Imagine There's No Country: Poverty, Inequality, and Growth in the Era of Globalization* (2002); *Devaluing Your Way to Prosperity: Misaligned Currencies and Their Growth Consequences* (forthcoming, 2010) and *Second Among Equals: The Middle Class Kingdoms of China and India* (2007, also forthcoming, 2010).

Lord Meghnad Jagdishchandra Desai studied at the University of Bombay, and obtained his PhD at the University of Pennsylvania. On 30th April 1991, he was created Lord Desai of St Clement Danes. Lord Desai has taught at the London School of Economics since 1965, he was made a Professor of Economics in 1983 and he established the Centre for the Study of Global Governance in 1992. His publications include: *A Basic Income Proposal in The State of the Future* (1998); *What should be India's Economic Priorities in a Globalising World* (1999); *Foreign Investment and Economic Development in Capital Regulation: For and Against* (1999); *Well Being or Welfare? in Public Policy for the 21st Century: Social and Economic Essays in Memory of Henry Neuberger*, (N. Fraser and J. Hills (eds.), 2000); *The Possibility of Deglobalisation in Globalisation, Inequality and Social Capital*, (W. Dolfsma and C. Dennreuther (eds.), 2001); *Marx's Revenge* and *The Resurgence of Capitalism and the Death of Statist Socialism* (2002). His latest publication is entitled *The Rediscovery of India* (2011). His research interests include economics, international political economy, economic history, South Asian studies and globalisation.

Nitin Desai, a graduate of London School of Economics (LSE), taught economics at two UK universities, worked briefly in the private sector, had a long stint as a government official in India and then joined the UN in 1990. In India he joined the Planning Commission in 1973, around the same time as Dr Vijay Kelkar, and worked there till 1988. Later he joined the Ministry of Finance as the Chief Economic Advisor (1988-1990). In the UN, which he joined in 1990, he was Under Secretary General for Economic and Social Affairs. After his retirement, he has been involved in a variety of public policy activities nationally and internationally. He is a member of the National Security Advisory Board and the Prime Minister's Council on Climate Change. He is a Distinguished Fellow of TERI and is an Honorary Fellow of the LSE. He writes a monthly column in the *Business Standard.*

Gursharan Dhanjal, MA, M.Phil, PhD from Delhi University and an expert in strategic affairs, is Editor & COO, Skoch Group. He is also Editor of *Inclusion*—a quarterly publication that focusses on development and inclusive growth issues. He has over 20 years of working experience ranging from academics to research and business journalism to consulting. He started his career as a Lecturer and taught at Delhi University for five years before joining Asia Business News (India)—Dow Jones, a premier broadcaster of business and financial news during mid-90s. He also worked for CNBC for over three years during the late 90s. He has led various research projects and field studies in financial inclusion, e-governance and ICT for development that included traversing across the country, collecting citizen voices for over eight years now. He also leads the video case study projects. His areas of expertise include research and rich media content. A prolific writer, Dr Dhanjal has contributed over 200 columns in leading national dailies and apart from several research papers in several journals of repute in addition to authoring a widely acclaimed book entitled *Tarapur: The Politics of Nuclear Age.* He has recently published another book in association with Sameer Kochhar entitled *Infrastructure and Governance.* He has contributed numerous papers that have been published in various books. He is member of the Working Group on ICT in Higher Education constituted by Planning Commission for the Twelfth Five Year Plan. He is a regular speaker at various public fora and institutions including IIT-Delhi and Delhi University where he is also a visiting faculty. He is also Member, Course Preparation Team for Master's Programme, School of Social Sciences, Indira Gandhi National Open University. His research interests include, nuclear non-proliferation, political systems, ICT for development, financial inclusion, education, public administration, conflict resolution and peace building.

Ravi Kanbur is T.H. Lee Professor of World Affairs, International Professor of Applied Economics and Management, and Professor of Economics at Cornell University. He holds a Bachelor's degree in Economics from the University of Cambridge and a Doctorate in Economics from the University of Oxford. He has taught at the Universities of Oxford, Cambridge, Essex, Warwick, Princeton and

Columbia. His vita lists over 200 publications, including in the leading economics journals such as *American Economic Review, Journal of Political Economy, Review of Economic Studies, Journal of Economic Theory,* and *Economic Journal.* Ravi Kanbur has served on the senior staff of the World Bank, including as Chief Economist of the African Region and Principal Adviser to the Chief Economist of the World Bank. He has also served as Director of the World Bank's *World Development Report*. The honours he has received include the Quality of Research Discovery Award of the American Agricultural Economics Association and an Honorary Professorship at the University of Warwick.

Sam Pitroda is an internationally respected development thinker, policymaker, telecom inventor and entrepreneur who has spent over four decades in information and communications technology and related human and national developments initiatives. Credited with having laid the foundation of India's technology and telecommunications revolution in the 1980s, Mr Pitroda has been a leading campaigner to help bridge the global digital divide. During his tenure as Advisor to Prime Minister Rajiv Gandhi in the 1980s, Pitroda headed six technology missions related to telecommunications, water, literacy, immunisation, dairy and oil seeds. He was also the founder and first chairman of India's Telecom Commission. In these roles, he helped revolutionise India's development policies and philosophies with a focus on access to technology as the key to social change. He was Chairman of India's National Knowledge Commission (2005-2009), an advisory body to the Prime Minister of India, set up to provide a blueprint for reform of the knowledge related institutions and infrastructure in the country. He is currently Adviser to the Prime Minister of India on Public Information Infrastructure & Innovations and has undertaken the ambitious task of providing a plan for creating digital infrastructure in the country for enhancing governance and improving delivery of public services. He is also the Chairman of the National Innovation Council (NIC), which is working on several initiatives to boost innovation performance in the country. He is also heading the Expert Group for Modernisation of Indian Railways constituted by the Ministry of Railways. He is also the Chairman of the Smart Grid Task Force set up under the aegis of the Ministry of Power, Government of India. He has also been appointed as one of the founding Commissioners of the United Nations Broadband Commission for Digital

Development. He holds close to 100 worldwide patents and has published and lectured widely in the US, Europe, Latin America and Asia.

Raghuram Rajan is the Eric J. Gleacher Distinguished Service Professor of Finance at the University of Chicago's Graduate School of Business. Dr Rajan is also currently an economic advisor to the Prime Minister of India. Prior to resuming teaching in 2007, he was the Economic Counsellor and Director of Research at the International Monetary Fund (from 2003). Since then, he has chaired the Indian government's Committee on Financial Sector Reforms, which submitted its report in September 2008. Dr Rajan's research interests are in banking, corporate finance, and economic development, especially the role finance plays in it. His 2003 book (with Luigi Zingales) entitled *Saving Capitalism from the Capitalists* was followed by *Fault Lines: How Hidden Fractures Still Threaten the World Economy*, which was awarded the Financial Times-Goldman Sachs prize for best business book in 2010. He is the President of the American Finance Association and a member of the American Academy of Arts and Sciences. In January 2003, the American Finance Association awarded Dr Rajan the inaugural Fischer Black Prize, given every two years to the financial economist under age 40 who has made the most significant contribution to the theory and practice of finance.

Yaga Venugopal Reddy was Governor, Reserve Bank of India, from 2003 to 2008. Subsequently, he was Member of the UN Commission of Experts to the President of the UN General Assembly on Reforms of International Monetary and Financial System. He is currently Professor Emeritus, University of Hyderabad, and Distinguished Professor, Indian Institute of Technology, Madras. He is also Honorary Fellow of the London School of Economics and Political Science. He is a Member of an informal international group of prominent persons on International Monetary Reforms, and is also on the Advisory Group of eminent persons to advise the Finance Minister of India on G-20 issues. He was Deputy Governor, Reserve Bank of India, for six years. Prior to being the Governor, he was Executive Director for India, Sri Lanka, Bangladesh and Bhutan at the International Monetary Fund since August 2002. Formerly, he was Secretary, Ministry of Finance, and Additional Secretary, Ministry of Commerce in the Government of India. He served Government of Andhra Pradesh, India in several capacities including Principal Secretary and Secretary—Finance and Planning, Collector and District Magistrate etc. He was also advisor in World Bank. Dr Reddy was honoured with the Padma Vibhushan Award in 2010. His book *India and the Global Financial Crisis: Managing Money and Finance* was among the best sellers in India (Orient Blackswan, 2009). His most recent publication is titled *Global Crisis, Recession and Uneven Recovery* (2011).

Hari Sankaran is Vice Chairman & Managing Director of Infrastructure Leasing & Financial Services Limited (IL&FS). After completing his Masters in Economics from the London School of Economics (LSE), Sankaran developed a career in the areas of project finance, infrastructure development and management, regulation and public policy. His primary interest has been to understand the relationship between communities, infrastructure development and economic growth. He has contributed several papers to some of the well-acclaimed books. Some of these include *Building from the Bottom: Infrastructure and Poverty Alleviation* (2010) and, *India on the Growth Turnpike* (2010)—both edited by Sameer Kochhar. He was recently conferred the Skoch Challenger Award for his contributions to education sector and infrastructure development.

Parthasarathi Shome is Director & Chief Executive, Indian Council for Research on International Economic Relations (ICRIER), New Delhi. He was Chief Economist, Her Majesty's Revenue & Customs (HMRC), United Kingdom (2008-2011) and Adviser to Indian Finance Minister (2004-2008). He served at the IMF (1983-2004) in various capacities, including as Chief of Tax Policy (1992-1995), and Director, IMF Singapore Institute (2001-2003). He was RBI Chair, ICRIER (1999-2001) and Director, National Institute of Public Finance and Policy (1995-1997), and Professor of Economics at American University Washington D.C. (1975-1983). His books are from Oxford University Press, Routledge and IMF. He has published in the *Journal of Economic Theory, Journal of Public Economics, Oxford Economic Papers, IMF Staff Papers,* and other international and national journals of Argentina, the Basque Region, India, Japan, Malaysia, the Philippines, Singapore and the United States. He has given fiscal technical assistance to over 30 countries in Africa, Asia, Europe and Latin America. He chaired India's Ninth Five Year Plan and Tenth Five Year Plan Task Forces on tax policy and administration. In 2000, he was awarded the highest civilian honour of the Brazilian government, 'Commander of the Order of the Southern Cross', for his contributions to

Brazilian tax reform. He did his PhD from Southern Methodist University in 1975. For his thesis on the burden of the corporation income tax, he received the National Tax Association of America award as an 'outstanding student of taxation and public finance'. He has Masters degrees from University of Rochester (1973) and Delhi University (1972). His BA Honours is from Calcutta University (1970) and high school matriculation from Madras University (1966).

N.K. Singh is a renowned politician, economist and former top bureaucrat. Presently he is a member of the Rajya Sabha from the state of Bihar. He serves on the Parliamentary Committee on Human Resource Development, the Committee on MPs Local Area Development Scheme, the Committee on Public Undertakings, the Consultative Committee on Finance, the Committee on Rules, the House Committee and the Parliamentary Forum on Global Warming and Climate Change. He has been among the country's top bureaucrats and handled important portfolios such as India's Revenue Secretary, Member of the Planning Commission, and Secretary to the Prime Minister. Mr Singh is on the governing bodies of research organisations like the Indian Council for Research on International Economic Relations (ICRIER), the International Management Institute (IMI) and the National Institute of Fashion Technology (NIFT). He has a wide range of national and international experience having interacted closely with multilateral organisations like World Bank, IMF, ADB, UNCTAD, GATT, WTO, UNDP and OECD. Additionally, he has taken up various international responsibilities in the UN, World Economic Forum, Indian Embassy (Tokyo), IMF etc. N.K. Singh has a Master's Degree in Economics and was teaching Economics at the prestigious St. Stephen's College, Delhi prior to joining the Civil Service. He has lectured widely at eminent universities and is currently also Short Term Senior Visiting Fellow at the University of Stanford. He has authored two books entitled, *Politics of Change* and *Not by Reason Alone* and has contributed several articles in the field of economics to leading Indian dailies, *The Financial Express, Hindustan* and *The Indian Express.* He is fond of photography, horticulture and Indian Classical music.

Duvvuri Subbarao assumed office as the 22nd Governor of the Reserve Bank of India on 5 September 2008. Prior to this appointment, Dr

Subbarao served as Finance Secretary to the Government of India from April 2007 to September 2008 and as Secretary to the Prime Minister's Economic Advisory Council from March 2005 to March 2007. As a member of the Indian Administrative Service (IAS), Dr Subbarao has been a career civil servant. Over the years of 1988-1998, he worked in various positions in State government of Andhra Pradesh and Government of India. Dr Subbarao was a Lead Economist in the World Bank (1999-2004), where he also task managed a flagship study on decentralisation across major East Asian countries which was acknowledged as innovative policy work. He received BSc (Hons) in Physics from the Indian Institute of Technology, Kharagpur and MSc in Physics from the Indian Institute of Technology, Kanpur. Subsequent to joining the civil service, he received an MS in Economics from Ohio State University (1978) and was a Humphrey Fellow studying public finance at MIT during 1982-83. He earned his PhD in Economics from Andhra University (1998). Dr Subbarao maintains a strong commitment to academic pursuits, and has written and lectured extensively on issues in public finance, decentralisation and political economy of reforms.

Roberto Zagha, a Brazilian national, is currently the World Bank Country Director for India. Prior to this assignment, he was a Senior Advisor in the World Bank Vice Presidency in charge of economic policies and poverty reduction strategies. His most recent work was Secretary of the Commission on Growth and Development which recently published *The Growth Report.* His previous work consisted of a review of the growth experience of the 1990s—a two-year programme whose results are summarised in three reports which review growth experiences, explore the current thinking on growth and the role of policies in growth strategies. Previous assignments in the Bank include Director for South Asia for the Bank department in charge of economic policies and poverty reduction in South Asia, Lead Economist for India, and several assignments in Central and East Africa, India, Sri Lanka, Argentina and Bolivia. He also was part of the core team for the *World Development Report* of 1991. Prior to joining the Bank, he taught at the University of São Paulo, Brazil, and worked as senior economist in the Economic Research Institute associated to the university in areas related to taxation and fiscal policies.

सत्यमेव जयते

डॉ. सी. रगंराजन

Dr. C. RANGARAJAN

अध्यक्ष
प्रधानमंत्री की आर्थिक सलाहकार परिषद्
विज्ञान भवन सौंध 'ई' हाल
मौलाना आज़ाद रोड
नई दिल्ली–110 011

CHAIRMAN
Economic Advisory Council to the Prime Minister
Vigyan Bhavan Annexe, 'E' Hall
Maulana Azad Road
New Delhi-110 011

Foreword

It gives me great pleasure to write the Foreword to this collection of essays in honour of Montek Singh Ahluwalia. Montek is decidedly one of India's most outstanding economists. His impact on policymaking in the last three decades has been immense. The note he wrote for the Prime Minister in 1990 which preceded the launching of reforms contained most of the ideas which were subsequently implemented. He was, thus, a pioneer as far as economic reforms are concerned.

After a brilliant academic record, Montek started his career in the World Bank. It was at this point he wrote several seminal articles touching on growth, inequality and poverty. On his return to India, he started advocating policies which could lead to the elimination of controls and restrictions which came in the way of faster economic growth. In the post-reform period, he steered the policymakers in the direction of creating a more competitive environment. Whether it be the reform of the fiscal sector or the financial sector or the external sector, his imprint is seen very much. More recently, he has been concerned with inclusive growth. A country like India requires social safety nets. We need to provide them without compromising on productivity and efficiency. Equity and efficiency have to be weaved together to produce a coherent pattern of development. Therein lies the skill of policymakers like Montek. In Montek we have a rare combination of intellectual brilliance, far sighted vision and commendable pragmatism.

At a personal level, I have known Montek for the last three decades. We have worked together on many policy issues. I value his association greatly. It has been a rewarding experience.

The articles included in this volume cover a wide range. Each article is written by an expert in the field. These articles edited ably by Sameer Kochhar constitute a fitting tribute to the immense contribution of Montek to India's policymaking.

(C. Rangarajan)

Preface

I was delighted to receive the updated monograph of the Festschrift that will be published on November 29, 2011 in honour of Shri Montek Singh Ahluwalia. It is a double treat: it says so much about the man whom we all praise and admire and it also contains so much knowledge and wisdom contributed by distinguished economists.

When I first came to Delhi in 1985 as a Member of Parliament, and subsequently became a junior Minister, Montek Ahluwalia had already acquired a large presence in the corridors of power and a formidable reputation as an economist. In the initial years, I could only watch him from a distance. What struck me immediately was his way with words, both the spoken word and the written word. He was precise, clear, cogent and convincing. Naturally, as a lawyer, I admired and envied these qualities.

We began to work together in 1991. When I joined the Commerce Ministry in 1991, he was the Commerce Secretary. Five years later, in 1996, when I became Finance Minister, he was the Finance Secretary. Eight years afterward, when I became Finance Minister under the UPA-I government, it was our privilege to request him to return to Government as Deputy Chairman, Planning Commission. Whether he was dealing with matters relating to international trade or finance or planning, Montek Ahluwalia was always the perfect embodiment of knowledge, reasoning, self-assurance and conviction.

Dr C. Rangarajan, in his Foreword, has referred to the note that Montek Ahluwalia wrote for the then Prime Minister in 1990 which charted the path for the economic reforms that were launched in 1991. He was my Secretary in the Commerce Ministry, but he was more than that. In a sense, he was also my teacher and guide. Together, we announced the first set of trade policy reforms in July 1991. Together, we travelled to the East, to the US and to Europe to speak to sceptical audiences that the reforms were for real and India would not look back or go back to the dirigiste regime. I would joke with our audiences that I would take all the difficult questions (who was the Prime Minister of India, what is the currency of India and so on) while the easy questions (tariff policy, exchange rate policy, non-trade barriers etc.) would be answered by Secretary Ahluwalia!

In 1991, when Dr Manmohan Singh, then Finance Minister, asked for the services of Montek Ahluwalia in order to appoint him as Secretary, Economic Affairs, although I was loath to do so, I let him go because I knew that his heart was in Finance. In retrospect, it was a wise decision, because when I succeeded Dr Manmohan Singh as Finance Minister of the United Front government, Montek Ahluwalia was in command in the Ministry of Finance and the transition from the Congress government to the United Front coalition government was smooth on matters relating to the Ministry of Finance. As Dr Y.V. Reddy has recorded in his essay, that was the period when a formal agreement was concluded between the Government and the RBI for ending automatic monetisation which laid the ground work for legislation on fiscal responsibility. Montek Ahluwalia was the key player on the Government's side. Dr Reddy has also recalled Montek Ahluwalia's contribution in enabling the RBI to build up reserves in its balance sheet. Earlier, in 1993, as recorded by Dr D. Subbarao, Montek Ahluwalia showed 'extraordinary competence and skill' in negotiating the settlement of the Rupee-Rouble deal with Russia.

Several authors who have contributed to the monograph have referred to Montek Ahluwalia's seminal treatise on 'Redistribution with Growth' published in 1974. Prof Ravi Kanbur has described it as 'the intellectual foundation of the McNamara years at the World Bank.' Dr Surjit Bhalla, paying tribute to Montek Ahluwalia's pioneering research on poverty and income distribution, has contributed an essay that concludes that, 'absolute poverty in India afflicts less than 5 per cent of the population' and, tongue-in-cheek, comments that the controversy about the efficacy of the Tendulkar poverty line 'says more about the content and conduct of the debate rather than the reality of poverty in India.'

N.K. Singh has captured the essence of Montek Ahluwalia. He has observed 'Montek has the conviction as well as the tenacity to "stay the course" with ideas which he deeply believes in. Political realities inject inevitable flexibility. But I have not seen him abandon ideas. He would shelve that temporarily to resurrect them when time is more opportune.'

Montek Ahluwalia has the distinction of being the longest serving Deputy Chairman of the Planning Commission. Dr Nitin Desai and Prof Meghnad Desai have recalled the contributions of the Planning Commission and of the individuals who worked in the Planning Commission in the last 60 years. The latter, in his inimitable style, has honoured Montek Ahluwalia with the observation that 'People matter in the formulation of policy. The good ones pass on smoothly. The bad ones cause havoc and leave their mark. Montek has been the smoothest of them all.'

Montek Ahluwalia had several choices before him at every stage of his career. That he always chose to come back and work in India, whenever there was an opportunity, marks him out among his contemporaries. The last time he did so was when he willingly gave up the honour of being the first head of the Independent Evaluation Office of the IMF and returned to India to join the Government. Prof Raghuram Rajan, a distinguished academic, rues that, 'it has been patently clear to me for many years that government's gain has been academia's loss.' All of us who are in government or who have been in government at one time or another can affirm that statement wholeheartedly. This Festschrift is indeed a well deserved tribute to the person, Montek Ahluwalia, who has given his best to the country and who, I am sure, will continue to give his best for many more years.

—P. Chidambaram
Minister of Home Affairs,
Government of India

Introduction

SAMEER KOCHHAR

I

When India's economy opened up in the early 1990s, a small number of people served as the architects of the reforms that led the country to its present economic renaissance. Among them is Montek Singh Ahluwalia, Deputy Chairman of India's Planning Commission. He works closely with Prime Minister Manmohan Singh to champion the reform process and ensure that it stays on track.

Montek Singh Ahluwalia, who was the first director of the Independent Evaluation Office (IEO) of the International Monetary Fund (IMF), took on his present job in June 2004. Before the IMF, he was a member of India's Planning Commission as well as a member of the Economic Advisory Council to the Prime Minister. Ahluwalia has previously held other government positions including finance secretary, Ministry of Finance; secretary, Department of Economic Affairs; commerce secretary; special secretary to the Prime Minister; and economic advisor, Ministry of Finance.

He is widely reckoned to be one of the brightest men in government. Only one of two non-IAS officers ever to be appointed finance secretary, he has supervised the content, tone and tenor of the nation's fiscal liberalisation programme under both finance ministers, Dr Manmohan Singh and Palaniappan Chidambaram.

Today, Montek Singh Ahluwalia is regarded as a world renowned economic policymaker.

Montek Singh is considered as the brain behind the successful governance of the country. Being the chief policy adviser to the Prime Minister, Ahluwalia has gained immense respect and reputation from his peers. This Oxford graduate has showcased his talent and knowledge in all policies ranging from economics to education. Moreover, Montek Singh has been the driving force in matters of the liberation programme for the last 16 years.

Prior to taking up his position at the IMF, Ahluwalia was a Member of the Planning Commission in New Delhi as well as a Member of the Economic Advisory Council to the Prime Minister. He had previously served as Finance Secretary, Ministry of Finance; Secretary, Department of Economic Affairs; Commerce Secretary; Special Secretary to the Prime Minister; and Economic Advisor, Ministry of Finance.

The process to get rid of stifling bureaucratic restrictions and outdated socialist economic policies accelerated in the early 1990s. 'A much more explicit change in policy occurred after 1991, with acceptance of the need to bring about a systemic change, *albeit* in a gradualist fashion,' Montek Singh mentioned in an article titled 'Planning Then and Now' (2008). 'The private sector was freed of much of the stifling controls that had been evolved over many years in the name of planning and rational allocation of scarce resources,' he further wrote about the liberalisation process initiated in the mid-nineties. 'Much greater room was allowed for entrepreneurs to respond freely to market forces with greater reliance on competition to increase efficiency,' Montek opined in the article. The Indian growth story has since accelerated gradually with planners like Ahluwalia making sure that the spurt is not ephemeral. There are number of bottlenecks, social issues, political compulsions and other factors which can impede the growth rate in a democratic setup like India.

The way Indian economy had shed shackles in the past two decades is clearly discernible and even stringent critics of the way things are moving in the South Asian country would not deny the growth. The acceleration has been significant while Ahluwalia has been in the Planning Commission's saddle. 'It has become one of the favoured destinations for foreign direct investment, and particularly in this decade, the expansion in the volume of foreign direct investment have been really quite remarkable, indicating the extent to which foreign investment perception investor perceptions have changed,' Ahluwalia wrote. 'In 2001, total foreign investment in India was about $4 billion, and in 2009-10, that had increased to $37 billion. So that's another indication of how the economy's been seen globally,' the Deputy Planning Commission chief added.

My first interaction with Montek dates back to 2005 when I extended an invitation to him to preside over the Third Skoch Challenger Award function and also give away the awards. As expected, like many others, he was also little perplexed by the name 'Skoch' and was not very sure as to where would he be going. I must say that it was not easy to convince him with the value proposition that I had and the awards that recognise people, projects and institutions that go an extra mile to make India better. We had Tarun Kumar Gogoi, Chief Minister, Assam on the one hand and Surojana Devi, an illiterate Gram Pradhan from a *mofussil* village in Uttarkashi called Darkaan—a first time Gram Pradhan who defeated her male rival of 16 years. At the very first instance she had solved both the drinking water as well as electricity problem in her village using up all her government grants. In her acceptance speech delivered in a mixed dialect, Surojana said that she had heard of computers and next she would like her *panchayat* to have one. I still remember Montek's words when he spoke from the dais after giving away the awards that the work done by Surojana Devi exemplifies commitment and dedication with her hand on the pulse. IT enablement not only brings transparency in government system but also hugely reduces the transaction costs, he added.

That was also the time when the government was increasing its focus on financial inclusion. That inclusive growth was always on top of his mind, Montek had said that the scaling up of operations and linking of bank branches is quite revolutionary and that change taking place, as a result, will be interesting to watch. He also lauded our efforts of recognising some such interventions that were being conferred the award. He said, 'I am in complete agreement that even within the government that this is something that needs to recognised and emphasised.'

Ahluwalia has been emphasising that the growth has to be gradual and there would be numerous challenges, which need to be taken care of. The Planning Commission economist recently identified energy, water management, urbanisation, climate change, and 'regional balance' as the five major roadblocks for the Indian planners drafting the 12th Five-Year plan. Surprisingly, he did not list corruption as one of the major stumbling blocks. '...all forms of corruption have actually disappeared. I'm not referring to petty bribes that people might have to pay, sort of grease money," Ahluwalia answered when Prof Gareth Evans posed a question about corruption in the 2010 K.R. Narayanan Oration on 'India's prospects in the post-crisis world' organised by Australian National University (ANU) on 29th November in Melbourne. 'But, you know, 20 years ago the corruption was around getting industrial licensing, getting import licences, getting foreign exchange permit; all of that has just more or less disappeared,' Montek Singh rationalised.

The Indian planning body is not only bothered by the aforementioned 'challenges' but a series of other impeding factors too. There is an ongoing process put in place by Ahluwalia to fast-track the planning process and remove the roadblocks to accelerate the growth rate even further.

In mid-2011, a meeting of about 150 officials of the Planning Commission was organised in New Delhi to discuss 40 major issues confronting the country. Various issues such as employment, agriculture and energy were reportedly discussed in the meeting attended by the top planners. This meeting is stated to be first such occasion when such rigorous, out of the box exercise was organised to vitalise the planning process. The top planners team is reported to have identified 15 issues including employment-led growth and also making markets work for the poor. The list of 15 issues would be cut short to 10 to form the basis of the Twelfth Five Year Plan.

The premier Indian planning body comes under further strain because of the rapid growth rate maintained by the most populous country in the world, China. While discussing the Indian growth story, one has to keep the perspective focussed and respect the differences too. 'The big difference between China and India, because in China the objective is a harmonious society. That's an end result objective. In India the objective is an inclusive society that is also very process-driven,' Ahluwalia writes about the so-called China-India rivalry.

One of Ahluwalia's favourite ideas when he was Planning Commission member in the Vajpayee government was that Yojana Bhavan should also have the powers to put policy proposals on sectoral and macroeconomic issues before the Cabinet. This fervour towards participatory planning is today evident as the Planning Commission invites comments on the Twelfth Plan via Facebook. A key figure in India's economic reforms from the early 1980s onwards. Ahluwalia's fingerprints can be found in policies from economics to education reforms and he has been a driving force in the liberalisation programme of the past 20 years or more. This Oxford-educated economist has spent 11 years with the World Bank in Washington before returning to India in 1979 to work as an economic adviser to the government. His commitment to poverty alleviation and inclusive growth can be found in his early writings and as Deputy Chairman of the Planning Commission. He has managed to translate this into the country's Plan process.

I recently asked him, the main thrust of the Twelfth Plan approach is 'inclusive growth' and rightly so—but how is this approach likely to be different from that adopted in the Eleventh Plan? He replied, 'it will be a continuation and strengthening, with some re-orientation and re-engineering based on experience. Inclusive Growth cannot be achieved in one Plan period. Inclusive growth means growth of a kind that the benefits flow to everyone and the participation in the benefits of growth is very high. This has many implications. What you do in agriculture is very important. The kind of hard infrastructure you build is also important for inclusion since the remote parts of the country, and small businesses generally, depend on general infrastructure. It also has relevance for social sector initiatives especially health, education and skill development. Without them, fast growth will be difficult to achieve and will certainly not be equitable if it somehow emerges. In short, we have to be active and innovative in many areas to achieve inclusive growth.'

I quizzed him further, 'what is happening to inclusiveness?' He said it is a relentless pursuit. Inclusiveness is a multidimensional phenomenon. Economists very often focus on poverty reduction but inclusiveness is much more than poverty reduction. It is for the first time that I felt that here is an economist with a heart who goes simply beyond numbers and statistics.

I met him again for making a documentary on his life and times and his contributions to the Indian reforms process. This accorded me a chance to see the personal side of him. Very much a family man, who regularly goes home for lunch and is joined by his wife Isher Judge Ahluwalia, his mother of over 91 years now and his two-year old grandson. He loves to spend his afternoons with his grandson, feeding him, playing with him, sharing stories with him, rather than take a siesta—which most people do. This is why Isher perhaps defines him as a man who is a combination of great mind and tremendous sense of fun.

His mother told me an interesting story as to why is he called Montek. It goes like this; he was very naughty and strong headed as a child. General Monty of world war fame was also known to be heady. So one day his mother quipped, 'this boy behaves like General Monty.' And he got his name! A lesser-known fact, but nevertheless, a name that remains most exclusive across the globe.

While researching Montek and his contribution to the Indian reforms process, I met up with several of his close associates, friends and colleagues. There was one thing common that everybody had to say that poverty reduction, decentralisation and participatory planning is something that has always been a priority for him. To quote a few, C. Rangarajan, Chairman to the Economic Advisory Council to the Prime Minister said that like any good economist, he knows that growth by itself is not adequate, we also need to address issues of poverty. Wajahat Habibullah, Chairman, National Minorities Commission added, he has been a considerable protagonist of the idea of public participation in governance which is of course at the heart of inclusive planning—that people must be involved in planning. Nandan Nilekani, Chairman, UIDAI, pointed out that he has brought in a lot of focus on inclusive growth in the Eleventh Plan. It is one thing to have eight per cent growth or so but it is equally important that everybody participates in that growth.

Sure enough, Planning Commission, for the first time since its inception embarked on participatory planning, wherein it invited suggestions and inputs through an open forum for the Twelfth Plan through its portal. In the process, it received over 30,000 responses.

To this Montek says, there is certainly no doubt that we need more decentralisation, the benefit of which comes from greater ownership, greater partnership, greater participation, greater accountability and local monitoring. The logical implication of this would be that money would go down to the district of lower level *panchayats*, the job of the ministry should be to give advice.

Born on November 24, 1943, in New Delhi, he studied at St. Patrick's High School, Secunderabad; Delhi Public School, Mathura Road and Bishop Cotton School, Shimla. He graduated with a BA (Hons) degree from St. Stephen's College, University of Delhi. He was a Rhodes scholar at Magdalen College, Oxford. He also studied for a BPhil in Economics at Oxford University, which the university later reclassified as an MPhil. While at Oxford, he was the president of the prestigious Oxford Union.

Ahluwalia, after graduating from University of Oxford, joined the World Bank during the tenures of Hollis Chenery and Robert MacNamara. At the age of 28, he became the youngest 'Division Chief' in the World Bank's bureaucracy.

His published work includes papers in professional journals and contributions to books. He was among 19 members chosen by UN chief Ban Ki-moon for a high-level advisory group on climate change financing, tasked with mobilising funds pledged during the Copenhagen meet to tackle global warming.

He has been a key figure in India's economic reforms from the mid-1980s onwards. For his outstanding contribution to economic policy and public service, he was awarded the Padma Vibhushan in 2011.

He has indeed made the Indian growth story possible by helping the stagnant Indian economy to catapult to a position of pre-eminence in the region. The hard work put in by Montek Singh has not gone totally unheralded as his planning genius is recognised by various global organisations. The IMF, where he has worked before, is one such body.

It is in recognition of his contributions to planning, reforms process and inclusive growth that he was conferred the Skoch Challenger Award for Lifetime Achievement in 2011. Humbled as he was while accepting the Award, he said, 'this is a recognition to see the hard work put together by so many architects of modern India finally coming to a fruition. To keep the economy growing at 9 per cent, the story of inclusion a few years later will be as illustrious as the story of growth during the past ten years or so has been.' Truly inspiring words that reinforce our conviction that treading the path of inclusive growth may be tough but once achieved, India's growth story would be substantially different from what it is today.

II

From a highly centralised planning system, the Indian economy is gradually moving towards indicative planning where the Planning Commission concerns itself with the building of a long-term strategic vision of the future and decide on priorities of nation. It works out sectoral targets and provides promotional stimulus to the economy to grow in the desired direction. It also plays an integrative role in the development of a holistic approach to the policy formulation in critical areas of human and economic development. In the social sector, schemes that require coordination and synthesis like rural health, drinking water, rural energy needs, literacy and environment protection have yet to be subjected to coordinated policy formulation.

Let us go back to the beginning. The Planning Commission was set up by a Resolution of the Government of India in March 1950 in pursuance of declared objectives of the Government to promote a rapid rise in the standard of living of the people by efficient exploitation of the resources of the country, increasing production and offering opportunities to all for employment in the service of the community. The Planning Commission was charged with the responsibility of making assessment of all resources of the country, augmenting deficient resources, formulating plans for the most effective and balanced utilisation of resources and determining priorities.

The First Five Year Plan contains one of the clearest early formulations of the need for planning and of the state's role in it. Planning, it pointed out, involves 'acceptance of a clearly defined set of objectives in terms of which to frame overall policies..., formulation of a strategy for promoting the realization of the ends defined..., and working out a rational solution to problems—an attempt to coordinate means and ends.' The launching of the First Five Year Plan in April 1951 initiated a process of development aimed not merely at raising the standards of living of the people but also opening out to them new opportunities for a richer and more varied life. This was sought to be achieved by planning for growth and social justice.

The guiding principles of Indian planning are in fact provided by these objectives. Within this framework, each five-year plan involves such directional changes to take into account new constraints and new possibilities. Two subsequent five-year plans were formulated till 1965, when there was a break because of the Indo-Pakistan conflict. Two successive years of drought, devaluation of the currency, a general rise in prices and erosion of resources disrupted the planning process and after three Annual Plans between 1966 and 1969, the Fourth Five Year Plan was started in 1969.

The Eighth Plan could not take off in 1990 due to the fast changing political situation at the Centre and the years 1990-91 and 1991-92 were treated as Annual Plans. The Eighth Plan was finally launched in 1992 after the initiation of structural adjustment policies. For the first eight plans the emphasis was on a growing public sector with massive investments in basic and heavy industries, but since the launch of the Ninth Plan in 1997, the emphasis on the public sector has become less pronounced and the current thinking on planning in the country, in general, is that it should increasingly be of an indicative nature.[1]

In his paper, Lord Meghnad Desai reviews the changing role of Indian planning, and the integral role of economists both from within and outside the Government. Viewed from this historical prism, we are presented with ideas in development planning, some that worked and some that did not. Nitin Desai brings us up-to-date with his paper on 'Planning in a Liberalised Economy'. He writes: 'The unique characteristic of the Planning Commission is that it is designed to take a comprehensive and holistic view of the real economy. It can look at the impact of policies on interconnected sectors, on regional balance, on poverty and employment, all dimensions that may escape scrutiny in a Finance Ministry centred economic policy system. This competence continues to be relevant even in a liberalised economy.' Desai also says that the role of the Planning Commission in Centre-state relations is vital. But it must move beyond the annual ritual of state plan discussions. Instead the goal of the discussions must be to make the states full partners in the planning exercise.

---

1. *http://planningcommission.nic.in/aboutus/history/index.php?about=aboutbdy. htm*

Centre-state relations is the topic of N.K. Singh's paper: 'The Planning Commission has increasingly become the only effective instrument which represents the view point of the States and transmits them to other Ministries in an overall framework.' Singh focusses on intergovernmental fiscal relations as these he feels constitute the most contentious issue of federal finances. He discusses the changing contours of fiscal federalism as it prevails in India and then outlines key issues that prevent smooth functioning and need to be revisited.

If one looks back at the evolution of the Indian state, the greatest long-term threat to Indian growth and development is the gradual deterioration of governance over the years. This must be reversed if India is to maintain its rapid development into an upper-middle income country.

Parthasarathi Shome in his essay provides a historical perspective to the concept of governance and its administrative and economic relevance. He notes that the 'lesson is that, in the prevailing era, governance by necessity embraces many aspects and concerns that tend to obfuscate the central issues that need singular attention for systemic correction. This assuages the developing countries claims for recognition of their long term structural concerns as a group while diluting away the need for advanced economies to take imperative macro-economic—financial and fiscal—tightening based on the introduction of strong and meaningful indicators and triggers reflecting the lack of development, leave alone, institution of the latter.' And there can be little argument with his conclusion that 'governance is a matter that exceeds government.'

Corruption is making headlines, for a variety of reasons, as we send this book into print. While efforts to induct transparency into government functioning and personnel continue at various levels. Kaushik Basu's paper puts forward a new idea for the control of one kind of corruption, namely, bribery, in India. Though in the domain of policymaking in India the proposal in this paper is novel, related ideas, which rely on creating divergent incentives among partners in crime, have been discussed in the past by economists and academic lawyers.

As indicated in the Planning Commission's presentation to the Prime Minister on April 21, 2011 and in the *Approach Paper, the Twelfth Five-Year Plan* is being developed with a targetted GDP growth rate of 9 per cent to 9.5 per cent, an increase in literacy rates to 100 per cent and an increase in expenditure on health from 1.3 per cent to 2.0 per cent of GDP between the plan's period from 2012 to 2017. In a boon for industry, the Planning Commission indicated that it aims to have industry and manufacturing-related activities grow by 11 per cent over the next five years, contrasted to 8 per cent over the previous Eleventh Five Year Plan. It also aims to undertake somewhat vaguely defined, but certainly well-intentioned, structural and regulatory reforms to facilitate investment. The presentation highlighted the Planning Commission's views that commercial energy demand is expected to increase by 7 per cent per year over the next five years. To address that increase in demand, the commission recommended that all methods of current energy production and distribution be developed, from coal to nuclear energy to solar and wind, and proposed that existing taxes on electricity should not be raised.

The Twelfth Five Year Plan is due to commence in 2012, a year after the population Census of 2011 was conducted. A great deal of fresh, authoritative information will accordingly be available as India's planners flesh out the prime minister's directive to aim for growth in the range of 9 to 9.5 per cent over the Twelfth Plan period, even while attempting to improve the distributive reach and ecological sustainability of this growth. Rapid economic growth has been one of the basic objectives of planning. The basic measure of economic growth is the continuous increase in real national income and per capita income. Each plan set for itself a target for raising national income and per capita income. The target ranged from 2.2 per cent per annum in the First Five Year Plan to 6.5 per cent in the Ninth Five Year Plan. The Tenth Five Year Plan proposed a target of 8 per cent GDP growth for the period 2002-2007. The actual achievement during the plans has been anywhere between 2.7 per cent and 6.8 per cent.

The growth of national income depends on a complex interaction of large number of variables, not all of which are amenable to government control. However, it is well known that the quantum of investment and the productivity of this investment, as measured in a simplified model by the capital output ratio, exercise an important influence on the overall growth rate.

The deficiency in investment and the higher capital-output ratios are only the immediate arithmetical explanations for the shortfalls in the growth targets. A further analysis is necessary to identify the factors, which would account for the departures from forecasts and targets for these two key magnitudes. Some part of the difference is attributable to a degree of unrealism in the forecasts; but in the case of investment and capital productivity, the explanation lies to a considerable extent in deficiencies in effective implementation of plans. The Indian planning process has always laid emphasis on measures to ensure sustainability of the development process not only in economic terms, but also in terms of social and environmental factors. Much of the measures adopted in the Agenda 21 of the United Nations Conference on Environment and Development (1992) already find reflection in the Indian plans.

The Ninth Plan was to carry this tradition further and consolidate on the creation of conditions for sustainable development. Rapidly growing population, urbanisation, changing agricultural, industrial and water resource management, increasing use of pesticides and fossil fuels have all resulted in perceptible deterioration in the quality and sustainability of the environment. It is recognised that environment protection does not only involve a prevention of pollution and of natural resource degradation, but has to be integrated with the overall development process and the well-being of people.

The Tenth Plan period (2002–03 to 2006–07) began modestly, but then saw the economy accelerating steadily to achieve an average growth rate of 7.7 per cent, for the Plan period as a whole, which is the highest ever achieved in any Plan period. In the last four years the growth rate averaged 8.9 per cent making India one of the fastest growing economies in the world. The transition to high growth is an impressive achievement, but we must not forget that growth is not the only measure of development. Our ultimate objective is to achieve broad- based improvement in the living standards of all our people. Rapid growth is essential for this outcome because it provides the basis for expanding incomes and employment and also provides the resources needed to finance programmes for social uplift. However, it is not by itself sufficient. We also need to ensure that growth is widely spread so that its benefits.

The objective of the Eleventh Plan was faster and inclusive growth and the initiatives taken in the Eleventh Plan period have resulted in substantial progress towards both objectives. Inevitably, there are some weaknesses that need to be addressed and also new challenges that need to be faced. Some of the challenges themselves emanate from the economy's transition to a higher and more inclusive growth path, the structural changes that come with it and the expectations it generates.

The acceleration in growth in the Eleventh Plan period compared with the Tenth Plan is modest, but it is nevertheless a good performance, given the fact that a severe global economic crisis depressed growth in two of these five years, and also that in the year 2009 India had the weakest monsoon in three decades. The slowdown in 2011-12 is a matter of concern, but it can be reversed if the investment climate is turned around and if fiscal discipline is strengthened.

Progress towards inclusiveness is more difficult to assess, because inclusiveness is a multidimensional concept. Inclusive growth should result in lower incidence of poverty, broad-based and significant improvement in health outcomes, universal access for children to school, increased access to higher education and improved standards of education, including skill development. It should also be reflected in better opportunities for both wage employment and livelihoods and in improvement in provision of basic amenities like water, electricity, roads, sanitation and housing. Particular attention needs to be paid to the needs of the SC/ST and OBC population, women and children as also minorities and other excluded groups. To achieve inclusiveness in all these dimensions requires multiple interventions, and success depends not only on introducing new policies and government programmes, but on institutional and attitudinal changes brought about, which take time.[2]

Reducing poverty is a key element in our inclusive growth strategy. Surjit S. Bhalla deals with the 'controversial, and now hot, issue of poverty in India.' Apart from examining the various dimensions of poverty, changing nature and definitions of poverty *per se*, Bhalla argues that purchasing power may perhaps not be a good, or true, indicator of poverty anymore. An important consequence of the focus on inclusion during the Eleventh Plan has been the much heightened awareness about

2. *Twelfth Five Year Plan Approach Paper*, August 2011, Planning Commission.

inclusiveness and empowerment amongst people. There is today a greater desire to access information about the rights and entitlements made available by law and policy, and eagerness to demand accountability from the public delivery systems.

An aspect of generating 'inclusive growth' is shifting the target of government aid to rural areas. Typically, large projects such as power generation, roads whereby freight can travel, and airports receive the lion's share of government subsidies, while rural infrastructure receives comparatively little. A recent op-ed piece in the *Wall Street Journal* by Saurabh Tripathi, a partner with Boston Consulting Group, echoed these sentiments. 'Rural infrastructure, which serves 70 percent of the population, doesn't get the attention it deserves. As the Planning Commission sets out to draft the country's planned investments for the next five years, it is important to take note of this gap, and the innovative solutions needed to fill it,' Tripathi wrote.

In fact, as Montek Singh Ahluwalia himself noted in his paper—*Prospects and Policy Challenges in the Twelfth Plan*—a key challenge in the Twelfth Plan is how to ensure creation of a sufficient number of productive jobs in the non-agriculture sector, in order to absorb the expected increase in the labour force and also absorb surplus labour that must be shifted out of agriculture.

The High Powered Committee for Estimating the Investment Requirements for Urban Infrastructure Services under the chairmanship of Isher Judge Ahluwalia concluded that India's economic growth momentum cannot be sustained if urbanisation is not actively facilitated. The existence of a robust physical infrastructure is widely recognised in policy circles, as a requisite for inclusive economic development.

For growth to be inclusive it must create adequate livelihood opportunities and add to decent employment commensurate with the expectations of a growing labour force. An oft repeated fact is that India's young age structure offers a potential demographic dividend for growth, but this potential will be realised only if the extent and quality of education and skill development among new entrants to the workforce is greatly enhanced. Hari Sankaran suggests the need for the creation of a 100 new habitations that will spur employment generation and invigorate an equitable growth in economic activity, would have to be selected from motley of Tier-II and Tier-III cities, *panchayat* clusters and the new cities proposed under schemes such as the DMIC. This should also encompass the new cities being developed by private actors, to create an overarching prospicience of development and employment creation, in the country.

In a recent article,[3] Montek Singh Ahluwalia provided his assessment of the Eleventh Five Year Plan's main accomplishments, and the prospects for improving growth performance in the Twelfth Five Year Plan, arguing that one of the emerging challenges is managing India's urban transition. A broad range of factors influence the growth of the urban population, notably differentials between average household incomes in urban and rural areas. The Chinese experience suggests if India succeeds in achieving its ambitious growth objectives, the rate of urbanisation could increase even more rapidly than currently expected.[4] An essential requirement for envisioning India's future in the new century is to recognise that the parameters which determine national development have changed in recent years and will change further in future.[5]

This will open up greater possibilities than ever before. A powerful set of catalytic forces is accelerating the speed of social change throughout the world. They include a rapid rise in levels of education, high rates of technological innovation and application, ever faster and cheaper communication that dissolves physical and social barriers both within countries and internationally, greater availability and easier access to information, and the further opening up of global markets. These trends are representative of a relative shift in the engines that drive development from manufacturing to the services sector and from capital resources to human and knowledge resources. Therefore, technology, organisation, information, education and productive skills will play a critically decisive role in governing the future course of development.

Sam Pitroda argues for a paradigm change. He writes that while India progressed along the path of economic liberalisation, the advancement in the realm of connectivity has accelerated. 'There is a primal requisite to

3. Ahluwalia (2011).
4. Bery (2011).
5. Gupta (2002).

create a whole new paradigm—one that is innovative, opens up new doors and challenges our traditional, hierarchical structures, by combining multiple layers of technology to access connectivity and information systems.' The role of planning immediately becomes evident when he says that a cross-cutting, multi-pronged strategy is needed to make India's innovation system better in meeting needs of the common people.

It is in this context that the National Innovation Council (NIC) constituted by the Prime Minister is trying to create a strategy for fostering innovations at the national, state and sectoral levels by focussing on five key parameters: platform, inclusion, ecosystem, drivers and discourse. The aim is to re-define innovations to go beyond formal R&D parameters, facilitate innovative solutions that lead to inclusive growth for the people and by the people, foster an innovation ecosystem across domains and sectors to strengthen entrepreneurship, focus on key drivers to ensure sustainability, durability and quality, and lastly, to expand the space for dialogue and discourse on innovation.

The Self Employed Women's Association or SEWA as a shining example of empowerment of women and marginalised and enabling them with a voice and participation has been dealt with at length in a chapter by Dr Gursharan Dhanjal and myself. Ahluwalia's conviction that the growth should not remain centralised and trickle down but also should be coupled with several centres of localised growth to positively impact numerous pockets, resonates well with all that SEWA has done in last three decades. Based on extensive interviews in the field, their paper highlights the positive effect of community and civil society participation in the development process and argues for greater empowerment at the grassroot level. Determination of policy is at different levels. They note that the building of powerful self-sustained institutions has helped SEWA to seize representation in various government bodies in the country and outside and influence policy changes.

Roberto Zagha seeks to bring nuances to the understanding of global imbalances and to identify deeper forces at work. First it reviews global imbalances over the last decade, and reminds us that global imbalances need not be destabilising. He highlights structural trends in the major economies that have contributed to global imbalances. Second, it looks back to financial crises in the last three decades, how they differ, or don't, from the current one, and what we can learn from them. Third, it concludes that the global crisis may be less the result of global imbalances than of what rendered them possible—a financial system that does not adequately evaluate and manage risks, and thus enables unsustainable trends to persist beyond prudence—and presents possible reasons for these shortcomings.

It is perhaps in the order of things, then, that Raghuram Rajan discusses how currency rates have a bearing on growth. He writes that the current jockeying over exchange rates has several important differences from that of the Depression years. Countries today are typically not trying to gain a short-term advantage through currency actions; instead, they are following entrenched domestic economic policy strategies. Stability, he says, will emerge when governments move to more sustainable domestic policy agendas, which are typically in their long-run interest.

Ravi Kanbur first met Ahluwalia in 1977 when he was at the World Bank. He along with his associate Sudhir Anand had just started careful, and critical, evaluation of the influential work of Montek and his colleagues at the World Bank which claimed to find evidence in favour of the famous Kuznets' 'inverted-U' hypothesis, that inequality first increases and then declines with development. Today, over 30 years later, he argues that even if the inverse-U is not to be found in the cross-section data, the broad forces in the dynamics of development identified by Kuznets and Ahluwalia continue to be present in the actual experience of individual countries, and are being confirmed by the time series evidence that has accumulated since the work of these two pioneers. It is these forces, and the policy interventions that shape them, which are central to the evolution of inequality during the course of development. 'It is only fitting that having started the post-Kuznets, literature on inequality and development, Montek is now at the heart of Indian policy making, addressing the distributional consequences of India's growth path.'

Any festschrift to Ahluwalia would undoubtedly be incomplete without some perspectives on banking and monetary matters. Reserve Bank of India Governor D. Subbarao recalls that as a Joint Secretary working under him, I obviously had an opportunity to interact with him on a continuous basis. But I must specially mention the extraordinary competence and skill that he showed in negotiating the settlement of the rupee-rouble debt deal in 1993 in which I had the opportunity to assist him. He goes on to give us some RBI perspectives on formulation of monetary policy, inflation targetting, macroprudential regulation and supervision, and debt management.

The future of the financial system is being debated globally since the financial system, as it existed in the recent years, had brought about a crisis in the global economy since 2008.

Y. Venugopal Reddy points out that the future of finance affects the totality of the economic life and, possibly political economy, and hence it is useful to explore some fundamental issues in order to appreciate how financial sector will evolve in future. He concludes that it is not appropriate to assume that state action will normally or automatically compensate for market failures. In a way, the problem in regulation of financial sector is not only technical but also one of political economy. The dynamics of relationship between state and market may be critical for designing a good financial system for future, he writes.

The most important area where government policy can help to accelerate development in a liberalised economy that relies upon private investment to achieve growth is the provision of basic economic and social infrastructure. This thought runs through many of the essays in this volume. The increasing success of the PPP model is in no small measure to the vision and encouragement provided by Montek Singh Ahluwalia. There are many other innovative touches he has brought to bear on Indian policy making, for the better which have been explicated in the following pages.

References

Ahluwalia, Montek Singh (2011). "Prospects and Policy Challenges in the Twelfth Plan", *Economic and Political Weekly*, May 21, at *http://epw.in/epw/user/loginArticleError.jsp?hid_artid=16089*

Bery, Suman (2011). *Coping with Unprecedented Urbanisation in India*. East Asia Forum. *http://www.eastasiaforum.org/2011/06/30/coping-with-unprecedented-urbanisation-in-india/*, June 30.

Gupta, S.P. (2002). *Vision 2020*. New Delhi: Planning Commission, http://planningcommission.nic.in/reports/genrep/pl_vsn2020.pdf

1 Policymaking for Indian Planning

The Role of Individuals and Ideas

MEGHNAD DESAI

Introduction

India has been a pioneering country and not just in the so-called Third World in building an analytical and policy apparatus to pursue a development programme for a long period. The Planning Commission is now 61 years old and has had its own existence as a separate institution of the Government of India outside the normal structures. It was set up by an Executive Order and is thus somewhat irregular and as many have complained, extra-Constitutional. Yet, it was an innovative response to the challenge of meeting the urgent needs of economic development for a newly independent nation.

Development in Theory and History

Development was declared as an objective of the independence movement ever since the Karachi Resolutions which were drafted by Nehru. Then in 1938, the National Planning Committee (NPC) was set up by Subhash Chandra Bose during his tenure as Congress President with Nehru in charge. The NPC continued its work during the War while Nehru and other Congress leaders were in prison and Bose was abroad under the secretaryship of Prof. K.T. Shah and submitted many reports which were more in the nature of stock taking than hard plan frame. But as Nehru revealed in his Discovery of India (1946), they had bold ambitions. 'That aim was declared to be to ensure an adequate standard of living for the masses, in other words to get rid of the appalling poverty of the people. The irreducible minimum, in terms of money, had been estimated by economists at figures varying from Rs 15 to Rs 25 per capita per month... We calculated that a really progressive standard of living would necessitate the increase of national wealth by 500 to 600 per cent. That however was too big a jump for us, and we aimed at 200 to 300 per cent increase within ten years.' (Nehru, *The Discovery of India*: 438)

Economics at the time of India's independence had not yet come to focus on economic growth as a subject on which it had much to say. Roy Harrod's London School of Economics (LSE) lectures 'Towards a Dynamic Economics' were published in 1949 and Evsey Domar's contribution though already published had not been discovered by his fellow economists. The Harrod-Domar growth theory with its simple calculus of a fixed capital output ratio and a constant saving-income ratio gave a mechanical answer to the growth possibilities a country had. Story goes that when K.N. Raj, recently graduated from LSE, went to work for the Planning Commission, he tried to tell Nehru that the achievable growth rate would be just about five per cent. This meant doubling income at best in 14 to 15 years rather than the target set by the NPC. Nehru is said to have been furious at the pessimism of this young economist. Luckily for India, Nehru did listen and unlike Mao did not launch his country on an impossible growth path which destroyed lives and industries in China during the Great Leap Forward. Yet, the task of forming a development policy was a new and challenging one.

Independent India had a continuity with the previous regime despite the bitterness of the Independence struggle. Nehru and Patel had appreciated the need for continuity and preserved the Army and bureaucratic structures including the steel frame of Indian Civil Service (ICS). But the British system of generalists entrusted with any and all tasks would not be the best for the technical aspects of economic policymaking. Hence, the Planning Commission has always had ways of recruiting experts and administrators from outside the ICS/IAS ranks as well as from within.

There being no hard theory of growth the policymakers had to fall back on whatever ideas they had inherited. Congress Party had an articulate critique of the effects of imperialism ever since its birth. Dadabhai Naoroji had written his *Poverty and Un-British Rule in India* (1901) and engaged in debates with Lord Curzon as to the impact of colonial rule on India. Naoroji was a pioneer in measurement of national income. Congress had a demand for an exchange rate of one pound to Rs 15 and for tariffs. A central idea was of course of the 'Drain'. This said that there was surplus aplenty in India but it was being drained off by the British. Once they were gone that surplus would be investible in India. Alas, the Drain which was around 5 per cent in the late 19th century had been shrinking in the first half of the 20th century. There were the Sterling balances (1.15 billion pounds about 100 billion in today's terms) accumulated as a result of India's contribution to the war effort. This was 'forced savings' but useful to cushion the impact of Partition in the early years. Sterling balances were spent 'as if there was no tomorrow', as C.D. Deshmukh complained later on when India hit resource constraint in financing the ambitious Second Five Year Plan (1956-1961).

Another idea similar to the foreign drain was the agricultural surplus that the cultivator had but was siphoned off by the landlords. Land reform was thus necessary to give land to the tiller and this would be sufficient to solve the rural poverty. The more radical elements in the Congress and the Socialist Party knew that the cultivating units were highly fragmented. But they had their faith that there would be a cooperative pooling of land by the farmers and large cultivating units would be more productive than small ones.

The assumption that there was an adequate supply of food grains was to prove too optimistic by the end of the fifties. Also research commissioned by the Research Programmes Committee of the Planning Commission had showed that small farms were more productive than large farms, thus, overturning what was an orthodoxy of the Left that farms should be large either by voluntary pooling or by collectivisation a la Soviet Union. Charan Singh the leader of the farmers in north India was able to defy Nehru in All India Congress Committee (AICC) elections in 1959 on the issue of cooperatives. Farm productivity was to be a burning issue in the last years of Nehru. [It was during the sixties that India stumbled upon the high yield variety seeds produced by the Rockefeller research centres and launched the Green Revolution under the leadership of C. Subramaniam.]

During the fifties, India attracted many foreign economists who came as guests of the Government of India and advised on the Plans. P.C.

Mahalanobis had submitted his highly original note, 'The Operational Research Approach to Planning in India' which contained a two-sector and a four-sector growth model. This attracted much attention both at home and abroad and many economists especially mathematical economists and econometricians were inspired to contribute to Indian efforts. The economists who came included Ragnar Frisch, Ragnar Nurkse, Oskar Lange, Michal Kalecki, J.K. Galbraith, Joan Robinson, Nicholas Kaldor (who also submitted his Report on taxation) and Milton Friedman.

Indian economists were encouraged to submit their comments and alternatives to the Mahalanobis model and a panel of economists as constituted to carry out the task. The Bombay economists Vakil and Brahmananda (1956) wrote their, *Planning for an Expanding Economy* which argued for a different approach to development based on an expansion of wage goods rather than the capital goods priority in the Mahalanobis model. The Bombay model was in the spirit of parallel ideas of harnessing surplus labour in rural areas and transferring it to the urban areas for industrialisation. W. Arthur Lewis wrote his seminal article 'Economic Development with Unlimited Supplies of Labour' in 1954. Ragnar Nurkse was also at that time advocating similar ideas in his *Problems of Capital Formation in Underdeveloped Countries* (1953).

Indian development plans were to ignore all these suggestions. The idea was that the priority was to build up the basic industries for capital good production before the economy could move on to consumption goods production. The latter were to be provided by small scale and cottage industries to the extent that the larger units could not fill the demand gap. It was also thought that employment would be taken care of by these small scale and cottage industries. There was a suspicion of foreign trade and the idea was to aim for self-sufficiency. India was one of the pioneers of Import Substitution Industrialisation (ISI) strategy. Arguably this choice of ISI tied India down to a relatively low rate of growth as compared to its Asian neighbours Malaysia and South Korea, but that is for another day.

The Planning Commission became the focus of efforts to build large input-output models which would support the plan projections. John F. Kennedy had committed USA to help India in its efforts even while he was a Senator in the late fifties, and prestigious academic institutions such as

Harvard and MIT were harnessed into this effort. P. Rosenstein-Rodan, Alan Manne, Hollis Chenery among others collaborated with young Indian economists such as Amartya Sen, Sukhamoy Chakravarty, Mrinal Datta-Chaudhuri in studying Indian planning. [The Centre of International Studies where this collaboration took place was later exposed as being financed by the CIA, much to the embarrassment of many. But its work was of a very high quality.]

Economists found they could always contribute to the formulation of development policy whether from within or without the Government. Thus V.K Ramaswami worked from within the Ministry of Commerce, but he wrote some brilliant academic pieces on tariffs and quotas. Jagdish Bhagwati who was a Professor at the Delhi School of Economics (DSE) often collaborated with Ramaswami on these subjects. Sukhamoy Chakravarty was inducted into advising the government by Indira Gandhi in 1971 and continued in one or other capacity till his early death in 1990. The tradition continues to this day with Kaushik Basu summoned from Cornell University (US) to become Chief Economic Advisor of India.

Civil Servants and Economists

India's experience in building and maintaining a cadre of professionals and civil servants dedicated to the task of policy formulation on development issue deserves a much more detailed treatment than I can give here. But as a tribute to Montek who as Deputy Chairman of Planning Commission has already had seven years, I want to explore the role of individual civil servants in development policymaking.

India has been lucky in having had a brilliant series of civil servants (ICS or IAS) or outside experts—academic economists or physicists (Pitambar Pant, Vikram Sarabhai) or statisticians (Mahalanobis) who have been trusted with the policymaking tasks on the economic front. Few other countries can claim such a stellar cast. Just consider C.D. Deshmukh (1896-1962) ICS who became the first Indian to be Reserve Bank Governor and later a distinguished Finance Minister between 1950-1956. There was Tarlok Singh, another ICS who was crucial both in refugee resettlement after the Partition but also a founder member of the Planning Commision whose Poverty and Social Change (1945) was a seminal contribution to the problems of development. Tarlok Singh was a LSE man while Deshmukh graduated from Cambridge with a Natural Science Tripos. P.S. Lokanathan was an academic who taught at Madras and later became a editor of *Eastern Economist*. He was the first executive secretary of Economic Commission for Asia and the Far East (ECAFE) and went on to found the National Council for Applied Economic Research (NCAER). One could add S. Bhoothalingam, ICS who played a crucial part in the Steel industry development.

In India, the expert economist could always find his way into the echelons of influence. Perhaps the best previous example of an outsider coming into the civil service ranks was Dr I.G. Patel. IG as he was universally known had a brilliant academic career at Bombay and Cambridge. He was also at Harvard during his PhD. IG came back to become principal of Baroda College but was then swiftly inducted into the Research Department of the newly set up International Monetary Fund (IMF). Here he did pioneering work with Edward Bernstein who headed the Department. IG returned to India in 1954 to work in Ministry of Finance and became the Chief Economic Advisor. He was later inducted into the civil service cadre to become Principal Secretary to the Ministry of Finance eventually spending 18 years in all between 1954 to 1972. IG went on to be the Governor of the Reserve Bank of India as well as Deputy Administrator of UNDP and Director of the LSE. Even after his return to India in 1990, IG kept up with the debate and rumour has it, that he was one of two or three people considered for the Finance Minister's job which finally went to Dr Manmohan Singh with such amazing results.

Deputy Chairmen

The Planning Commission has always stood outside the main framework of the Government of India and has been able to recruit experts from a wide variety of fields. Nehru set a precedent when as Chairman of the Planning Commission he submitted the report on the First Five Year Plan (1951-1956) to the Prime Minister, i.e., himself, thus making clear that he was not ex-officio Chairman. Yet, every subsequent Prime Minister has taken on the post of Chairman of the Planning Commission. It is the Deputy Chairman who is the full time *de facto* head of the Planning

Commission. The Deputy Chairman's position has been occupied by many outstanding people.

Gulzarilal Nanda was Vice-Chairman of the Planning Commission when it was first set up. He was elected to Lok Sabha in 1952 and became Minister for Planning, Irrigation and Power. Later in the fifties, he was designated as Deputy Chairman of the Planning Commission. He had been a professor of Economics in his 20s and spent much of his early life as a trade unionist in Ahmedabad and later on a prominent leader of the Indian National Trade Union Congress. He was twice made interim Prime Minister for 13 days each after the deaths of Nehru and Shastri.

There was Asoka Mehta, a politician with an academic or better perhaps an intellectual bent, who served as Deputy Chairman of Planning Commission in the early 1960s. As a Socialist, Asoka Mehta had been critical of the Congress's approach to planning. He wrote a series of critical essays 'On the Political Compulsions of Planning in India' (which appeared in the Socialist Party magazine *Janata* during the early 1950s) advocating widespread use of British style nationalised industry boards which the LSE Prof. William Robson had written about. Earlier in 1951, he had written 'Who Controls India's Economy? A Continuing Pattern of Concentration of Wealth.' He was the economist intellectual of the Socialist, later the Praja Socialist, Party. But in Opposition, he could find little use for his talents. This was especially so because the Party kept on splitting and dividing. At the end of 1950s, Nehru found a use for him when he was asked to chair a committee inquiring into the question of food grains availability in 1958. This was when the Second Five Year Plan had run into a resource constraint and India began to experience food price inflation for the first time since the War. He joined the Planning Commission as Deputy Chairman in 1963 and later joined Congress Party. Asoka Mehta was also to write an influential report on Panchayati Raj during the Janata Government of 1977-1979.

Perhaps a more unusual appointment was that of Prof. D.R. Gadgil. He had written a pioneering thesis at Cambridge published as Industrial Evolution of India and then was the first Director of the Gokhale Institute of Politics and Economics in Poona (now Pune) founded in 1930 by Rao Bahadur R.R. Kale who was his father-in-law. Gadgil remained at Gokhale

Institute till his retirement, a stretch of 35 years at the helm. He established Gokhale Institute as an outstanding place for applied economic research. On his retirement, he became Deputy Chairman of Planning Commission in 1967. Gadgil was an unusual appointment because he was not a supporter of Congress Party and had reservations about Mahatma Gandhi's economics and politics. He was also not a mathematical or technical economist in the style of the economics then becoming dominant. His tenure coincided with the Plan holiday of 1967/68 and the drafting of the Fourth Five Year Plan which was launched in 1969. India had been forced to devalue the Rupee under pressure from the World Bank and there was some prospect of large scale aid to sweeten the bitter pill. As it happened, Lyndon Johnson did not like Indira Gandhi's stance on the Vietnam war and the aid never arrived. Indira Gandhi obviously approved of Gadgil as he was a pretty firmly rooted economist and a radical one at that without being a Marxist. Gadgil's tenure ended in 1971 and he died almost the day after his retirement on the train returning to Poona. Gadgil is remembered also for his early advocacy of cooperatives in irrigation which he helped implement at Pravaranagar in Maharashtra. The initial experiment was such a success that subsequently irrigation and sugar cooperatives grew up to be a powerful force in the economy and the politics of Maharashtra.

Another academic who was also Deputy Chairman was Prof. D.T. Lakdawala. He was a public finance specialist and had been at the University of Bombay in the company of C.N. Vakil, M.L. Dantwala and P.R. Brahmananda. He left Bombay to join Gujarat University in 1968 and then set up the Sardar Patel Research Institute in Ahmedabad. Like Gadgil, Lakdawala was an applied economist with a shrewd eye for practical detail. He became Deputy Chairman of Planning Commission during the brief Janata Government 1977-1979. Here again was someone with no political profile but perhaps his association with Gujarat was crucial for Morarji Desai, the Janata Prime Minister to choose him as Deputy Chairman. Like Gadgil again Lakdawala was an institution builder and after leaving Sardar Patel to join the Planning Commission, he set up the Institute of Social Sciences (ISS) in Delhi which hosts the Lakdawala Memorial Lectures. The distinctive planning philosophy which the Janata government could have pursued with a Gandhian twist was never to be realised as the Government fell within two years. Madhu Dandavate, another Socialist politician was also Deputy Chairman during the 1990s. In two stints in 1990 and again between 1996 and 1998. He had also been Finance Minister in the V.P. Singh government.

Of course, the most distinguished member of this select club of Deputy Chairmen of Planning Commission must be Dr Manmohan Singh, the sole person to be Deputy Chairman and Chairman of Planning Commission. Manmohan Singh's career in international organisations like UNCTAD and the South Commission as well as an economist in the Government of India plus his stint as Reserve bank Governor makes him the complete Indian economist par excellence. No one else to my knowledge has occupied all these positions even if we don't count his current job.

Conclusion

This somewhat scattered essay on the people and the ideas in development planning in India scarcely does justice to the person being honoured. Yet, it is a story not often told. People matter in the formulation of policy. The good ones pass on smoothly. The bad ones cause havoc and leave their mark. Montek has been the smoothest of them all.

References

Lewis, W. Arthur (1954). *Economic Development with Unlimited Supplies of Labour.* Manchester School.

Nurkse, Ragnar (1953). *Problems of Capital Formation in Underdeveloped Countries.* Blackwell.

Vakil, C.N. and P.R. Brahmananda (1956). *Planning for an Expanding Economy.*

2 Planning in a Liberalised Economy

NITIN DESAI

Montek S. Ahluwalia has been at the centre of policymaking in India for over three decades now. He came to the Government of India from the World Bank where he had worked closely with Hollis Chenery and specialised in matters relating to poverty and redistribution. After coming to India he has been associated more with the gradual shift from socialist orthodoxy that has characterised Indian planning at least from the early eighties. The high point of course came in 1991 when he was the principal bureaucrat working with Dr Manmohan Singh in the great bonfire of controls. His substantial achievements as one of the principal architects of the liberalised economy are justly celebrated. More recently he has bent his energies at transforming the venerable and graying professorial institution that we call the Planning Commission and he has had a longer tenure as Deputy Chairman than anyone else in the past 50 years.

The Planning Commission has been around for about 60 years and over these years its influence in shaping the rate and pattern of growth has fluctuated. One can distinguish four phases. An exuberant youth that lasted from 1950 to 1965, an awkward adolescence from 1965-1980 when it tried to change as often as the confused politics of this period required, a depressed middle age from 1980 to 1990 when it struggled to remain relevant and now after 1991 a period of maturity, as it tries to reinvent itself to remain relevant in a liberalised economy. A synoptic view of the past, present and future of the Planning Commission is the subject of this contribution to honour its current head who has faced the challenge of defining a role for planning in a liberalised economy.

The Past

The first phase from 1950 to 1965 was the period when the Commission was most effective in shaping policy. It had the ear of an all-powerful Prime Minister, a clearly articulated strategy for development, immense influence over the states, but kept a certain distance from the private sector. The central element of this vision was the gradual articulation of socialist goals.

The First Five Year Plan focussed less on socialism and more on breaking out of stagnation when it said: 'The modern world is changing so rapidly that it is not enough to think in terms of slow changes and marginal adjustments, a minor shake-up here and a little cementing elsewhere. An underdeveloped country which has suffered long from the effects of cramped development desires inevitably to progress rapidly and in many directions; the aim of planning must be to make this possible.'[1]

Even its vision of planning controls is more in terms of price controls rather than direct controls on investment: 'Controls in a word are the means by which Government maintains a balance between various sectional interests. Under certain circumstances the accent may be on the maintenance of certain price ceilings, and through these of the real purchasing power of the incomes accruing to certain classes. Under other conditions, the enforcement of minimum prices might be a necessary corollary to a policy of ensuring a reasonable rate of return on effort in certain lines of economic activity.'[2]

The major change came later in the Second Plan, which is perhaps the most uncompromising statement of the ideology that guided this first phase of planning typified in the following passages from the Plan: 'These values or basic objectives have recently been summed up in the phrase "socialist pattern of society". Essentially, this means that the basic criterion for determining the lines of advance must not be private profit but social gain, and that the pattern of development and the structure of socio-economic relations should be so planned that they result not only in appreciable increases in national income and employment but also in

1. Planning Commission (1951), Chapter 1, Para 5.
2. *Ibid.*, Chapter 1, Para 42.

greater equality in incomes and wealth. Major decisions regarding production, distribution, consumption and investment—and in fact all significant socio-economic relationships—must be made by agencies informed by social purpose.'[3]

The planners were never really as powerful as this passage would have required. In theory, their direct role in the allocation of funds for public investment both by the Centre and the states and the growing share of the public sector in investment should have done this. But in practice, the private sector in India stoutly resisted the discipline of planning and subverted the licence-permit system to make easy profits. The planners had only a modest influence on the detailed design of the foreign trade and investment licensing system or over credit or foreign exchange allocations. The responsibility for these rested with the Finance, Commerce and Industry ministries and these were generally headed by powerful politicians who would not be dictated to by Yojana Bhavan.[4]

The droughts of the mid-sixties changed all this and the second confused phase of Indian planning started in 1965 and lasted till 1980. The vision of an industrialisation led growth strategy faded with the need to give priority to agriculture. The sharp cutback in industrial investments hit the public sector particularly hard. The political environment changed with the emergence of non-Congress governments in some states. The power of the Centre weakened. The dominant ideology of development went through sharp changes—priority for agriculture and rural development to start with, replaced by 'Garibi Hatao' and some doctrinaire socialism as Indira Gandhi took on the old guard and a semi-Gandhian populism, focussed on rural development under the Janata government. These swings in ideology were driven largely by political forces outside the Commission, whose experts had to lurch from one ideological mindset to another, very much like some confused adolescent.

The first two phases lasting about 30 years was when development policy was designed to respond to market failure rather than working with the market. But it was never quite as dirigiste as later critics have

3. Planning Commission (1956), Chapter 2, Para 3.

4. Chibber (2003).

suggested. In practice, the departures from a market mechanism were not as widespread and one can discern broadly three modalities of intervention.

- In the field of infrastructure and large industry, an emphasis on public ownership, direct regulation of private investment through licensing, price and distribution controls and coordination of specific investment decisions through the planning/licensing mechanism. This was the sphere in which departures from a market mechanism were most widespread.
- In the field of agriculture, village and small industries, private ownership with indirect measures to influence decisions through fiscal and monetary measures and public spending on infrastructure and support services, but with some direct intervention through procurement and distribution operations for some products.
- In the field of redistributive measures, a limited use of direct redistribution through land reforms, a progressive fiscal policy and job reservations and greater dependence on public spending on social consumption, subsidies targetted at the poor and rural employment programmes.

The big bone of contention amongst economists of diverse persuasions is the planner's emphasis on import substituting industrialisation. This, it is argued, led to inefficiencies in resource use as measured by the variance in effective rates of protection and it failed to exploit opportunities for labour intensive export production which could have led to a faster growth in manufacturing employment. The economic rationale for this rested on a pessimism about the prospects for exports that prevailed in the early fifties and the possibility that export oriented investments would have required a much more welcoming attitude to foreign capital. This latter possibility was not welcome to most Indian capitalists and to the political leadership influenced by the anti-colonial fervour of the freedom struggle. Hence, the reasons for the import substitution bias are ultimately political. In any case it represented a continuation of a trend that had started much earlier as the driving force of Indian industrialisation before independence was the replacement of imports, typified in the heroic story about the foundation of Tata Steel.

The stress on public sector and industrial licensing was a little different. There was a certain distrust of industrialists and a socialist passion that guided this, even though many politicians were close to and even financed by domestic industrialists. This is what changed in the eighties as the political class was now willing to openly support the case for domestic liberalisation. What as the reason for this fairly quick change of attitude? Was it the failure of socialist initiatives like the takeover of the wholesale trade in food grains? Did the emergence of new politically savvy industrialists who had benefitted from the restraints on more established industrial houses make the difference? Was it the growing power of money in an electoral process that had become much more competitive? Or was it the growing influence of a new set of advisers?[5]

The Planning Commission struggled to maintain its relevance in the changed environment of the eighties and one of the areas that it stepped into with some aplomb from the mid-seventies onwards was the social cost benefit analysis of public investment. Even though the formal responsibility for the approval of public investment was with the Finance Ministry, it deferred virtually the entire responsibility for guiding the discussion to the Planning Commission, perhaps to protect itself from political pressures, which the Commission, at that time, was better placed to resist. The other area of influence for the Commission in this period was energy policy whose importance in development strategy was greatly increased by the oil crisis of 1973-74 and 1979-80. It exercised this influence mainly through a couple of high profile policy committees and to some extent through the foothold it had secured in public investment approvals.

The link between the regulatory environment and economic performance[6] is tenuous given the break in growth performance that occurred around 1980-81. This acceleration of GDP growth in the eighties was not the product of any radical change in the role of the Government in regulating investment and production decisions though some changes were made, the most important being the tax reforms presented in the 1985-86 budget.

5. See Kohli (2006), Sengupta (2004), Sengupta (2008) and McCartney (2010).

6. Desai (2008).

The Present

The big change in the policy regime came after the near bankruptcy of the country in 1991, that forced the newly elected Congress government to go to the IMF. The 1991 reforms presented by Dr. Manmohan Singh in his budget saw massive changes in the licence-permit system with a near complete dismantling of industrial licensing and quantitative trade restrictions. Sharp reductions in tariff rates and major changes in the foreign investment policy. Capital market controls were transferred to an independent regulatory body, SEBI, and stock trading was modernised by the pioneering work of the National Stock Exchange. These changes have been very well decribed in a several writings by Montek S. Ahluwalia[7] and other economists who were associated with the reform process.

The demolition of the licence-permit raj was precipitated by the payments crisis. But it was also the product of a climate of opinion that had built up in the decade before, fed by influential official reports prepared by the early supporters of deregulation like L.K. Jha, M. Narasimhan, Abid Hussain and Vadilal Dagli. Those who blame the bureaucracy should note that the first three, who were civil servants, were more radical in their proposals than Dagli, who was the editor of a pro-business periodical.

However, the growth performance of the economy in the decade after liberalisation did not look much better than the performance in the eighties. There was a short-term growth boom and a marked slowdown after 1995-1996, when the stock market collapsed and Indian industry had to cope with the sudden exposure to international competition. Infrastructure growth continued to be inadequate relative to need. The weather related slowdown in the agricultural economy also played a role in depressing growth. But there were some spectacular success stories in info-tech exports and the beginnings of the telecom boom.

The acceleration of growth after 2004 has lasted for quite some time and must be attributed to some underlying systemic change. One major structural change was the rapid growth in corporate savings from around 4 per cent of GDP to 8 per cent of GDP. This fuelled a huge increase in corporate spending. The second factor was the widening of the base for

7. Ahluwalia (2002) and (2006).

rapid export growth. The restructuring of Indian industry that came after the opening of the economy in the nineties surely helped. One example of this is the emergence of the auto component industry as a major source of export growth after it restructured to meet the demands of the new car producers. The third factor possibly was the vast sums poured into rural India under the NREGA and Bharat Nirman programmes that may have fuelled a consumer goods boom.[8]

The impact of the reforms on the role of the Planning Commission was quite substantial. The shift from public investment as the primary source of investment in infrastructure and core industries to a growing dependence on private investment in these areas meant a shift in the locus of influence from the Planning Commission-Finance Ministry to the sectoral ministries. The private sector responds to business opportunities, not to goals and targets set by the Government. The capacity to micro-manage relative profitability with fine changes in tax rates has been reduced by the very necessary simplification and rationalisation of the indirect tax structure. What determines relative profitability now is increasingly a function of regulatory policies that are implemented by the sectoral ministries and the sectoral regulators. Even in the area of infrastructure, with the growing reliance on public-private partnerships (PPPs), the role of the sectoral ministries is enhanced.

At the same time, the Indian economy is becoming more open and the Indian corporate sector is more vulnerable to global competition. A new element is the global ambition of many corporate houses who want to become multinationals. In this environment, the corporate sector needs coherence in investment even more than before. Its profitability and survival depends on upstream requirements, particularly infrastructure, coming up as planned. It also depends on the sequencing and timing of the opening to the world economy. Take for instance the liberalisation of capital market flows. Clearly, the cautious policies of the Finance Ministry and the Reserve Bank helped to insulate the Indian economy from the upheavals in the global financial system 2008 onwards.

The reform process has basically altered the relationship of the Government with the corporate sector, which now has much more

8. Desai (2010a).

independence in its decision-making. The opening of the economy has also increased greatly the salience of macroeconomic stability as a key policy goal so as to reassure private savers and investors about the safety of their capital from expropriation through inflation. The third element is the substitution of ministerial regulation by supervision by supposedly independent regulatory authorities. All of these are still work-in-progress. Delicensing is a reality but politically exercised controls to protect the environment, or forests or public health or natural resources remain a space where rent-seeking behaviour, both by the politicians and their corporate cronies, is possible. Macro stability has been enshrined in law; but the reality of unsustainable deficits and inflation continue. Statutory regulators have been established for infrastructure sectors; but the political system has not accepted the idea of independence and impartiality in policy implementation.

The Future

From an institutional perspective, the reform process has shifted the levers of power over the real economy to the Finance Ministry and the sectoral ministries. The Finance Ministry, however well qualified its personnel may be as economists, tends to focus on the financial superstructure. This is its job and it is best it sticks to it. The sectoral ministries are in effect lobbies for the sector interest when they work honestly and for favoured client corporates when they do not. The unique characteristic of the Planning Commission is that it is designed to take a comprehensive and holistic view of the real economy. It can look at the impact of policies on interconnected sectors, on regional balance, on poverty and employment, all dimensions that may escape scrutiny in a Finance Ministry centred economic policy system. This competence continues to be relevant even in a liberalised economy.

In fact we need an effective Planning Commission even more now than in the past. An economy that is growing at a cracking pace of 8 per cent plus can quite quickly run into supply bottlenecks, particularly for non-tradable infrastructure and labour skills. A more open economy with even agriculture depending heavily on foreign trade will be more vulnerable to external shocks and anticipating and coping with these coherently will require the broad view of the real economy, that is the special competence of the Planning Commission.

The Planning Commission will undoubtedly continue to prepare economy-wide macro projections though the role of these projections in a liberalised and open economy is open to question. One also finds the animated debates about the choice of growth rates a little surreal. Governments do not determine growth rates in an open market economy. They set policies which influence investment and other choices made by private entities that determine the growth outcome and the real debate should be about these policies rather than some supposed choice of outcomes.

The primary task of planning is still to address potential areas of market failure. In the present context the challenge for the Planning Commission is to develop a consensus on the role of public policy with regard to the following:

- Poverty and inequality,
- Infrastructure development,
- The global competitiveness of Indian producers,
- Human capital, particularly labour skills,
- Scientific and technological capacity,
- The environment,
- The response to economic shocks.

These areas of public policy require systematic and planned intervention by public authorities. Good planning means that the competencies and capacities for doing this are strengthened in specific part of the Central or state administration responsible for that area of policy formulation. But these separate policies are interconnected and need to be driven by a common vision.

In today's India, where the public sector does not dominate the core areas of the economy and the power of the Central government is increasingly constrained by powerful state governments. Policies to be effective must also enjoy a broad measure of support amongst all stakeholders. The Planning Commission wields very little by way of executive power and its influence in the liberalised economy of today depends on its credibility in the eyes of the corporate sector, the state governments, foreign investors and the many NGOs and community organisations that work at the ground level. This is where the Planning Commission, with its battery of expert members, can play a truly important role.

A Planning Commission that is designed to do this must be substantially different from what it is at present. It must lay less emphasis on its role as a glorified Joint Secretary (Plan Finance) dealing with the minutiae of plan budgeting for the Centre and the states. There are other things that it does which needs much more capacity and this includes perspective planning and analytical work, monitoring and evaluation of policy and programme impact, and international economic analysis.

It has always associated industry, academia, trade unions, NGOs and other stakeholders with the processes of plan formulation. This must be extended to become a part of its regular work even in the years in between plan formulation. Its members have a substantial public standing and should be deployed for this purpose and to provide a presence in public debates on development. The risk of occasional embarrassment by some loose cannon should not worry the Government which is surely able to manage minor mishaps.

The Planning Commission cannot become a mere research institution and talk-shop. Even if the role of direct public investment has come down, the role of public policies that affect private decisions has gone up. The Plan framework and the policy reviews undertaken by the Commission can be made to matter if it is made an obligatory basis for policy formulation by all entities in the Central and state administration.

Is this possible in today's political environment? Will a powerful minister from a coalition partner defer to the experts in the Commission? How will states, led by opposition party chief ministers, take to direction from the Planning Commission?

The maintenance of planning discipline at the Centre is largely a matter of how 'coalition dharma' evolves as our political system adjusts to this reality. If it is based on a jointly agreed Common Programme then the discipline can be maintained by an effective Prime Minister, at least to the extent to which the Common Programme and the Plan are compatible. But if coalitions are based simply on a sharing of spoils with each coalition partner free to run its ministries as semi-independent fiefdoms, then it is not just planning but the long-term prospects for sustaining high and equitable growth that is at risk. Planning cannot impose coherence if politics becomes incoherent.

But all is not lost even in this sorry eventuality. A Commission that keeps its doors open to corporates, academia and civil society can act as forum for articulating the public interest partly by providing space for critical comments on the more egregious departures from good policy by venal or misguided ministers and partly by adding its own, more tactfully formulated, suggestions for change.

Centre-state relations cannot be handled simply by the emergence of a sound 'coalition dharma'. Many of them will be run by political parties who are not a part of the coalition at the Centre. Today the states are being run by powerful chief ministers. Some of them are fiscally not heavily dependent on Planning Commission grants. The role of the Planning Commission in Centre-state relations is vital. But it must move beyond the annual ritual of state plan discussions.

The orientation of the dialogue with state governments must be changed. Fiscal discipline, which was the staple of these discussions for long, will have to come from the norms and rules set by bodies like the Finance Commission and RBI. The real challenge is to go beyond a mindset where the officials of the Central government sit in judgment on the work of the officials in the state government, often with little or no impact. Instead the goal of the discussions must be to make the states full partners in the planning exercise. Consider the priority areas for planning mentioned above. At least four of these poverty, infrastructure, human capital and environment—depend largely on the policies of the states and the competencies of the state administration. A Commission that truly cares for outcomes in these areas must spend as much time and effort talking to the state governments as it does in talking with the corresponding Central ministries.

In some ways the idea of a 'coalition dharma' based on a Common Programme can be extended to cover possible role of planning in managing

Centre-state relations. But for this to happen the Commission and the Central government must listen to the views of the states on national matters including the national plan. The National Development Council can provide the frame for this and much more use can be made of the modality of Empowered Groups of Chief Ministers to address national issues.

Our polity needs safety valves like this if a plural and federal democracy is to survive. A redesigned Planning Commission can help to keep together a fragmented polity around a set of shared values and goals. More specifically it should:

- keep together the coalitions that will rule at the Centre,
- act as a honest broker between the Centre and the states,
- engage the corporate sector in meeting national development goals, and
- keep the polarised forces in civil society engaged in the policy dialogue.

Beyond this political role, the Planning Commission must continue its classical role of being an often unpopular countervailing body, acting as a lobby for the poor and a lobby for the future. This is its real value in an economic and political environment where the short-term interest of the powerful tend to prevail.

References

Acharya, Shankar, Isher Judge Ahluwalia, K.L. Krishna and Ila Patnaik (2006). "Economic Growth in India, 1950-2000", in Kirit S. Parikh (ed.), *Explaining Growth in South Asia.* New Delhi: Oxford University Press.

Ahluwalia, Montek (2002). "Economic Reforms in India since 1991: Has gradualism worked?", in *The Journal of Economic Perspectives* 16(3).

———. (2006). "India's Experiences with Globalisation", in *The Australian Economic Review* 39(1).

Chibber, Vivek (2003). *Locked in Place: State-building and Late Industrialisation.* Princeton: Princeton University Press.

Desai, Nitin (1988). "Development Planning in India: A Review", Paper presented at seminar on *India since Independence.* New Delhi: Indian Council of Social Science Research, New Delhi: December 26-30. (*mimeo*, available on request from the author at *nitin-desai@hotmail.com)*

———. (2004). "Why Planning Matters Even More Now", in *Business Standard,* September 16.

———. (2008). "Economic Growth and Regulatory Reform", in *Competition and Regulation Report.* New Delhi: CUTS Institute of Regulation and Competition.

———. (2010a). "Sustaining High Growth", in Sameer Kochhar (ed.), *India on the Growth Turnpike: Esays in Honour of Vijay L. Kelkar.* New Delhi: Academic Foundation.

———. (2010b). "Demographic Dividend or Debt?", in Sameer Kochhar and M. Ramachandran (ed.), *Building from the Bottom: Infrastructure and Poverty Alleviation.* New Delhi: Academic Foundation.

Kohli, Atul (2006). "The Politics of Economic Growth in India 1980-2005", in *Economic and Political Weekly* 41(13): 1251-1259; 42(14): 1361-1370.

McCartney, Matthew (2010). *Political Economy of Growth and Liberlaisation in India 1991-2008.* London, New York: Routledge.

National Commission for Enterprises in the Unorganised Sector (2009). *The Challenge of Employment: An Informal Economy Perspective*. New Delhi: Government of India.

Planning Commission (1951). *First Five Year Plan*. New Delhi: Government of India.

———. (1956). *Second Five Year Plan*. New Delhi: Government of India.

Sengupta, Mitu (2004). *The Politics of Market Reform in India.* Toronto: University of Toronto Press.

———. (2008). "How the State Changed its Mind: Power, Politics and the Origins of India's Market Reforms", *Economic and Political Weekly 43(21):* 35-42. *May 24-May 30.*

Virmani, Arvind (2004). "India's Economic Growth: From Socialist Rate of Growth to Bharatiya Rate of Growth", *Working Paper* No. 122, ICRIER, February. *www.icrier.org/wp122.pdf*

———. (2004). "Sources of India's Economic Growth: Trends in Total Factor Productivity", *Working Paper* No. 131, ICRIER, May. *www.icrier.org/wp131.pdf*

3 Centre-State Relations
The Forward Path

N.K. SINGH

Montek Singh Ahluwalia's contribution to the modernisation of the Indian economy is by any reckoning path breaking. His sound grounding in theoretical economics has been combined and refined with successive policymaking roles. His quest for seeking policy prescriptions distinguishes him from others of comparable standing in his own profession. As the key economic advisor of Mr Rajiv Gandhi, he was closely associated with the liberalisation programme which commenced during the Rajiv era. In the Commerce Ministry, he worked closely with former Commerce Minister P. Chidambaram to liberalise India's trade economy. Later, moving to the Ministry of Finance both Montek and myself worked closely with Manmohan Singh and later with P. Chidambaram and Yashwant Sinha. This period saw the design and successful execution of the far reaching economic reforms programme beginning 1991. Montek has the conviction as well as the tenacity to 'stay the course' with ideas which he deeply believes in. Political realities inject inevitable flexibility. But, I have not seen him abandon ideas. He would shelve them only temporarily to resurrect them when time is more opportune.

In his first stint in the Planning Commission as a Member he tried to restructure the working of the Planning Commission. In his Second stint as Deputy Chairman of the Planning Commission he has overseen the evolution and implementation of the Eleventh Five Year Plan (2007-2012) as well as the draft of the Twelfth Five Year Plan (2012-2017). His ideas in strengthening infrastructure, priority for social sector and workable models of public-private partnership (PPP) has proved to be structural and innovative.

In more than one way, the Planning Commission is about Centre-state relations. Planning Commission has increasingly become the only effective instrument which represents the view point of the states and transmits them to other ministries in an overall framework. That is why this piece written by me is on 'Centre-state relations'. This is indeed in the proximate domain of the Planning Commission.

Montek has never shirked controversies and nor smothered dissent. It is his congenial style which has enabled consensus building. Seeking consensus is the only forward path for implementing the daunting unfinished agenda of economic reforms.

Centre-state relations have come centre stage. This relationship has evolved significantly in two dimensions. First, the issue of inter-governmental fiscal relations and the second, the matrix of coordination on issues of governance. Managing internal insurgency, combining credible enforcement with development and weaning insurgents back into the mainstream of development pose complex challenges. This paper however, concentrates on economic issues and particularly intergovernmental fiscal issues. Intergovernmental fiscal relations constitute the most contentious issue of federal finances. The essence of federal system is that the Centre and the state governments should be independent in their respective spheres of action and each layer of the government should be provided with sources of raising adequate revenues to discharge the functions entrusted to it under the constitution with the ultimate objective of maximising the welfare of citizens. These arrangements should not only be stable but flexible enough to adapt to the changing economic realities. India is the largest and probably the most diverse democratic country with a federal form of government. The fiscal arrangements in India have evolved in accordance with the centralisation inherent in the constitutional arrangement. In the economic sphere, liberalisation and globalisation have necessitated greater fiscal decentralisation. On the political front, factors such as the end of single party rule, emergence of coalition of parties in power at the Centre and increasing importance of regional parties in the political affairs of the country have forced greater decentralisation. The 73rd and 74th Constitutional amendments to empower local governments is an important enabling factor in the evolution of a more decentralised federal structure in India. Nonetheless there are contradictions in view of foreclosing large resources of the Central sector by the Planning Commission and making them available to the states based on adherence to multiple conditionalities. There is therefore a centrifugal approach in the amendments mandating fiscal transfers. On the other hand the continuation of large number of centrally sponsored schemes (CSSs) from foreclosed resources of Central sector tend to accentuate the inherent centripetal bias.

In the past six decades that have gone by, both the polity and economy of India have undergone profound changes, posing new challenges for government at all levels. A number of new issues have come to the fore in the wake of economic reforms and there are developments outside the realm of economic reforms. There is now an increased role of states and local governments in managing the developmental programmes and to deliver most of the public services. The growing regional imbalances both interstate and intrastate are matters of serious concern and are counter to the objective of realising the goal of inclusive growth. The strategy consisting of area-specific programmes and the area-specific tax exemptions have so far failed to address the problems adequately. In this context it is pertinent to look at the evolution, challenges and possible reform areas concerning fiscal federalism in India.

Evolution of Fiscal Federalism in India

Evolution of fiscal federalism in India can be traced back to the Government of India Act, 1919. This Act secured for the provinces a greater degree of financial autonomy by abolishing the 'divided heads' of revenue effecting a complete separation between the Central and provincial heads. Under the 1919 Act, heads of specific revenue departments were assigned wholly to the provinces, while the Centre retained responsibility for the revenues administered by the remaining department heads. The framework set up in 1919 remained unaltered until the Government of India Act, 1935. Subsequent reviews of the financial situation kept the structure of Centre-state relations unchanged while altering their respective shares of centrally collected revenue. A principal objective of these endeavours was to equip the provincial governments with greater financial resources. It was not until the enactment of the Constitution in 1950 that a Finance Commission was appointed to overhaul the financial system of the Indian federation and make recommendations about the distribution of revenues between the Union and the states. The Constitution provides that the distribution between the Union and the states of the net proceeds of taxes that are to be divided between them and the allocation between states of the respective shares of such proceeds shall be done on the recommendations of a Finance Commission that is appointed every five years. The commission also recommends the principles that should govern grants-in-aid to the states. The grants are both a means to assist development schemes in states lacking adequate financial resources and an instrument to exercise control and coordination over the states' welfare schemes.

The framers of the Indian Constitution adopted in 1950 opted for a centralised quasi-federal system. This system worked well at a time when there was homogeneous single party governments in almost all the states and the Centre. However, the framers of the constitution could not have anticipated the subsequent emergence of heterogeneity in polity and the decline in institutions as well as changes in the economy that have eroded the rationale for unitary and quasi-federal features of the constitution. It is in this context that a fresh look at intergovernmental relations assumes crucial importance. Both procedures and institutions need restructuring to meet the new developmental challenges. The Constitutional scheme which by and large has stood the test of time may require an imaginative appraisal and appropriate interpretation to be able to support the realisation of the vision articulated in our Constitution.

Changing Contours of Fiscal Federalism in India

The Centre-state relations in India have always contained the seeds of conflict and distrust. Apart from the regular appointment of the constitutionally mandated Finance Commission every five years, the Government has also constituted several commissions in the past to deal with the issue of Centre-state relations. Prominent among the commissions appointed by the Government of India which examined the Centre-state financial relations are the First Administrative Reforms Commission (1966), Commission on Centre-State Relations or Sarkaria Commission (1983) which submitted its report in 1988, the National Commission to Review the Working of the Constitution (2000) and the M.M. Punchhi Commission (2007). Among these, the mandate of the Sarkaria Commission was specific to the task of comprehensively reviewing the whole gamut of Centre-state relations. The First Administrative Reforms Commission highlighted the need for a new balance between the national and state level requirements following the developments since Independence. In matters of finance and planning, the commission recommended greater role for states. A realignment in the roles of the Planning Commission and the Finance Commission with a greater role for the latter was recommended by the Commission. The First Administrative Reforms Commission also recommended setting up of an Inter-State Council (ISC) under Article 263 for resolution of conflicts between the Centre and the states. The Sarkaria Commission was the first national level commission to have comprehensively reviewed the Centre-state relations. The main issues considered by the commission in the area of financial relations broadly related to correspondence between the resources and responsibilities of states, autonomy of states in raising resources from their mineral wealth, shrinking of divisible pool of Central taxes following the levy of cesses and surcharges, enactment of Central Sales Tax in 1956, administered prices, impact of the pay revision by the Centre, lower exploitation of revenue potential of taxes under Articles 268 and 269, increasing Central transfers outside the purview of the Finance Commission and increasing expenditure of the Union government on the subjects listed in the State List. The National Commission to Review the Working of the Constitution (NCRWC) made a number of recommendations with regard to the Constitutional provisions having a bearing on financial matters. It recommended a specific enumeration of services that may become amenable to taxation by the states and advocated a Constitutional amendment to enable states to levy and collect certain taxes, now levied and collected by the Union for augmenting the resources of states. It also recommended the establishment of an authority called the 'Interstate Trade and Commerce Commission' under Article 307 to ensure removal of barriers to interstate trade and commerce. The Commission for Centre-State Relations headed by Justice M.M. Punchhi has recently submitted its report. The commission has recommended a comprehensive review of all transfers to states with a view to minimising the component of discretionary transfers, particularly those channelled through CSSs. It has also recommend higher Central transfers to backward states to enable them to improve their physical and human infrastructure. To bring greater accountability in fiscal legislations, the Commission has suggested an annual assessment by an independent body. Existing Central legislations where the states are entrusted with the responsibility of implementation have been recommended to be suitably amended providing for sharing of costs by the Central government. The Commission has recommended that maintenance of macroeconomic stability is the responsibility of the Union and that states should be properly compensated for any additional expenditure they bear or revenue loss they suffer on account of measures taken by the Union to maintain macroeconomic stability. It has also recommended that there should be much better coordination between the Finance Commission and the Planning Commission through synchronisation of the periods covered by the Finance Commission and the Five Year Plan.

Major Issues of Contemporary Relevance in Fiscal Federalism

Federal Constitutions everywhere are characterised by an imbalance between the functional responsibilities and the financial powers at different levels of government. The Indian Constitution, while expressly vesting the Centre with greater powers of taxation, also provides for an institutional mechanism—the Finance Commission—to determine the share of the states in the Central tax revenues by way of correcting this imbalance. In deciding on the devolution of taxes and the provision of grants, the Finance Commission is required to address the vertical imbalance (between the Centre and the states) as also the horizontal imbalance, the one between the states with varying fiscal capacities but similar responsibilities in the provision of public services. The Centre gets a little over 60 per cent of the total revenues. The states are thus left with less than 40 per cent of the revenue while their share in revenue expenditure averaged about 57 per cent. On the horizontal imbalance front, the most disadvantaged are the 11 small, mountainous states which are classified as 'special category' states with very little production activity or capacity to raise revenues from the sources assigned to them. But even the remaining 17 'general category' states have significant differences in size, revenue raising capacities, efforts, expenditure levels, and fiscal dependence. The Constitution recognises that the states' tax powers are inadequate to meet their expenditure needs and therefore provides for the sharing of Central tax revenues.

There is a clear vertical imbalance between: (1) the powers of taxation assigned to the Union and the states and (2) the social and economic responsibilities assigned to the states. That is, the states' responsibilities exceed their own-source revenues. This arrangement is intended to permit each layer of government to do what it is thought to do best; that is, it recognises that the Centre is perhaps in the best position to collect certain kinds of taxes and to expend and redistribute tax revenues for equitable purposes nationwide, while states and local governments are in the best position to manage developmental programmes and to deliver most services because they are closest to the people. Furthermore, the Finance Commission, the Planning Commission and the National Development Council provide mechanisms for periodically correcting this imbalance and for allowing the states to better discharge their responsibilities. As conceived, the Union and the states together form one organic whole for the purposes of utilising the resources. The Union is intended to play the role of equaliser between the greatly disparate states that constitute the Indian Union.

A notable feature of fiscal federalism in India is the existence of multiple channels for transferring funds. At present, about 40 per cent of Central revenues (tax and non-tax) is transferred to the states, and this includes the grants they get from the Planning Commission and the Central ministries. Although the sharable pool has been enlarged (thanks to the 80th Constitution Amendment) to include all Central taxes, the relative revenue accruals of the Centre and the states have not seen any major change. Presently the Finance Commission transfers constitute about 60 per cent and those by the Planning Commission constitute about 20 per cent of the devolution meant for the states from the sharable pool. In addition to the above two channels, various Central ministries give specific-purpose transfers to states with or without matching requirements. While the devolution of the Finance Commission are formulae-driven, there is an element of discretion in the devolutions of the Planning Commssion and the Central ministries.

The transfer system is beset with many problems. Multiple transfer channels sometimes work at cross purposes, creating serious problems of focussing the transfers on fiscally disadvantaged states. The methodology adopted by the Finance Commission transfers—that of filling the gaps between projected revenues and expenditures—has not only created serious disincentives, but also results in inequity. The system does not attempt significant equalisation, as projections of expenditures for poorer states are made from a low base. As the projected gaps are filled through transfers, disincentives are created for tax effort and expenditure economy. The distinction made between plan and non-plan transfers also has segmented the budget with adverse consequences on fiscal management. Furthermore, the proliferation of specific purpose transfers has led to inefficiency in expenditure management. These problems have significantly politicised the transfer system. The intergovernmental policies and institutions in India evolved in the context of a public sector dominated, heavy industry based industrialisation that was implicit in the planned development strategy. With economic liberalisation and the opening up of the economy, significant changes in fiscal federalism have become imperative. Given the increasingly globalised economy, the state governments are required to be efficient in their predominant role of providing social services and their equal role of providing physical infrastructure. In addition, the fiscal system has to deal with the issue of ensuring fiscal discipline at sub-national levels to arrest the deteriorating situation of higher state deficits and debt accumulation. The emergence of a coalition government at the Centre and the states has led to competitive populism, disregarding the fiscal consequences. These factors have all had an adverse impact on fiscal management.

There is no doubt that the present mechanism of Centre-state consultations have ceased to be meaningful. Inter-State Council has not served its original objectives. National Development Council has become a ceremonial body which is not presented with hard policy choices to be made and does not permit meaningful interaction. To create functional institutional entities is now a contextual necessity. The degree of fiscal bias in devolution of resources in one form or the other or selection in the location of Central investments, are not free from political predilections depending on the hue of the state governments and their friendliness with the coalition of the Central government. Important decisions by the Central government which impact the states fiscally rarely precede consultations with them. For instance fiscal concessions in tax policies, both direct and indirect, or various exemptions take away large corpus (as much as half of the collected revenues) of funds which would otherwise form part of the common divisible pool to be shared with the states.

The states have legitimate reasons to ask and worry, of at whose expense are these concessions being given since they are being denied what would otherwise be part of their share and with no prior consultations, much less consent. This is not to take away the Budget making powers of the Central government but with Centre and states as common stake-holders, a meaningful consultative mechanism between them is necessary. For instance, extension and deepening of implicit and explicit subsidies or preferring populist schemes in current fashion which have an impact on the fiscal health of states are also decided with no consultations. If states are expected to behave in a fiscally responsible way, is it fair that Central government's own policies should remain above any discussion or reproach? Why can't the states discuss the Central government's fiscal policies as much as those of the states themselves subjected to by the Centre?

The present structure of inherent biases, political predilection and differential criteria make the present structure of Centre-state relations an unequal one. The political appetite in coalition governments for constitutional changes may be low. Lot of things can be done within the existing framework and through administrative action to create new and a more meaningful mechanism for Centre and states dialogue. But who will take the lead? The present Central leadership given the other distractions may not show much urgency and inclination to consider, consult and act in concert with the states to seek a fair and rational redressal of the present embedded inequities. While reflection brings up several areas in need of reform, the most enduring point is that such reform is eminently possible.

The existing fiscal transfers system in India requires structural reforms concerning both its vertical and horizontal dimensions. These concerns primarily revolve around the following key questions:

First and foremost, the structure of financial devolution. While the recommendations of the constitutionally mandated Finance Commission have lent stability, the same cannot be said of other devolutions. The additional plan flows from the Centre are not statutorily defined and bilateral consultations between states and the Planning Commission are not devoid of quasi-political considerations. Looking at the somewhat opaque manner in which various ministries allocate funds to states, it is difficult in one place to collate all the funds which any state has received in a fiscal year and relate them to principles based on either equity or efficiency. The access to externally aided funds is a further complication, and despite differences in absorptive capacity or efficiency of utilisation, political preference or directional encouragement to lending agencies adds to the distortion. Looking at the transfer system, several improvements seem possible—not only governance and fairness, but also efficiency in integrating the myriad forms of transfers that exist today. Higher transparency and coordination would protect these funds from the winds of politics and improve utilisation.

Second, absence of well-functioning institutional mechanism. The National Development Council which meets occasionally to approve the Five Year Plans, its Mid-term Review or on special subjects and the Inter-State Council which was to play a central role in dispute resolution have not served their purpose. The bodies like Planning Commission, Finance Commission and the Boards of the Reserve Bank of India and other financial institutions have neither worked with effective representation of the states, nor have their decisions succeeded in providing a fair deal to the states. In fact, these bodies have functioned ceremonially and almost as an extension of the Union government.

Third, given the pace of change, on how to deal with recalcitrant states on issues which are in the domain of states but have national implications? Everyone knows there is lack of adequate reforms in power, education, health and agriculture, which lie in the purview of the states. If education or health system in a state continues to suffer, what recourse does the Central government have? This raises the larger issue of how to balance devolutions from being performance-driven rather than entitlement outcomes and the need to harmonise considerations of equity with efficiency when the two may lead in the opposite direction.

Fourth, several international treaties and trade agreement have serious implications for the states, especially with respect to state subjects like agriculture. International treaties and agreements on matters like climate change, various trade agreements under WTO and free trade agreements

(FTAs) with other countries and regions have direct bearing on the economy of states. In all such cases, consultation with the states and concurrence of the Inter-State Council must also be made mandatory.

Fifth, vertical imbalance remains the basic problem in Centre-state financial relations. While the major responsibilities in the sphere of development expenditure have been given to the states, the more important powers of revenue-raising have been given to the Centre. For instance, annual development expenditure borne by the states taken together is much more than of what is borne by the Centre. In contrast, the share of the states in total revenue receipts is only one-third, with almost two-third going to the Central government.

Sixth, is the issue of inadequate Central transfers. This mismatch between the greater responsibilities for undertaking development expenditure lying with the states on the one hand, with greater powers of revenue mobilisation lying with the Centre on the other, has not been met through commensurate resource transfers from the Centre to the states. In fact, the share of net Central transfer in terms of devolution of Central taxes and grants as a proportion of total revenue receipts of the Centre has declined over the years.

Seventh, restrictions on borrowing by states. The share of total market borrowing to which the states may be entitled is dictated by the Centre. The share of market borrowing of the states has now fallen sharply to around 15 per cent, with more than 85 per cent of the market borrowing being cornered by the Centre. Within the bounds of acceptable debt profile the states need greater flexibility for contracting debt. Of course, these are turbulent times and the overall debt profile as well as the Debt/GDP ratio need to be kept within the bound of prudence.

Eighth, the issue of tax concessions. The resource mobilisation effort continues to be severely constrained by myriad tax concessions by the Centre. The latest Budget documents show that revenues in excess of Rs 4 lakh crore were foregone on account of the various tax exemptions. These tax concessions, especially the ones on corporate taxes, not only cause enormous revenue losses, but also distort the patterns of investment and growth and aggravate regional imbalances.

Ninth, the proliferation of CSSs, whose design and implementation are totally determined by the Centre without adequate consultation with the state governments, is another serious problem. The excessively centralised and rigid formats of these schemes often make them ill-suited for the specific needs of the states. Since the state governments have to bear a part of the expenditure behind such schemes in most cases, they find it difficult to make proper allocation of their own resources keeping their own priorities in view. The increase in the number of CSS, though largely funded by the Central government, has implications for states in terms of higher expenditure commitments. There is cost sharing by states in a number of CSS. In respect of some CSS, there has been an increase in the share of the states in funding. For instance, under the Sarva Shiksha Abhiyan (SSA), there has been an increase in the matching contribution of states from 15 to 40 per cent. There are proposals now to increase the share further to 50 per cent. While the Centre's funding of SSA is financed through the proceeds of education cess, states have to finance their share through their normal budgetary resources.

Tenth, in a federal setup like India where regional variations in terms of per capita income, tax base and population are quite large, the equalisation component of Central transfers assumes greater significance. The equalisation component of transfers is quite important in federations like Canada where they have been mandated constitutionally since 1982 to ensure that sufficient resources are available to the provincial governments for providing comparable levels of public services at comparable levels of taxation. The Australian system of equalisation transfers is based on the criteria of cost differentials and equal efficiency in the provision of goods and services across provinces. The Australian equalisation differs from the Canadian equalisation due to the reference to efficiency and standard of services. In the Indian context, since different agencies dealing with transfers follow different approaches, without much coordination, a unified approach to transfers has not been developed. The net outcome of this segmentation has been that transfers have been far from equalising.

Eleventh, the fiscal capacities of the states as measured by the per capita income continue to vary widely even after six decades of federal financial devolution and economic planning. The disparity between the highest and the lowest is in the ratio of 4:1. As a consequence, there is an uneven provision of public services across different states, including 'merit goods' such as education and health services. This interstate inequality on account of differences in fiscal capacity is further compounded by two factors. The states with low income levels have a large population. It means they have to transfer huge additional resources if there has to be any impact at all. Further, some states have certain 'cost disabilities' because of the vastness of the area or other geographical and climatic factors. An explicit equalisation methodology is yet to be developed to tackle this systemic problem.

Finally, there are several other issues which are important for Centre-state relations. One of the areas where political predilections influence decision-making is the decision for undertaking large Central investments in public sector or projects in states. There is a tendency where a homogeneous government receives a larger proportion of Central investment. These include Central investment in CPSUs, railways, national highways, ports, airports, major irrigation projects, present scheme of the National Calamity Relief Fund, interstate competition over mineral resources and issue of revision of royalties on an ad-valorem basis etc. Principles of equity and efficiency should equally apply to these transfers. It is also important to involve the states in the policies of credit disbursement by the banks and financial institutions. In each of these issues, the interests of the Centre and states are involved, and it is necessary to ensure interstate balance in taking decisions.

Federal fiscal imbalances have become endemic during the last two decades and have assumed alarming proportions recently. For this state of affairs, the constitutional provisions can hardly be blamed. Broadly, the causes have to be sought in the working of the political institutions. There are shortcomings in the transfer system. For example, the 'gap-filling' approach adopted by the Finance Commission and the soft budget constraints have provided perverse incentives. The point, however, is that these deficiencies are capable of being corrected without any change in the Constitution. In this context there are few propositions those are implementable. First alter the mandate of finance commissions to allow it to consider issues and efficiency of public sector entities which can impact (and indeed have done so) finances at the Centre and state. Second, unify all devolutions by doing away with discretionary transfers and multiple

CSSs. Third, constitute a Fiscal Policy Review Council consisting of the Prime Minister, Finance Minister and the Chief Ministers as well as experts to examine fiscal issues from an overall macro viewpoint which will enable participative engagement of Centre and the states and also enable the states to question policies of the Central government. Fourth, there is wide ranging debate on the restructuring of the Planning Commission. There are several ideas in this context. Prof. T.N. Srinivasan has suggested to reconstitute the Planning Commission as a Fund with both the Centre and the states as its stakeholders which can borrow loanable funds like Development Bank to provide resources for long-term finance. This may not be very workable. It may be recalled that the colonial government of India had set up a Department of Planning and Development in 1944, and at its instance, the then Central and provincial government had put together a number of development schemes. Based on best international practices the Department of Planning and Development must become more functioning. The Planning Commssion could become a national think-tank and a body of experts which can generate alternative ideas, options in our overall Plan strategy. It could in this fashion become the advisory body to the Department of Planning and Development. One aspect must be kept in mind that the Planning Commission primarily works as a bridge between the Centre and states and therefore a more effective body than the ceremonial National Development Council (NDC) needs to be constituted for an overall restructuring of the institutional mechanism.

The last 60 years has seen fundamental changes both in our own economic strategy as well as the global configuration. Global interdependence in multiple ways in terms of access to information, technology, and capital have altered earlier concepts of sovereignty and sub-sovereign entities. Domestic political compulsions arising out of not only economic reforms but the heterogeneity of polity lend complexity in the decision-making process. The altered dynamics of Centre-state relations have not been reflected in processes and procedures which governs the matrix of this complex relationship. Postponing or not revisiting some of these fundamental issues will make Centre-state relations increasingly unworkable.

References

Bagchi, Amaresh and Pinaki Chakraborty (2003). *Towards a Rational System of Centre-State Revenue Transfers in India: An Exploration*. National Institute of Public Finance and Policy.

Fjeldstad, O.H. (2001). "Intergovernmental Fiscal Relations in Developing Countries: A Review of Issues", *CMI Working Paper*.

Fraschini, Angela (2006). "Fiscal Federalism in Big Developing Countries: China and India", *POLIS Working Paper* No. 66, January.

Gupta, Arnab, Ramkishen S. Rajan and Reza Y. Siregar (2004). *Fiscal Federalism in India: Exploring the Budgetary Implications of Political Alignment and Institutional Quality*. February.

Heller, Peter S. and M. Govinda Rao (2007). "A Sustainable Fiscal Policy For India: An International Perspective", *Reserve Bank of India Occasional Papers* 28(1).

Kincaid, John and George Alan Tarr (2005). *Constitutional Origins, Structure and Change in Federal Countries*. International Association of Centers for Federal Studies.

Kurian, N.J. (2008). "Equalising Transfers through the Finance Commission", *Economic and Political Weekly* 43(29), July 19–25.

Rajaraman, Indira (2004). "Fiscal Developments and Outlook in India", *NIPFP-IMF Conference Paper*, January.

Rao, M. Govind (2005). *Changing Contours in Fiscal Federalism in India*. National Institute of Public Finance and Policy.

Rao, M. Govinda and Nirvikar Singh (2004). *Asymmetric Federalism in India*. National Institute of Public Finance and Policy.

Rao, M. Govinda and Tapas K. Sen (2011). "Federalism and Fiscal Reform in India", *National Institute of Public Finance and Policy Working Paper* No. 84.

Shah, Anwar (1998). *Fiscal Federalism and Macroeconomic Governance: For Better or for Worse?*. World Bank.

Singh, Nirvikar (2007). "The Dynamics of Reform of India's Federal System", *MPRA Paper* No. 2282, March.

Singh, Nirvikar and Garima Vasishtha (2004). *Some Patterns in Center-State Fiscal Transfers in India: An Illustrative Analysis*. National Institute of Public Finance and Policy. September.

Singh, Nirvikar and T.N. Srinivasan (2006). "Federalism and Economic Development in India: An Assessment", *SCID Conference on Economic Reform in Asia*, May.

Sinha, Aseema (2004). "The Changing Political Economy of Federalism in India: A Historical Institutionalist Approach", *India Review* 3(1), January.

Wallack, Jessica and T.N. Srinivasan (2005). "Analysing Federalism: Stylised Models and the Political Economy Reality", in *Federalism and Economic Reform: International Perspectives*. Cambridge, UK.

4 Governance: History, Contemporary Debate and Practice

PARTHASARATHI SHOME

There are three aspects of governance that stand out categorically in the literature. First, it has not only been addressed but also written about and instructed upon exhaustively in ancient treatises by philosophers, scholars and administrators. Second, while there is a long list of probable definitions of governance that has appeared in the relevant literature over the years, an exact concept does not exist. Rather, there is an intuitive appeal with a certain degree of convergence on what it should represent though, even there, some have challenged emerging premises. Third, the matter of governance is among the most widely addressed in contemporary discussion and debate in domestic environments and multilateral forums, with countries revealing renewed interest and commensurate action in unilateral cross-border interventions to globally align the concept and practice of governance. This paper is a sweeping review of governance as an ever emerging concept with administrative and economic relevance, as a preoccupation with a considerable degree of historicity, and as a contemporary instrument with wide ranging domestic and cross-border political connotations.

A Commonly Understood Consideration of Governance

Deconstructing the Standard Definition of Governance

While various short editions of Webster's dictionary link governance directly with government,[1] in longer editions (Webster's II, 1984), it is described as 'the act, process, or power of governing: Government' and 'the

1. Collegiate editions between 1944-1996 equate governance with government, a single composite term.

state of being governed.' In contemporary discussion, however, the concept has been much elaborated, with an exhaustive list compiled by Weiss (2000) that includes definitions from the International Institute of Administrative Services, Institute of Governance Ottawa, OECD, Tokyo Institute of Technology, World Bank, UN Development Programme, UN Secretary General, and others. The upshot is clear, that governance has moved beyond government, and now stands to represent a much wider concept. Yet, while, therefore, there is now a good understanding of governance, conceptually it is not closed.

Such an emergent concept, reflecting various available claims and interpretations, needs to recognise, first, particular characteristics of government as necessary components of governance and, second, consciously include civil society as an actor in the conduct of governance. The OECD (1995) defines governance as the relationship between the ruler and the ruled that creates an environment in which economic agents can operate smoothly, and a system that manages resources, distributes benefits, and resolves conflict. The Commission on Global Governance (1995) refers to its overall objectives as respect for human rights and the rule of law, strengthening of democracy, promotion of transparency and capacity in public administration.[2] The World Bank (1994) posts three similar pillars: form of political regime, process of exercise of authority in management of resources, and capacity of governments to design, formulate and implement policies and discharge functions. The research community have emphasised how various interests, in particular civil society—that comprises community based institutions, unstructured groups and the media—are accorded a place and role in decision-making through interaction with government. As we review next, we will find that these cognitive aspects were generally known in the early tenets and practices of governance.

A Historical Sweep of Governance: Its Existence from Ancient Times

Astonishment and appreciation abound over the fact that, in the annals of ancient history, precepts of governance had been promulgated.

---

2. Attributed to Kofi Annan, then UN Secretary General.

Upon pondering the matter, however, this should not be too surprising. By definition, every time a war has been won, even after rapacious conquests, a government had to be formed by the victorious not only for the welfare of its own citizens but often inclusive of the conquered. Governance has also been perceived as essential to avert war. And covert governance has been espoused to prevent dissension from within. Such human traits, from times immemorial, helped establish and practise the craft of governance around the centrality of government. In the same manner, galactic generations of the future are likely to find it remarkable that primitive denizens of earth could steel themselves for governance for much of their epoch until they almost self-destructed before finally being assimilated into extra-terrestrial populations, thereby creating new races for new frontiers in a cycle of historical repetition of earth's own history (Spielberg, 1977).

Travelling back, Indian epics, the *Ramayana* and *Mahabharata*, that emerged in the 'evolved' Hindu tradition, are both replete with guidance for governance while, much later, Kautilya's *Arthashastra* written during the Maurya period, comprises direct instruction for how to govern. Further to the East, Lord Shang of China and, to the West, Plato of Ancient Greece, provided comparable treatises, *albeit* founded on different tenets of governance, reflecting the mores of society in which they lived and foresaw. Subsequent to Hinduism and Buddhism, 'declared' religions which were founded in rural societies, also stipulated rules and guidelines for living, for example, in the Bible, *Guru Granth Sahib*[3] and the *Quran*. In combination, they comprise a formidable set of insights into governance through the manner of living, interacting, administering, and dying in those societies of yore. A quick review of a select few should, therefore, be illuminating in the context of the evolution of governance.

The most utopian description of governance, as recounted in the *Ramayana*, is possibly *Ramrajya*, or the 'Rule of Ram', in which there were no lies since people did not know dishonesty and where the virtuous,

---

3. Gentle and compassionate shall be governance, instructs the scripture of the Sikh religion. Governance aspects in the Bible and *Quran* are more commonly known, though the political advancement of the Sikhs was also carefully charted with practices of governance under Guru Gobind Singh and consolidated later by Maharaja Ranjit Singh who ruled over most of Punjab that straddles present day India and Pakistan.

godlike king[4] represented his people through every aspect of kingship. It incorporates specifications by Rama regarding limbs of the state including the king, ministers, friends, treasure, territory, forts and army. Evils attendant on royalty include hunting, daytime siesta, lust, inebriation, pride and other diversions, details of war and fortifications, expedients including making peace, liberality, sowing dissension, and chastisement. Muniapan and Satpathy (2010) assert that the seven books in Valmiki's *Ramayana* contain multiple dimensions of life and governance including 'philosophy, spirituality, politics, economics, sociology, culture, literature, language, poetry, (and) technology.' (p.645)

Rama leaves for the forest and assigns Bharata,[5] his brother, to govern in his absence. Rama implores Bharata to take the responsibilities of the art and craft of governance. To cite a select set of issues:

- On fiscal prudence, income distribution and the vulnerable:

> O, Bharata! I hope you pursue wealth, religion and the delights of the senses, dividing them according to time. I hope your income is abundant and your expenditure, minimum... I hope you do not eat by yourself...and share it with your friends...I hope your treasure does not reach undeserving people. I hope you are regularly giving your army the daily provisions and suitable salary without any delay... I hope that you seek to conciliate by gifts, a loving mind and polite words, the aged, the children and the foremost physicians...I hope you are not honouring the materialistic *brahmanas*, my dear brother! Thinking themselves to be learned and reaching to their logical acumen, these men of perverted intellect preach meaninglessly...Are you cherishing all those who live by agriculture and cattle rearing, O, dear brother, ...providing them what they need and abstaining from what they fear? All the citizens are indeed to be protected by the king through his righteousness.

- On the cabinet and administration:

> The source of victory indeed comes from a concealed counsel by ministers who are well versed in political sciences and who hide their thoughts within themselves...I hope you are appointing ministers who are eminent, incorruptible,...of good family, full of integrity...I hope you do not

4. Rama is like Vishnu in bravery, godlike in benevolence and justice, attractive like the full moon, equals the earth in perseverance but is like the conflagration fire in his wrath.
5. Note that Bharata is also the address for ancient India.

deliberate alone nor indeed with numerous men...I hope the decision arrived at by you through such deliberation does not flow to the public (even before it is carried out). I hope that superior servants are assigned superior works only, mediocre servants in mediocre works and inferior servants in inferior works...the best is who accomplishes more than the duty entrusted, mediocre is he who never attempts to do more...even though he is capable, and the worst is he who does not carry out the order.

- On diplomacy:

I hope other kings know your entire undertakings only after they have been successfully completed...but not your proposed undertakings...I hope a knowledgeable man, wise (and) skilled endowed with presence of mind and who knows how to speak the point is selected as an ambassador by you. (Muniapan and Satpathy, 2010: 651-59).[6]

The popular understanding of the *Mahabharata*[7] is as an epic of sacrifice and war, of which the *Bhagwat Gita*, or the 'Song of God', in which He relates to Man the occasional justification, art and conduct of war, is the most universally familiar. However, as the longest known epic produced by humankind, it constitutes 18 *parvas* or books spanning major other facets of societal governance. For example, the *Rajdharma* or kingship/statehood focus of *Shantiparvam* relates to peace and is the counsel of Bhishma, sage and uncle to the Pandavas, the victors over their cousins, the Kauravas, at the Kurukshetra war. This part is a treatise for post-conflict government formation and its functioning, with details of the role and responsibilities of a dutiful king and the sphere of state activity, its contents spread over 130 chapters (Sharma, 2003).

The qualities of the king in *Mahabharata* should include intellect, renunciation, awareness of the enemies' weaknesses, capacity to be fair and just, ability to make quick decisions and, last but not least, good appearance (Basham, 1967). The king should follow the path of, and derived his authority from, *dharma* or righteousness at the cost of severe punishments in life and thereafter. The king should be powerful, though

6. However, one aspect of Rama's governance remains controversial, that of *Agnipariksha*, or test by fire, of Sita, his wife, to test her chastity, at the behest of his citizens. Sita, in her vicissitude, eventually is received back by Mother Earth who had gifted her to mankind. Hence the question remains, how far should the responsibility of a ruler extend to represent his people even to his own, or his family's detriment.

7. Or, the Greatness of India.

the course of royal life is to be determined and charted by priests reflecting their superiority of knowledge and reason over physical prowess. Statehood being the seed of stability, Bhishma advises that a king, who maintains social order, should be positioned in a nation prior to its citizens acquiring family or wealth.

In terms of economic progress, the king should encourage the development of commerce and industry, impose appropriate taxes within prescribed limits of income,[8] institute penalties for tax evasion, and ensure the welfare of his subjects. In carrying out his responsibilities, the king should be advised by a five-member council, with particular attributes and characteristics, while there should be a 37-member cabinet comprising different castes, commensurate with expertise and portfolios. The king should be vigilant and may have to engage in espionage to read the activities of enemies and to assess the moods of his subjects.

The king should be firm but, unless *Rajadharma* was practised genuinely, 'the *Mahabharata* explicitly sanctions revolt against a king who is oppressive or fails in his function of protection, saying that such a ruler is no king at all, and should be killed like a mad dog,' (Basham, 1967: 88-89 in Sharma, 2003). Anarchy should be prevented at any cost. Indeed, a kingless state might even invite an invading king to prevent it.

Kautilya's *Arthashastra* appeared in a later era. It emerged in the process of consolidation of small kingdoms in the vicinity of Magadha around 500 BC that linked the power of the state to governance, the central objective being internal peace, with economic wealth and military power assuming a central place. The essential elements of the Mahabharata's *Shantiparvam* are also found in the *Arthashastra*, with two crucial differences. First, the latter is not a work of political philosophy while the former could be perceived to be so (Niaz, 2008). Second, the latter does not sanction or recommend the removal of the king, leave alone in the forbidding manner suggested in the former, though the king is described in the latter as a servant of the state who should have no personal preference (Sharma, 2005).

8. Sharma (2008) describes in some detail the specification of a six percent income tax in Kalidasa's Abhignanshakuntalam, reputed to be Adiparva, or earlier epoch, of the Mahabharata. Tax revenue inculcates responsibility in the king and is to be used for the pursuance of the common good, that is, provision of basic amenities and security.

The *Arthashastra* ruler was the 'embodiment of the state', diligent, and a just and efficient administrator. He had to be vigilant, would conduct inspection tours, and rely on a secret service. Ruthlessness might be a necessary evil. The ruler should thus perform 14 hours of official work, most of which he would spend with advisers, civil servants, military officers and spies. Complementing efforts at the top, supervision of the state machinery required several hundred senior officials including councillors, governors, generals, department heads and chiefs of espionage. Supervisors cascaded down to villages in groups of 800, 400, 200, 10 and one. The remuneration of officers by category and level was fixed. The principal aim of the state was the accumulation of material strength in a prevailing environment of anarchy in the Indian subcontinent.

Kautilya emphasised economic and financial discipline. To quote Niaz (2008: 5-6):

> Although taxes on land were the largest source of revenue, the efficient operation of state-owned businesses, the promotion of domestic and international trade, anti-corruption measures, and strict accounting procedures, merited the sovereign's attention...the ruler and his servants had sound factual knowledge of the economic assets controlled by the state. They must also have the means to punish violations of taxation discipline with fines, confiscations and imprisonment. This discipline extended to a host of indirect taxes on leisure activities, such as liquor and gambling, as well as service charges for irrigation, transport and technical support. Royal monopolies over mines were particularly critical.
>
> Financial discipline was to be maintained through budgeting, accounting, auditing and espionage, with senior officers held personally liable for any major discrepancies. ...The ruler (should) reward upright financial administrators who increase the revenues without resorting to heavy-handed or arbitrary measures...A country can indefinitely sustain a moderate level of taxation. ...An overly high level of taxation destroys the basis of future productivity, deprives people of their subsistence and provokes rebellion, thereby making the state vulnerable to external pressure. (Thus) laxity in financial administration breeds chaos and disintegration of the country.

Kautilya's emphasis on internal management rather than on diplomacy revealed his apparent conviction that the existence of a state depended far more on its internal political dynamics and economic equilibrium rather than on foreign influences. The relevance of his writings carries on intact as the imperatives of economic and financial discipline and of political disequilibria reverberate across the globe today.

The need for firmness in statecraft is pervasive in historical texts. Lord Shang[9] who lived during the era of the Warring States when decentralisation to feudal heads was occurring, cautions in his *Book*, 'Benevolence and righteousness are not sufficient for governing the empire' while Plato, in *Laws*, indicates, 'For that state in which the law is subject and has no authority, I perceive to be on the way to ruin' (Spengler, 1969: 450). This is the basis for Spengler's contemporary hypothesis that,

> increasing political stimulation of man's wants beyond his capacity to supply them has generated forms of disorder. Wants generated by political means are bound to outstrip a community's economic capacity to satisfy such wants and hence must give rise to increasing frustration of man's expectations. This ascendance of political over economic want-generation, together with the disorder which comes in its wake, may be numbered among the progeny of the two Pelopennesian wars which sundered the world of European civilization and polity between 1914 and 1945 (Spengler, 1969: 451).

The observation resonates strongly in India's prevailing politico-economic environment, as if foreseen by Spengler while placing it in historical context. And, interestingly, while Kautilya wrote over a large, expansive and consolidating land empire, Plato's world reflected the concerns of small sea facing city states, and Sheng's comprised the preoccupations with unfolding federalism; these early thinkers from across the known world all found common solace in ultimately emphasising the need for, if not praising, the incipient importance of authority, severe if called for, the non-application of which would result in anarchy, possibly the ultimate sin that a society could commit. In this sense, they seemed to have come close to Webster's 'governance is government' concept view while attaching important responsibilities to the ruler though not providing conditions for his ouster unlike in the case of the *Mahabharata*.

In more recent times, perhaps the most well developed system of governance established by Indians was that by the Mughals. Their fiscal system was comprehensive, 'taxation being justified as the monarch's reward

9. Shang Yang (390 BC–338 BC) was an important statesman of the state of Qin during the Warring States period of Chinese history.

for the government and protection of his subjects' (Grapperhaus, 1998: 141). Land comprised the main tax base as well as import and export duties, and tributes from controlled states. There was *jizya*, a progressive income tax on non-Muslims with an exemption for minimum wagers. Akbar, the Great Mughal, was uncomfortable with religious segregation and abolished it. Aurangzeb, his great grandson reinstated it. *Mansabdars*, or rankholders were civil servants whose remuneration could take two forms, salary plus fringe benefits, or the allotment of a *jagir* or land area from which tax could be collected which was, however, shared with the monarch. The *jagir* system of compensation was, therefore, preferred by and large by the ruler. Here too, Grappelhaus confirms, '...the slightest weakness of the imperial authority could give cause for rebellions. ...order was therefore maintained, i.e. the taxes were collected with a rod of iron, with the assistance of the army' (p.138). Historical experience, therefore, confirms the supremacy of power in the practice of governance up until recent times.

Contemporary Domestic and Global Governance: Increasing Complexity

Keeping in mind the time machine of man and ideas, how has the debate over the governance precept progressed? It is remarkable how, since the Second World War, the dimensions of governance could be viewed to have undergone quite a sea change. In the modern era, domestic governance is no longer a matter of domestic interests or dictates alone but has become a matter of global concern. Weiss (2000) points to the appearance of a divergence in laying down the objectives of good governance in international policy debates and emergent, if ephemeral, views.

The most important divergence is perhaps that between the UN system on the one hand and the Washington Consensus (WC) comprising the World Bank, the IMF and region multilateral banks on the other. The UN could be said to have been more statist or normative than the WC's more positivist approach. The UN emphasised the need to incorporate the complexity that must be attached to the overarching concept of governance. Thus, empowerment to institute democracy and freedom become politico-civic dimensions of governance. By the early 1990s, there was a new course that was being charted to include legislative and judicial reform, corruption and human rights.

The Washington Consensus, by contrast, was more prone to consider such matters in the periphery of efficiency in resource allocation and economic growth, a premise that presumed automatic political conditionality irrespective of the individual environment. In fact, shrinking government was established as the stance of global governance from the Reagan-Thatcher era. That position changed when visible, vocal and virulent protests from civil society at WTO and Bank-Fund meetings at Seattle and Washington in 1999-2000 made it impossible for the meetings to function. It became transparent that a qualitative understanding of the environment in which societies function is crucial before prescribing and obliging them to adopt purely neo-classical rationalist policies. And, despite continuing differences, a baseline common UN-WC approach that good governance does not mean less, but quality, government, emerged. This has included electoral assistance, human rights advancement and attention to alleviation of corruption.

In particular, Kaufmann *et al.* (2003) of the World Bank developed a set of indicators for the perception of governance using several hundred individual variables, drawing from 25 different data sources constructed by 18 organisations. These are then used for cross-country comparisons. Authors Kaufmann, Kraay and Mastruzzi use, a statistical methodology, *albeit* with some caveats, across more than a 100 countries. They base their questions on:

- Voice and accountability.
- Political stability.
- Government effectiveness.
- Regulatory quality.
- Rule of law, and
- Control of corruption.

Reflecting the scale and importance of the exercise, the break-up of these questions is listed in Annexure A-4.1. The detailed nature of query in the construction of governance indicators is obvious. This endeavour has provided a new range of possibilities for comparisons of the quality of governance across countries. Thus, perceptions of governance become quantitatively comparable through this methodology.

The preoccupation with multiple facets of governance by every multilateral institution in the absence of a carefully synchronised division of responsibilities can, and do indeed, lead to unmanageable menus of tasks for each. Thus, while the UN-WC combine may be rightly perceived to be awareness in the right direction, it is the consistency of policies that matters rather than each institution having to address every aspect of governance in the programme formulation for member countries. For example, in propounding humane governance, Haq (1999) may have propounded the most comprehensive of all concepts of governance incorporating economic, political and civic aspects, though questions of realism persist as to whether such a premise is achievable without a long-term roadmap beyond the familiar ephemeral memories of functioning societies. This becomes obvious from a reading of how humane governance is conceived. To quote Weiss (2000: 805):

> Humane governance involves those structures and processes that support the creation of a participatory, responsive and accountable polity (that is, good political governance) embedded in a competitive, non-discriminatory, yet equitable economy (that is, good economic governance). That requires the resources contributed by people to be ploughed back to serve their own basic human needs, which will in turn expand the opportunities open to them; people must be given the ability to self-organise (that is, good civic governance). Bounded together by such principles as "ownership", "ecency", and "accountability", the components of humane governance are inextricably linked.

The issues become more incommodious in the context of global governance. The inter-connectedness of individual economies with the inexorable advent of globalisation through rapid progress in international trade, telecommunications and finance inarguably characterises a new industrial revolution. Under the growing burden of multitasking, the risk of getting submerged in multiple goals and objectives deepens. Today, the Group of Twenty (G-20) nations has witnessed an increase in its overall and, in particular, its development, agenda as reflected in the Framework for Strong, Sustainable, and Balanced Growth. This has resulted in a wide agenda comprising objectives, actions and outcomes for the Group as a whole (G-20, 2009; Hersh, 2010; Ahluwalia, 2011).[10] In turn, the process of resolution of issues is clearly taking longer than that desired in the prevailing crisis laden global economic and financial environment.

On the international political front, the onslaught of cross-border terrorism not only led countries to unilaterally introduce tax and non-tax legislation to combat money laundering that became identified as the closest financial link to terrorism, but there were active and successful attempts to multilateralise those actions (IMF, 2010 and 2011).

The impact of civil war from Africa—Rwanda, Sudan—to Europe—Yugoslavia—and the dissolution of the Soviet Union, in combination resulted in a complexity that the world had hitherto not experienced in their resource cost, or in the generation and influx of refugees. Even reformist economic movements such as in the extension of the European Union clearly led to cross-border challenges not only in the coordination of macroeconomic policies and eventually untenable cross-border subsidies but also in the regulation of free cross-border labour movements across heterogeneous economies including a horrendous rise in human trafficking (Salt, 2000; UN General Assembly, 1999). The world had quintessentially undergone a metamorphosis and the boundaries of governance had easily crossed national boundaries with global dimensions, in a growing list of concerns with transnational consequences.

Ramifications of the new developments are anticipated by authors such as Cerny (1995) to be the disablement of prevailing political frameworks from their ability to provide an already familiar range of public goods (Weiss, 2000). Thus, the growing complexity of international markets has made state based collective action for global public goods

10. The Framework for Strong, Sustainable, and Balanced Growth was launched in the Pittsburgh Summit. The launch of the Framework and also the Mutual Assessment Process (MAP) were mentioned in Points number 5 and 6 of the Leaders' Statement. To elaborate:

> 5) Framework for Strong, Sustainable, and Balanced Growth. To put in place this framework, we commit to develop a process whereby we set out our objectives, put forward policies to achieve these objectives, and together assess our progress; and
>
> 6) We call on our Finance Ministers and Central Bank Governors to launch the new Framework by November by initiating a cooperative process of mutual assessment of our policy frameworks and the implications of those frameworks for the pattern and sustainability of global growth. (G-20, 2009).

provision infeasible and unrealistic. This would certainly have been fully observed, if not experienced by states in the 2008-09 global financial crisis that turned into an economic crisis. Despite the awareness that it is only structural reform in global finance that can reverse the collapse of the global economy in the medium to long term, the introduction of financial regulation at the global level has been exceptionally challenging as revealed by the inability of the G-20 Frameworks Committee to shift away from broad macroeconomic indicators to focus instead on global financial indicators that would more successfully rein in runaway destabilising speculation in international financial markets (Shome, 2012a). This has to do directly with the relative powers behind the formation of ideas and their implementation that safeguard self-interest at the cost of global equilibrium and growth. Instead of ensuring the introduction and implementation of financial regulation, consideration of more distortive forms of tax and non-tax means of capital controls—such as financial transactions taxes and direct capital controls as used by Chile—are being considered (Shome, 2012b).[11]

G-20 is the most recent common platform to have emerged in the context of global governance. Its revival reflected the sudden global financial crisis in 2008-09 that witnessed deep financial turmoil with a global reach and contagion, leading to economic recession and negative economic growth in advanced economies. Exiting global recession requires systemic correction of international finance through exchange of information, and indicators to trigger unilateral and multilateral action that would help provide stability and minimise volatility in global financial and inter-related commodity markets. These have been reflected in

11. Chile introduced capital controls in the form of unremunerated reserve requirements (URRs) which was operative between early 1991 and late 1998. Initially borrowers were required to keep 20 per cent of any foreign borrowing in a one-year interest-free deposit with the central bank. In response to the changing external environment and to prevent attempts at evasion, there were changes in the proportion of inflows to be kept as URR, the class of inflows covered and the currency in which the deposits were to be kept. In late 1992, the proportion was increased to 30 per cent. In 1995, financial transactions involving less than $200,000 per person per annum became exempt from the reserve requirement. Decline in capital inflows following the East Asian crisis led to the relaxation of the regime. In mid-1998, the requirement fell from 30 per cent to 10 per cent and, later that year, it was abolished.

objectives (Shome and Rathinam, 2010: 103-04) expressed by emerging economies such as India:

- Rebalancing global governance by reforming global financial institutions.
- Reforming the global financial and monetary systems to provide better financial safety nets.
- Checking global macro-imbalances.
- Ensuring lines of credit and export finance to developing countries.
- Checking any protectionist measures and
- Widening the current agenda to include development issues.

It is the inclusion of the last objective that has expanded into nine pillars:

- Infrastructure.
- Human resource development.
- Trade.
- Private investment and job creation.
- Food security.
- Growth with resilience.
- Financial inclusion.
- Domestic resource mobilisation, and
- Knowledge sharing.

that have challenged the singular focus that is needed to address the most crucial faultlines that should be addressed for restoring stability in financial flows. The lesson is that, in the prevailing era, the widely accepted concerns of global governance appear to embrace so many aspects and issues that they compete with the central issues that demand singular attention for achieving systemic correction. The broadening of objectives assuages the developing countries that claim recognition of their long-term structural concerns as a group. However, it carries the danger, and perhaps the reality, of diluting the immediacy of instituting strong and meaningful global indicators that should automatically trigger tightening/loosening macroeconomic—financial and fiscal—policies that most advanced economies should be implementing now in future.

To conclude, clearly governance is much wider and more challenging than government. It is challenging enough in the context of a domestic state where governance can be imagined as an outer circle around the centre of an existing government. At the global level, such conceptualisation is necessarily more complex in the absence of a global government. Yet, global governance has taken shape and form in an expanding set of manifestations and actors. Good global governance has to function and progress around a non-existent global state, mainly through intergovernmental relationships. Further, not only are governments' participants but, increasingly, 'international NGO's, grassroots and citizens' movements, multinational corporations and the global capital market' (Weiss, 2000), have to be included as relevant actors as necessitated by their increasing visibility and role. This poses an extraordinary set of challenges that are chastening, making progress slow and, perhaps, somewhat understandable.

Microfoundations of Governance

Finally, it would be incomplete not to touch upon a use of the governance concept in economics that is based on its microfoundations. Weiss (2000) surveys this aspect in some detail. He recognises that Boas (1998) had pointed to this particular use of governance as a term in relation to the study of micro-behaviour of firms in the business economics literature. The leading exponents of the rich discourse from this aspect have been Dixit (2004), Williamson (2002, 2005), and some others. Williamson (2005), drawing from early economists like Adam Smith, Chester Irving Barnard, Friedrich Hayek, Kenneth J. Arrow and Gérard Debreu, explains that, at a micro level, governance relates to the 'study of good order and workable arrangements' (p.1).

Williamson (2005) elaborates that good order is not just spontaneous but also intentional. It is, in other words, not merely ensuring the flow of the market, but devising workable arrangements in the form of contracts and mechanisms to mitigate contractual hazards. Thus, 'as against simple market exchange, governance is predominantly concerned with *ongoing contractual relations for which continuity of the relationship is a source of value...* Maladaptation to disturbances is where the main costs of governance reside' (p.2). For example, in an early paper, Ratti and Shome (1977) showed how, in the presence of uncertainty, the usual rule for an auctioneer, that of searching for a set of relative prices at which excess demand in each market is zero, is no longer appropriate.

What is of interest is that in the industrial organisation literature, governance continues to form a microcosm of its overarching, commonly used concept. Thus, the broad governance rubric and the microeconomic use are not counter-positioned from each other. The latter is a manifestation of the former, in its attempt to suggest ways to preserve order and ensure contracts in an environment that is otherwise uncertain and could be lawless.

The four pillars on which this literature on the economics of governance rests are: governance, transactions costs, adaptation and interdisciplinary social science (Williamson, 2005: 3). Governance refers to 'working rules, problems of organization, and ways the organization of activity is stabilized.' (Commons, 1950: 21). Thus, 'governance is the means by which to infuse order, thereby to mitigate conflict and realize mutual gains' (Williamson, 2005: 3). Arrow (1969) recognises transactions costs as an obstruction to economic activity, a premise of possible market failure quite ignored in the neo-classical literature. This second pillar incorporates and neutralises the ramifications of such transactions costs (or externalities). Adaptation, the third pillar, refers to communication of information when the market mechanism does not work but has to be adapted through 'conscious, deliberate, purposeful' means that facilitates the process such as the use of administration (Barnard, 1938: 9). Finally, inter-disciplinary social science, the fourth pillar, emphasises economic organisation as more complex than economic theory would make one believe. Thus, 'the mission of neoclassical economics is to understand how the price system co-ordinates the use of resources, not the inner workings of real firms' (Demsetz, 1983: 377). For that, one needs to have a wider interdisciplinary approach.

In sum, at the industrial organisation oriented microeconomic firm level literature, governance expands the concern of determining order and minimising lawlessness beyond market determination, just as in the broader governance literature, the term incorporates many wider and deeper aspects than the term government.

Conclusion

Governance is a matter that exceeds government. Human history from across the globe has been concerned with matters of governance from times immemorial. 'Evolved' and 'declared' religions are quintessentially founded on matters of governance. A sweep of history reveals a central emphasis on authority and able decision-making, buttressed by a cabinet and intelligent fiscal system, a forceful army and use of espionage for the success of government and, surrounding it, a recognition of justice, fairness and equanimity towards farmers and the vulnerable. Strong punishment usually awaits a ruler and the ruling class if governance fails due to negligence or defeatism.

In modern times, governance has incorporated many aspects of egalitarianism. Multilateral institutions have become increasingly interested and policy-focussed on issues of domestic governance in a country context, though they have not always agreed or have a common platform on what comprises governance. The World Bank has gone beyond the single country premise and constructed an index of the perception of governance based on an elaborate quantitative exercise that could arguably be used for cross-country comparisons. The latest global governance concern has witnessed the re-emergence of the Group of 20 (G-20) from the ashes of the 2008-09 global financial and economic crisis. Competitive incorporation of objectives to respond to concerns of global governance, has challenged the G-20 to successfully arrive at the correct set of mutual assessment indicators and commensurate action to enable emergence from the crisis.

The overarching rubric of governance has been extended into firm level inquiry in an environment in which the smooth operation of markets has failed and price determination has eluded the equilibrium. Here, governance refers to the adaptability of the framework to go beyond the market auction system and generate equilibrium through administrative or other facilitative mechanisms. The search for global equilibrium by the G-20 could be viewed as a blow-up of this approach to achieving equilibrium in an environment of market failure.

References

Ahluwalia, Montek (2011). "The G20: A New Experiment in Global Governance", in *Festschrift in Honour of Prof. Lord Meghnad Desai.* London: Palgrave, Macmillan.

Arrow, Kenneth J. (1969). "The Organization of Economic Activity: Issues Pertinent to the Choice of Market versus Nonmarket Allocation", US Joint Economic Committee, 91st Congress, First Session, *The Analysis and Evaluation of Public Expenditure: The PPB System.* Vol.1. Washington D.C.: US Government Printing Office. pp.39-73.

Basham, A.L. (1967). *The Wonder that was India.* New Delhi: Rupa and Co. Reprinted in 1995.

Barnard, C. (1938). *The Functions of the Executive.* Cambridge, Massachusetts: Harvard University Press.

Boas, Morten (1998). "Governance as Multilateral Bank Policy; The Cases of the African Development Bank and the Asian Development Bank", *European Journal of Development Research* 10(2): 117-34.

Cerny, Philip G. (1995). "Globalization and the Changing Logic of Collective Action", *International Organization* 49(4): 595-625.

Commons, J. (1950). *The Economics of Collective Action.* Madison: University of Wisconsin Press.

Commission on Global Governance (1995). *Our Global Neighbourhood.* New York: Oxford University Press.

Demsetz, H. (1983). "The Structure of Ownership and the Theory of the Firm", *Journal of Law and Economics* 26(2): 375-90.

Dixit, Avinash (2004). "Lawlessness and Economics: Alternative Modes of Governance", *Gorman Lectures in Economics.* Princeton: University College, London, Princeton University Press.

G-20 (2009). "G-20 Leaders Statement: The Pittsburgh Summit". Available at *www.g20.utoronto.ca/2009/2009ccommuniqué0925.html*

Grapperhaus, Ferdinand H.M. (1998). "Taxation in the Empire of the Great Mughals", in *Tax Tales From the Second Millennium.* Amsterdam: International Bureau of Fiscal Documentation. pp.109-158.

Haq, Mahbub ul (1999). *Human Development in South Asia 1999: The Crisis of Governance.* Human Development Centre, Oxford: Oxford University Press.

Hersh, Adam (2010). "Monitoring Commitments and Compliance of the G20 Framework for Strong, Sustainable, and Balanced Growth", *New Rules for Global Finance.* January 13. Available at *www.new-rules.org*

IMF (2010). "Germany: Report on Observance of Standards and Codes—FATF Recommendations for Anti-Money Laundering and Combating the Financing of Terrorism", *IMF Country Report* No. 10/79. Washington, DC.

————. (2011). *Anti-Money Laundering and Combating the Financing of Terrorism (AML/CFT)—Report on the Review of the Effectiveness of the Program.* Prepared by the IMF's Legal Department, Washington, DC.

Kaufmann, Daniel, Aart Kraay and Massimo Mastruzzi (2003). "Governance Matters III: Governance Indicators for 1996-2002", Policy Research Working Paper, Washington D.C.: World Bank Institute, World Bank. June 30.

Muniapan, Balakrishnan and Biswajit Satpathy (2010). "The Relevance of *Valmiki Ramayan* in Developing Managerial Effectiveness", *International Journal of Indian Culture and Business Management* 3(6): 645-68.

Niaz, Ilhan (2008). "Kautilya's *Arthashastra* and Governance as an Element of State Power", *Strategic Studies* 28(2): 1-16. Islamabad: The Institute of Strategic Studies.

OECD (1995). *Participatory Development and Good Governance*. Paris.

Ratti, Ronald A. and Parthasarathi Shome (1977). "On a General Equilibrium Model of the Incidence of the Corporate Tax under Uncertainty", *Journal of Public Economics* 8: 233-38 (June).

Salt, J. (2000). "Trafficking and Human Smuggling: A European Perspective", *International Migration* 38(1): 31-54.

Sharma, Sanjeev Kumar (2003). "Good Governance in Ancient India: Remembering Kingship in *Shantiparvam* in *Mahabharat*", *Journal of Political Science and Public Administration* 6(1): 109-23. India.

____________ (2005). "Indian Idea of Good Governance: Revisiting Kautilya's Arthashastra", *Dynamics of Administration* 17(1-2): 8-19. India.

____________ (2008). Spheres of Public Governance in Ancient India: Reflections on *Abhignanshakuntalam* of Kalidasa", *Journal of Political Studies* 2(1): 6-16. India.

Shome, Parthasarathi (2012a). "Fiscal Stimuli and Consolidation", in Olivier J. Blanchard, David Romer, Michael Spence, and Joseph E. Stiglitz (eds.), *In the Wake of the Crisis: Leading Economists Reassess Economic Policy.* Cambridge, Massachusetts: International Monetary Fund, M.I.T Press.

————. (2012b). "Financial Transactions Taxes", in *Essays in Honour of Raja Chelliah.* New Delhi: Sage Publications. pp.11-36.

Shome, Parthasarathi and Francis Xavier Rathinam (2010). "India's Expectations from G-20", *Global Financial Stability: A Dialogue on Regulation and Cooperation.* Bonn: Federal Ministry for Economic Cooperation and Development. Shorter version at *http://www.voxeu.org/index.php?q=node/6127.*

Spengler, Joseph J. (1969). "Kautilya, Plato, Lord Sheng: Comparative Political Economy", *Proceedings of the American Philosophical Society* 113(6): 450-57.

Spielberg, Steven (1977). *Close Encounters of the Third Kind.* Hollywood, California.

UN General Assembly (1999). "Revised Draft Protocol against Smuggling in Migrants by Land, Air and Sea, Supplementing the United Nations Convention against Transnational Organized Crime", Article 2 [AC/254/4/Add. 1/Rev.3], UN General Assembly. 23 November.

Webster's II (1984). *New Riverside University Dictionary*. Boston: Houghton Mifflin Company.

Weiss, Thomas G. (2000). "Governance, Good Governance and Global Governance: Conceptual and Actual Challenges", *Third World Quarterly* 21(5): 795-814. Taylor & Francis, Ltd. October.

Williamson, Oliver E. (2002). "The Theory of the Firm as Governance Structure: From Choice to Contract", *Journal of Economic Perspectives* 16(3): 171-95.

————. (2005). "The Economics of Governance", *American Economic Review* 95(2): 1-18. Richard T. Ely Lecture at the American Economic Association.

World Bank (1994). *Governance, The World Bank's Experience.* Washington D.C.

Annexure A-4.1

State Capacity Survey (Developed and Developing Countries), 2000-2002

Voice and Accountability

- To what extent does the state and/or its allied groups engage in repression of its citizens?
- In carrying out internal security tasks, to what extent does the state rely on tactics commonly considered illegitimate in the international community?

Political Stability

- Assess the degree to which the decline or collapse of central political authority posed a threat to political stability in this country.
- Assess the degree to which political protest posed a threat to political stability in this country.
- Assess the degree to which ethno-cultural and/or religious conflict posed a threat to political stability in this country.
- Assess the degree to which external military intervention posed a threat to political stability in this country.

Government Effectiveness

- Rate the administrative and technical skills of the country's civil service (occupying middle and higher management roles).
- Rate the efficiency of the country's national bureaucracies overall.
- Rate the efficiency of the country's local-level government bureaucracies overall.
- Rate the effectiveness of coordination between the Central government and local-level government organisations.
- Rate the state's ability to formulate and implement national policy initiatives.
- Rate the state's effectiveness at collecting taxes or other forms of government revenue.
- Does the Central government produce budget in a timely manner?

contd...

...contd...

- Do local governments produce budgets in a timely manner?
- Rate the state's ability to monitor socioeconomic trends, activities, and conditions within its borders.
- Rate the state's ability to create, deliver, and maintain vital national infrastructure.
- Rate the state's ability to respond effectively to domestic economic problems.
- Rate the state's ability to respond effectively to natural disasters.

Regulatory Quality

NA

Rule of Law

- For the most part, is the state seen as legitimately representing its citizens?
- Rate the state's adherence to the rule of law, considering the country as a whole.

Control of Corruption

- Rate the severity of corruption with the state.
- To what extent do the country's primary political decision-makers engage in patterns of nepotism, cronyism and patronage?
- To what extent do the country's civil service (occupying middle and higher management roles) engage in patterns of nepotism, cronyism and patronage?
- To what extent do patterns of nepotism, cronyism and patronage undermine the state's ability to exercise the basic functions of government effectively?
- To what extent do patterns of nepotism, cronyism and patronage distort broad patterns of economic development?

Country coverage was 108 in 2000 and 98 in 2002.

Source: Kaufmann *et al.* (2003: 68).

5 Why for a Class of Bribes the Act of Giving a Bribe should be Treated as Legal

KAUSHIK BASU

Preamble

In selecting a paper for Montek Singh Ahluwalia's festschrift, I faced a quandary. I could try to write a paper in one of the many fields in which he has contributed through his writings and outstanding lectures. The risk was that it would be a shadow of what he did with such flair. I decided, instead, to present a paper that I wrote a few months ago, as a discussion paper, on a very different subject—the control of corruption. The paper had generated a huge amount of controversy with serious comments in *The Indian Express, The Telegraph, Le Monde, The Economist,*[1] and several other newspapers, web chat groups and television channels.[2] Given the surprising level of interest in the paper, I had been thinking of revising it at some future date with the intention of publishing it in some academic journal. When I heard of this festschrift for Montek Ahluwalia, I decided I would make the revisions now and present it to him. Though this is not a field of research with which one associates his name, it can be construed as a tribute to him for one important reason. During my term in government, I have come to believe that he has a level of tolerance for different kinds of ideas and opinions and a relish for intellectual argument and discourse, which is rare in government. So I decided that presenting him a paper,

1. Dreze (2011); Mitra (2011); Seabright (2011); The Economist (2011).
2. The reader may also like to see the comment by Narayana Murthy on this proposal for controlling corruption, as reported in *The Economic Times: http://economictimes.indiatimes.com/tech/software/infosys-chairman-narayana-murthy-backs-kaushik-basus-proposal-to-make-bribe-giving-legal/articleshow/9299479.cms*

from which many politicians would like to keep a safe distance, would be both a tribute and a nice test of the limits of his tolerance.

The Thesis and the Proof

This paper puts forward a new idea for the control of one kind of corruption, namely, bribery, in India. In describing this as 'new', I am aware that as a research idea it is sufficiently obvious not to be thought of as novel. It constitutes a standard exercise of backward-induction reasoning in two-period games. Yet, in the world of policymaking this kind of analysis is new—this became more evident by the angry reaction to the original version that I made available on the web—and I am convinced that this kind of 'law and economics' analysis needs to be used in conjunction with civil society activism, if we really want to control corruption and do so in ways that are morally acceptable.

Bribery is rampant in India. It is a scourge that deserves to be banished. Tackling this is a problem, that has to be a joint effort of all wings of the government and also of all political parties and even civil society. While it is not possible for a single person or even a single ministry to cure this malaise, one can think of small steps which, taken together, can add up to something substantial. It is in this spirit that this paper is being written. Though in the domain of policymaking in India the proposal in this paper is novel, related ideas, which rely on creating divergent incentives among partners in crime, have been discussed in the past by economists and academic lawyers (see, for instance, Schroth and Bostan, 2004; Spagnolo, 2006; Buccirossi and Spagnolo, 2006; Apesteguia *et al.*, 2011; Bigoni *et al.*, 2011; Rose-Ackerman, 2011).

What the paper puts forward is a small but fairly radical idea of how we can take one step towards cutting down the incidence of bribery. There are different kinds of bribes and what I am concerned with in this paper are bribes that people often have to give to get what they are legally entitled to. I shall call these 'harassment bribes'. Suppose an income tax refund is held back from a taxpayer till he pays some cash to the officer. Consider a case where to buy a regular train ticket you are told that you have to pay some money under the table. Suppose government allots subsidised land to a person but when the person goes to get her/his paperwork done and receive documents for this land, she/he is asked to pay a hefty bribe. Consider the case of an exporter who has fulfilled all formalities but is asked to make an illegal payment before getting a customs clearance. These are all illustrations of harassment bribes. Harassment bribery is widespread in India and it plays a large role in breeding inefficiency and has a corrosive effect on civil society.[3]

The central message of this paper is that we should declare the act of giving a bribe in all such cases as legitimate activity. In other words, the giver of a harassment bribe should have full immunity from any punitive action by the state.

It should be clarified that the act of bribery is still being considered illegal, and the total punishment meted out for bribery may still be the same. That is, if under the old system, the bribe giver and the bribe taker are fined Rs x each, what I am suggesting is that we fine the bribe taker 2x and the bribe giver 0. In other words, what is being argued is that this entire punishment should be heaped on the bribe taker and the bribe giver should not be penalised at all, at least not for the act of offering or giving the bribe. It is recommended that we in fact go further and say that, in the event of a case of bribery being established in the court of law, the bribe taker is required to give the bribe, to the extent that its size can be uncovered, back to the giver.

The main argument of this paper is that such a change in the law will cause a dramatic drop in the incidence of bribery. The reasoning is simple. Under the current law, discussed in some detail in the next section, once a bribe is given, the bribe giver and the bribe taker become partners in crime. It is in their joint interest to keep this fact hidden from the authorities and to be fugitives from the law, because, if caught, both expect to be punished. Under the kind of revised law that I am proposing here, once a bribe is given and the bribe giver collects whatever she/he is trying to acquire by giving the money, the interests of the bribe taker and bribe giver become completely orthogonal to each other. If the act is revealed, the bribe giver will go scot free and will be able to collect his bribe money back. The bribe

3. For surveys of bribery and corruption, especially in the context of developing countries and in particular India, see Bardhan (1997) and Dasgupta (2011).

taker, on the other hand, loses the booty of bribe and faces a hefty punishment.

Hence, in the post-bribe situation it is in the interest of the bribe giver to have the bribe taker caught. Since the bribe giver will cooperate with the law, the chances are much higher of the bribe taker getting caught and that way the bribe giver can get back the money she/he gave as bribe. Since the bribe taker knows this, he will be much less inclined to take the bribe in the first place. This establishes that there will be a drop in the incidence of bribery.

Indeed, under the new law, when a person gives a bribe, she/he will try to keep evidence of the act of bribery—a secret photo or jotting of the numbers on the currency notes handed over and so on—so that immediately after the bribery, she/he can turn informer and get the bribe taker caught. The upshot of this is not that the bribe taker will get caught but, more often, he will not take the bribe in the first place in anticipation of getting caught.[4]

Since the argument is being made here for harassment bribes, it can reasonably be expected that, if a change in the legislation is made in the manner suggested in this paper, there will be a sharp drop in the incidence of harassment bribery.

Institutional Details

In India, the main law concerning bribery is a 1988 legislation called the Prevention of Corruption Act, 1988. According to this law, bribe taking by a public servant and bribe giving are equally wrong and, in the event of conviction, both are punishable by anywhere between six months and five years' imprisonment and they shall also be liable to fines. For the most part, the act of giving and taking a bribe are treated on par under this law. As Section 12 states, 'Whoever abets any offence [pertaining to bribery],

4. This use of rationality calculus as in Becker (1968) may be questioned by some. I myself believe that trying to understand crime by assuming relentless self-interested behaviour on the part of all individuals is inappropriate. There are moral individuals and their existence makes a large difference to how behaviour in society at large plays out (see Guha and Guha, 2011). However, once one is analysing the behaviour of those who have chosen to be engaged in an act of corruption or bribery, it seems reasonable to analyse the outcome by utilising standard rationality calculus.

whether or not that offence is committed in consequence of the abetment, shall be punishable with imprisonment for a term which shall be not less than 6 months but which may extend up to five years and shall also be liable to fine.' It may be added here that the giving of a bribe is treated by lawyers as abetment to the crime of bribery, and so bribe giving is covered under this section.

There is, however, an exception to the bribe giving or abetment law in the form of Section 24 of the Prevention of Corruption Act, 1988. I reproduce this section in full here:

> Notwithstanding anything contained in any law for the time being in force, a statement made by a person in any proceeding against a public servant for an offence under sections 7 to 11 or under section 13 or section 15, that he offered or agreed to offer any gratification (other than legal remuneration) or any valuable thing to the public servant, shall not subject such person to a prosecution under section 12.

However, this section has a lot of ambiguity. In a case, three years ago, *Bhupinder Singh Patel vs. CBI*, 2008 (3) CCR 247 at p. 261 (Del): 2008 Cri LJ 4396, it was ruled that this exemption would apply only if the bribe giver could establish that the bribe was given unwillingly and in order to get the public servant trapped. But the word 'unwillingly' is itself so ambiguous that the use of this judgment as precedence is not easy either.

As a consequence, Section 24 is increasingly becoming a clause meant for those wanting to carry out a sting operation to trap a public servant in the act of bribe taking and seeking protection from the law. This was clear from a ruling of the Delhi High Court in *Bharadwaj Media Private Limited vs. State*, 2008 146 DLT 108 (Del): 2008 (1) CCR 11: 2008 (2) Crimes 244.

What this paper argues for is a much clearer statement concerning the legality of the bribe giver's action in the context of harassment bribes. In other words, this would amount to a revocation of Section 12 in the case of harassment bribes. In addition the law should say that once the fact of bribery is established in court, the amount of the bribe has to be returned to the person who gave the bribe.

One problem with the new law is the following. Once it is completely clear that a bribe giver has immunity from our bribery law, it is true that many more people will be willing to give bribes. However, since, every time a person gives a bribe, after that it will be in the interest of the bribe giver to expose this act of corruption (since by that not only will she/he not be punished but she/he will be getting back the money that she/he gave as a bribe) the bribe taker will not want to take the bribe. Since the crime of bribery cannot occur without both sides, the giver and the taker agreeing to undertake this act, the fact of greater desire on the part of the bribe giver to give a bribe under the new law will be of little consequence. This paper predicts that the end result will be a sharp decline in the incidence of bribery.

For the sake of clarity, let me emphasise what to the careful reader will be obvious anyway. It is not being argued here that the (harassment) bribe giver be pardoned in retrospect. A retrospective pardon is like an amnesty; and barring rare exceptions, amnesties are not worth it. They encourage corrupt behaviour by raising hopes of future pardon and corrodes society's morals.

What is being argued is that the law should be changed, so that, at the time of committing harassment bribery, both parties know that the giver has immunity and that the taker not only has a heftier penalty but also has to return the bribe. If we simply grant clemency to the bribe giver *after* the crime has been committed, none of the benefits being talked about here will be achieved.

One can today get a snapshot view of harassment bribery across the nation thanks to the innovative work by the not-for-profit organisation, Janaagraha, and its remarkable website, *ipaidabribe.com*. It illustrates well how citizens are often compelled to give a bribe; and by bringing such practices out of the closet, the idea is not to take away the guilt from such actions but the reverse, to discourage the very act of bribery. The legal change that this paper suggests will simply strengthen this kind of action, by strengthening the voice of the harassed bribe giver and increasing the penalty on the bribe taker.

The argument in this paper is founded in both strategic and moral precepts. The strategic element consists of breaking the bond between the bribe giver and the bribe taker in the post-bribe scenario.[5] This is

5. This amounts to creating incentives for the whistle blower (see Apesteguia *et al.*, 2011).

reminiscent of the old 'Sati' laws in India. In their eagerness to put an end to the practice, the British had declared illegal not only abetment but also the witnessing of 'Sati'. This was all fine, except that, when the charge of 'Sati' came up and the courts looked around for witnesses, they invariably did not find any. The only way to change this was to distinguish between the abettor and the innocent bystander.

The moral precept lies in the recognition that even if a particular action involving two parties is considered a crime, we must be prepared to distinguish between the victim and the perpetrator of the crime. In cases of dowry, for instance, not to distinguish between the taker and the giver, seems not only to be foolish (from the point of view of strategic economic theory, as argued above) because that makes both parties partners in crime and for that reason harder to uncover proof of the crime, but also morally unjustified. Surely, we must separate out the roles of the dowry giver and the dowry taker and not hold the former culpable. To me this is not just good economics but morally the right way to go.

Non-Harassment Bribes

I have confined the above analysis to harassment bribes.[6] The question that naturally arises is about other kinds of bribe, for instance, the kinds of bribery that are believed to occur when government gives out big development contracts. Should the bribe giver be given full immunity in such cases? The simple answer to this is a 'no'.

But what should be the optimal policy be in such cases? We need to give this much greater thought and subject it to formal law and economic analysis before we have an answer. The main problem arises from the fact that in such cases the bribe giver is likely to have got something by giving a bribe that she does not deserve to get. Hence, in the event of bribery being

6. Also, we ignore here the fact that in a society with widespread corruption there is the problem of 'bribe hierarchy', that is, the possibility that even after one gets caught taking a bribe one may be able to escape by bribing the very person or agency that caught you taking a bribe. This immediately opens up another layer of the same problem. What these 'towers of bribery' do to a society is discussed in Basu *et al.* (1992). In a fuller analysis of policy change, it is critical to pay attention to these towers of bribery and how we can strategise to break them down.

established in a law court, the issue remains about the bribe giver being in possession of an object that is not supposed to be in her/his possession.

A full answer to how the law should treat such cases will have to await further analysis. But I am inclined to believe that even in such bribery cases there ought to be an asymmetric treatment of the bribe taker and the giver. In particular, the punishment meted out to the bribe taker should be substantially greater than on the giver. This will mean that the collusive bond between the bribe taker and the giver will be weakened and the bribe giver will be more likely to cooperate with the judiciary in exposing the crime than under the current circumstances.

Further, it may well be argued that the public servant who takes the bribe is the gate keeper who violates his responsibility and sells off the property that she/he is supposed to protect. Since bribery is not a case of theft but of collaboration between two agents, the primary moral responsibility for the same rests on the shoulder of the bribe taker. Of course, if the bribe giver uses threats to induce the public servant to take a bribe that becomes a criminal act in itself.

Caveats

It is worth being clear that giving immunity to the bribe giver, even when this is restricted to harassment bribes, will not cause bribery to vanish altogether. This is because of the interests of the serial bribe giver, that is, a person who regularly meets with government officials and is asked or offers to pay a bribe or the agent who acts as go between in crimes of bribery. For such a bribe giver, reputation is a matter of great importance, as game theory emphasises and people with common sense know. In other words, a serial bribe giver, planning to aid the judiciary in trapping a bribe taker, will have to weigh the cost of his loss of credibility among the officials with whom he interacts repeatedly and give bribes against the gain of getting her/his bribe money back.

What is being argued here is that the legal amendments being suggested in this paper will not remove all incentives to bribery. But to the extent that it does create mistrust between the bribe giver and the taker in the post-bribery situation, it means that the comfort zone within which bribery occurs in today's world will cease to exist and the upshot will be a decline in the incidence of bribery. However, the fact that the changes in the law suggested in this paper will diminish the incidence of bribery should not lull us into the sense that there are no other actions needed to tackle this ubiquitous phenomenon. Among these is the effort to use e-technology to make procedures rule-based and to minimise the interface between ordinary citizens and the public servant. Fortunately, important steps along these lines have been initiated in recent times.

If we want to put a virtual end to bribery and corruption, what we really have to rely on are individual values and character traits. As I had argued in a paper many years ago (Basu, 1983), human ingenuity is so great that no matter how many plugs we put in to stop corruption, people will almost invariably find a way around it.[7] One of the most acute observations on this go back by two millennia—Kautilya's *Arthashastra* (p.281), where we find this wonderful but cynical observation: 'Just as it is impossible to know when a fish moving in water is drinking it, so it is impossible to find out when government servants in charge of undertakings misappropriate money.'

In the scheme I am suggesting, one problem that will open up is that public servants may be vulnerable to blackmail and false charges of bribe-taking. We could try to plug this loophole by increasing the punishment for blackmail and false accusation. What all this underlines is the fact that there is nothing fool-proof in economic policy design.

If we want to really get at corruption, what we need to build up are values of honesty and integrity in society. In the language of the *Arthashastra,* we have to wean fish off water. This has received so little attention and even to make such an argument sounds like moral claptrap because mainstream economics has taught us that human beings are endlessly self-seeking. In truth, they are not. Honesty, pro-social preferences and a sense of right and wrong constitute a part of the human

7. It may be pointed out here that the game theorist's ingenuity is also so remarkable that we can technically create models whereby we can create complex models of good compliant behaviour which do not rely on individual moral commitments. For a very skillful model of this see Myerson (2004). Importantly, Myerson manages to illustrate the powerful role of institutions in these kinds of situations. It shows, that trying to understand human behaviour without recognising the important role of institutions and collective beliefs, can easily lead us to erroneous conclusions.

psyche (Hauser, 2006), even though we can create societies where such traits are barely visible.

It is possible to go further and argue that we cannot have an efficient market economy unless human beings are endowed with a minimal amount of integrity and pro-sociality (Basu, 2011). Because of the propensity of economics to ignore these traits, these are under-researched areas. But if we want to substantially cut down the incidence of corruption, such as bribery, and want an efficient and vibrant economy, alongside getting our laws and economic policies right, we need to work on building up appropriate social and cultural traits, which provide the foundations for such an economy.

References

Apesteguia, Jose, Martin Dufwenberg and Reinhart Selten (2011). "Blowing the Whistle", *Economic Theory* 48(1).

Bardhan, Pranab (1997). "Corruption and Development: A Review of Issues", *Journal of Economic Literature* 112.

Basu, Kaushik (1983). "On Why We Do Not Try to Walk Off Without Paying After a Taxi Ride", *Economic and Political Weekly* 18 (November).

———. (2011). *Beyond the Invisible Hand: Groundwork for a New Economics.* Princeton: Princeton University Press and New Delhi: Penguin Books.

Basu, Kaushik, Sudipto Bhattacharya and Ajit Mishra (1992). "*Notes on Bribery and the Control of Corruption*", *Journal of Public Economics* 48.

Becker, Gary (1968). "Crime and Punishment", *Journal of Political Economy* 76.

Bigoni, Maria, Sven Olof Fridolfsson, Chloe Le Coq and Giancarlo Spagnolo (2011). "Trust, Salience and Deterrence: Evidence from an Antitrust Experiment". University of Bologna. (*mimeo*)

Buccirossi, Paolo and Giancarlo Spagnolo (2006). "Leniency Policies and Illegal Transactions", *Journal of Public Economics* 90: 1281-97.

Dasgupta, Arindam (2011). "Corruption", in K. Basu and A. Maertens (eds.), *New Oxford Companion to Economics in India.* New Delhi: Oxford University Press.

Dreze, Jean (2011). "The Bribing Game", *The Indian Express*, April 23.

Guha, Ashok and Brishti Guha (2011). "The Persistence of Goodness", *Journal of Institutional and Theoretical Economics* (forthcoming).

Hauser, Marc (2006). *Moral Minds: How Nature Designed Our Universal Sense of Right and Wrong.* New York: Harper Collins.

Kautilya (1992 edition). *Arthashastra.* Edited by L.N. Rangarajan. New Delhi: Penguin Books.

Mitra, Ashok (2011). "The Unquiet Grave", *The Telegraph*, April 22.

Myerson, Roger (2004). "Justice, Institutions and Multiple Equilibria", *Chicago Journal of International Law* 5.

Rose-Ackerman, Susan (2011). "The Law and Economics of Bribery and Corruption", *Annual Review of Law and Social Science* (forthcoming).

Schroth, Peter and Daniela Bostan (2004). "International Constitutional Law and Anti-Corruption Measures in the European Union's Accession Negotiations: Romania in Comparative Perspective", *American Journal of Comparative Law* 52.

Seabright, Paul (2011). "Should Corruption be Legalized?" (my translation from the French), *Le Monde*, 24 May.

Spagnolo, Giancarlo (2006). "Divide et Impera: Optimal Leniency Programmes", *Discussion Paper* No. 4840. London: Centre for Economic Policy Research.

The Economist (2011). "Novel Way to Combat Corruption: Who to Punish", *The Economist*, 5 May.

Acknowledgements and Disclaimer: I briefly spoke about the main idea behind this paper in my inaugural remarks at a conference organised by the National Institute of Public Finance and Policy in New Delhi on 15 March; and, subsequently, put it up as a working paper on the web. What is presented here is a marginally revised version of that paper. I am grateful for comments and criticisms received from Merijn Bosnan, Supriyo De, Sean Dougherty, Arun Duggal, K.P. Krishnan, H.A.C. Prasad, Ramesh Ramanathan, Ajay Shah, Shekhar Shah, Giancarlo Spagnolo, T.C.A. Srinivasa-Raghavan and Yang Yen Thaw. I am also grateful to Sayali Phatak and Jyoti Sagar for drawing my attention to some of the relevant legal literature. The ideas presented in this paper are personal and do not necessarily reflect the views of the Ministry of Finance, Government of India.

6 Does Kuznets Still Matter?

RAVI KANBUR

Introduction

I first met Montek Ahluwalia in Oxford in 1977. The impressions we had of each other were, I am sure, asymmetric. I was in awe of him. He was the youngest ever 'Division Chief' at the World Bank, the well known co-author of *Redistribution with Growth* (Chenery *et al.*, 1974), in many ways the intellectual foundation of the McNamara years at the World Bank. He had come to Oxford from the World Bank on a recruiting visit. I was a graduate student. But I was a graduate student with great interest in his work on income distribution.

I had just finished my B.Phil and had embarked on a D.Phil. My doctoral work was on the theory of risk taking and income distribution, but I had separately also started work with Sudhir Anand on the empirics of income distribution and development. In particular, Sudhir and I had started a careful, and critical, evaluation of the influential work of Montek and his colleagues at the World Bank (Ahluwalia, 1976 a, 1976 b and Ahluwalia *et al.*, 1979) which claimed to find evidence in favour of the famous Kuznets 'inverted-U' hypothesis, that inequality first increases and then declines with development.

Montek's work had refreshed and brought up to date the classic work of Simon Kuznets (1955), by formulating his hypothesis in the context of modern development theory, and testing it using cross-section data from developing as well as developed countries. The Anand-Kanbur critique questioned the empirical foundations of the Ahluwalia findings (Anand and Kanbur, 1984, 1993a and 1993b). We argued that if appropriate econometric techniques were used, no 'inverse-U' was found in the cross-section data that formed the basis of the Ahluwalia *et al.* work. And if there was no 'inverse-U', the policy conclusions that might flow from it would not stand up either.

As a 'young turk' development economist, I revelled in the critique we had advanced. It helped make my career. But now, 35 years after Ahluwalia and more than half a century after Kuznets, I am less sure. I am not of course saying that our technical critique was not valid—in its own terms it was a perfectly legitimate econometric assessment of that body of World Bank based research. But it was a cross-section critique of a cross-section finding. The validity of the critique is quite consistent, of course, with the hypothesis being valid as a time series proposition. The increase of inequality during the spurt of high growth in many developing countries over the past quarter century is the key factor that has given me pause for thought. Maybe Kuznets still matters, after all.

But in my view Kuznets still matters, also because of the Kuznets (1955) paper itself. The paper is little read these days, but I think scholars of inequality and development would benefit greatly from reading it carefully. As I will argue, the paper contains within it not only the famous 'inverse-U', but a whole range of arguments and intuitions about the evolution of income distribution during the course of development. Many of these have been rediscovered, and many remain to be developed by modern day analysts. One of the objectives of my contribution to Montek's Festschrift is to bring the many dimensions of the Kuznets (1955) paper to a current readership.

The outline of the paper is as follows. Section II revisits Kuznets (1955) and shows that the paper is truly a classic—it set out the issues very clearly, and anticipated developments in the literature decades before they happened. Section III takes up the story of the Ahluwalia and post-Ahluwalia literature, which left us, I think, uncertain about the empirical support for the inverse-U. Section IV comes up to date with assessment of the evolution of inequality in fast growing countries over the past two decades, and it argues that the time series experience provides support for the processes of distributional change hypothesised by Kuznets. Section V concludes.

Kuznets in the Original

Very few people these days actually read the original Kuznets (1955) paper. It is a magisterial *tour de force,* comparable to and in many ways related to Lewis (1954), another Nobel Prize winning paper. He starts with a clear statement of the problem:

> The central theme of this paper is the character and causes of long term changes in the personal distribution of income. Does inequality in the distribution of income increase or decrease in the course of a country's economic growth? What factors determine the secular level and trends of income inequalities? (Kuznets, 1955: 1).

Showing himself to be the careful empirical economist he was, Kuznets sets out the data requirements for answering these questions:

> First, the units for which incomes are recorded and grouped should be family-expenditure units, properly adjusted for the number of persons in each—rather than income recipients for whom the relations between receipt and use of income can be widely diverse. Second, the distribution should be complete, *i.e.,* should cover all units in a country rather than a segment either at the upper or lower tail. Third, if possible we should segregate the units whose main income earners are either still in the earning or already in the retired stages of their life cycle—to avoid complicating the picture by including incomes not associated with full-time, full-fledged participation in economic activity. Fourth, income should be defined as it is now for national income in this country, *i.e.,* received by individuals, including income in kind, before and after direct taxes, excluding capital gains. Fifth, the units should be grouped by *secular* levels of income, free of cyclical and other transient disturbances... Furthermore, if one may add a final touch to what is beginning to look like a statistical economist's pipe dream, we should be able to trace secular income levels not only through a single generation but at least through two—connecting the incomes of a given generation with those of its immediate descendants (Kuznets, 1955: 1-2).

He then comes to the observed trends, in other words, he looks to time series data to trace the evolution of inequality over the course of development:

> Forewarned of the difficulties, we turn now to the available data. ...[T]he trends in the income structure can be discerned but dimly, and the results considered as preliminary informed guesses... In the United States, in the distribution of income among families (excluding single individuals), the

> shares of the two lowest quintiles rise from 13 per cent in 1929 to 18 per cent in the years after the second world war (average of 1944, 1946, 1947, and 1950); whereas the share of the top quintile declines from 55 to 44 per cent, and that of the top 5 per cent from 31 to 20 per cent. In the United Kingdom, the share of the top 5 per cent of units declines from 46 per cent in 1880 to 43 per cent in 1910 or 1913, to 33 per cent in 1929, to 31 per cent in 1938, and to 24 per cent in 1947; the share of the lower 85 per cent remains fairly constant between 1880 and 1913, between 41 and 43 per cent, but then rises to 46 per cent in 1929 and 55 per cent in 1947. In Prussia income inequality increases slightly between 1875 and 1913-the shares of the top quintile rising from 48 to 50 per cent, of the top 5 per cent from 26 to 30 per cent; the share of the lower 60 per cent, however, remains about the same. In Saxony, the change between 1880 and 1913 is minor: the share of the two lowest quintiles declines from 15 to 14 per cent; that of the third quintile rises from 12 to 13 per cent, of the fourth quintile from 16 per cent to about 18 per cent; that of the top quintile declines from 56 per cent to 54 per cent, and of the top 5 per cent from 34 to 33 per cent. In Germany as a whole, relative income inequality drops fairly sharply from 1913 to the 1920's, apparently due to decimation of large fortunes and property incomes during the war and inflation; but then begins to return to prewar levels during the depression of the 1930's.... Even for what they are assumed to represent, let alone as approximations to shares in distributions by secular income levels, the data are such that differences of two or three percentage points cannot be assigned significance. One must judge by the general weight and consensus of the evidence—which unfortunately is limited to a few countries. It justifies a tentative impression of constancy in the relative distribution of income before taxes, followed by some narrowing of relative income inequality after the first world war—or earlier (Kuznets, 1955: 4-5).

I have quoted extensively from Kuznets (1955), and will continue to do so in this section and in this paper, because I would like to give readers a sense of the care and circumspection with which Kuznets made his claims. Since few scholars now read the original paper, they also miss the fact that many of the issues we grapple with in the modern literature were in fact raised in the original paper:

> Three aspects of this finding should be stressed. First, the data are for income before direct taxes and exclude contributions by government (e.g., relief and free assistance)...[T]he distribution of income after direct taxes and including free contributions by government would show an even greater narrowing of inequality in developed countries... Second, such

> stability or reduction in the inequality of the percentage shares was accompanied by significant rises in real income per capita...a reduction in inequality of the shares means that the per capita income of the lower-income groups is rising at a more rapid rate than the per capita income of the upper-income groups. The third point can be put in the form of a question. Do the distributions by annual incomes properly reflect trends in distribution by secular incomes? ... [D]istributions by longer-term average incomes might show less reduction in inequality than do the distributions by annual incomes; they might even show an opposite trend (Kuznets, 1955: 5-6).

Thus, Kuznets (1955) introduced the 'modern' questions of: (i) inequality of pre-tax *versus* post-tax income, (ii) inequality *versus* poverty when there is significant growth in mean income and (iii) the implications of volatility for measured inequality.

Moving to the second of his two overarching questions, the causes of inequality trends, Kuznets has a highly sophisticated and detailed discussion of a range of explanations that will repay close reading. The explanation which has become best known to development economists is what Anand and Kanbur (1993a) call the 'Kuznets process', a well defined process of distributional shift as population moves from agricultural (rural, traditional) to non-agricultural (urban, modern) sectors during the course of development. Kuznets' paper was in fact his Presidential Address to the American Economic Association in 1954, and in the same year Arthur Lewis (1954) published his celebrated paper on dualistic development which presented the logic of such population shifts. Kuznets (1955) translated this to the distributional realm, providing a numerical illustration to make his basic point:

> The numerical illustration is only a partial summary of the calculations, showing the shares of the lowest and highest quintiles in the income distribution for the total population under different assumptions. The basic assumptions used throughout are that the per capita income of sector B (nonagricultural) is always higher than that of sector A; that the proportion of sector A in the total number declines; and that the inequality of the income distribution within sector A may be as wide as that within sector B but not wider. With the assumptions concerning three sets of factors—intersector differences in per capita income, intrasector distributions, and sector weights—varying within the limitations just indicated, the following conclusions are suggested: ... [E]ven if the differential in per capita income between the two sectors remains constant

> and the intrasector distributions are identical for the two sectors, the mere shift in the proportions of numbers produces slight but significant changes in the distribution for the country as a whole. In general, as the proportion of A drifts from 0.8 downwards, the range tends first to widen and then to diminish (Kuznets, 1955: 12-15).

So there it is—the famous Kuznets inverted-U: 'the range tends to first widen and then to diminish.' Though much has been done to formalise the process, the assumptions and the conclusions through specific models (for example, Anand and Kanbur, 1993a), it is worth seeing the hypothesis at the creation, so to speak.

Although we must now stop this exploration of the Kuznets' paper, he does not stop here. In the second half of the paper, there is a rich discussion of the limited data for developing countries and its implications for the development discourse. Truly, this classic paper is worth revisiting!

U or not U?

Two decades after the Kuznets (1955) paper, Ahluwalia (1976b) launched a furious debate about the applicability of the 'inverse-U hypothesis' to developing countries. There were, of course, other papers, (for example, Adelman and Morris, 1973; Paukert, 1973; Robinson, 1976), but it is Ahluwalia (1976b) which stands as the originator of the modern literature on inequality and development. Here is how he saw his task:

> The relationship between the distribution of income and the process of development is one of the oldest subjects of economic enquiry... The purpose of this paper is to explore the nature of this relationship on the basis of cross country data on income inequality. The use of cross country data for the analysis of what are essentially dynamic processes raises a number of familiar problems. Ideally, such processes should be examined in an explicitly historical context for particular countries. Unfortunately, time series data on the distribution of income, over any substantial period, are simply not available for most developing countries. For the present, therefore, empirical investigation in this field must perforce draw heavily on cross country experience (Ahluwalia, 1976b: 307).

The central and striking estimation in Ahluwalia (1976b) was that of a log-quadratic relationship between inequality and per capita income in the cross-section of countries. Here is how the main conclusions are summarised at the end of the paper:

> (i) There is strong support for the proposition that relative inequality increases substantially in the early stages of development, with a reversal of this tendency in the later stages... (ii) There are a number of processes occurring *pari passu* with development which are correlated with income inequality and which can plausibly be interpreted as causal. These are intersectoral shifts in the structure of production, expansion in educational attainment and skill level of the labour force, and reduction in the rate of growth of population... (iii) The cross section results do not support the stronger hypothesis that the deterioration in relative inequality reflects a prolonged absolute impoverishment of large sections of the population in the course of development... (iv) Finally, the cross section results do not support the view that a faster rate of growth is systematically associated with higher inequality than can be expected given the stage of development achieved (p.338).

It was the first finding which was central to the subsequent literature, and helped to structure the debates of the coming decades, right up to the present. Hedged though it was by a multitude of caveats in the paper itself, the Ahluwalia (1976b) findings provided a hard target for critiques, much as they provided an anchor for subsequent policy discourse. This is such a huge literature that it is simply not possible to summarise it. Suffice it to say that in my view the consensus is that the Kuznets inverse-U cannot be found in cross-section data. Anand and Kanbur (1993b) conducted a thorough analysis based on the Ahluwalia (1976b) data set itself:

> The object of this paper has been to undertake a critical appraisal of the empirical literature on inequality and development, and particularly the influential examples of it due to Ahluwalia (1976b) and Ahluwalia et al. (1979). Their results are central to this literature, since they have served to confirm the Kuznets U-hypothesis and have been used as the basis of projections of inequality and poverty (including by the World Bank). We have tested for the robustness of Ahluwalia's estimates with respect to variations in functional form and data set, and find them to be lacking. A rigorous statistical methodology is used for testing non-nested functional forms against one another, and it is found that alternative forms which are equally well supported by the data imply very different shapes for the inequality-development relationship... We have indicated the deficiencies of the data used in this literature and constructed a minimally consistent data set from the original sample of 60 countries. Estimates of the inequality-development relationship for this data set are striking. Not only do the data reject the log-quadratic form in favour of a straight quadratic form, but the preferred form displays a *reversal* of the commonly accepted U-hypothesis (Anand and Kanbur, 1993b: 41-42).

In the late 1990s a new data set by Deininger and Squire (1998) set off another frenzy of duelling estimations. Although by this time some observations made over time were becoming available, it is perhaps fair to say that the nature of the exercise still remained cross-sectional in nature. In my view it is equally fair to say that the broad consensus is one of lack of empirical support for the inverse-U relationship between inequality and development—this is the view taken, for example, by Fields (2001), in his survey of the literature up to turn of the millennium (see also Piketty, 2006).

What is the relevance of the existence or otherwise of an inverse-U in a cross-section of countries? The answer, surely, has to be 'not very much in and of itself.' It can only be significant as an indication of a time series phenomenon, which in turn highlights fundamental underlying development processes. Of course, Ahluwalia (1976b) is well aware of this:

> The results presented above therefore should not be viewed as definitive either in defining the prospects facing particular developing countries or in providing unambiguous policy guidelines. They are best viewed as a useful documentation of empirical regularities—the so-called "stylised facts" of cross country experience. More ambitiously, they can also be viewed as providing some clues to the mechanisms through which the development process affects the degree of inequality. They can be no more than clues precisely because the essential complexity of a dynamic process, and its great variety across countries, cannot be adequately captured in a single equation. (Ahluwalia, 1976b: 338)

Of course, despite these caveats, the reason why the Ahluwalia (1976b) findings took on such significance in the debates was precisely because they were interpreted as intertemporal causal relationships (for example, they were used as the basis for projections by Ahluwalia, Carter and Chenery (1979). In fact, two interesting lines of argument emerged. One said that since there was a 'natural tendency' for inequality to increase in the early stages of development, it was appropriate for policy interventions to mitigate the negative consequences of this increase. Another said that since inequality would eventually turn down, it might be worth waiting out the initial increase, and not use measures to hold back the initial inequality increase. This was especially true if these measures led to a decrease in the growth rate, which would only postpone the turning point of the inverse-U. This second strand of argument was strengthened by the third of Ahluwalia's findings, also present in the Kuznets (1955) simulations, that despite inequality increase, the absolute incomes of the poor did increase because of the effects of growth.

Both of thc above arguments rely on the inverse-U being a 'law'. We now know that the initial confidence placed in an inverse-U in cross-section data was misplaced. But what about country-specific time series evidence and its policy interpretation? We now turn to that topic.

Kuznets in the New Millennium

It is worth recalling that the central empirical information deployed by Kuznets (1955) in his classic paper was time series information on the United States, United Kingdom and Germany. Even for these, he only picked up a declining trend, not an inverse-U. The increasing portion of the inverse-U was hypothesized on the basis of theory and simulations. His paper did have a whole section devoted to developing countries, but he only had a single snapshot for three countries—India for 1949-50, Ceylon in 1950 and Puerto Rico in 1948. He confined himself to level comparisons between developed and developing countries, extrapolating every now and then to draw conclusions on how inequality in developing countries might evolve:

> Is the pattern of the older developed countries likely to be repeated in the sense that in the early phases of industrialization in the underdeveloped countries income inequalities will tend to widen before the leveling forces become strong enough first to stabilize and then reduce income inequalities? While the future cannot be an exact repetition of the past....if and when industrialization begins, the dislocating effects on these societies, in which there is often an old hardened crust of economic and social institutions, are likely to be quite sharp-so sharp as to destroy the positions of some of the lower groups more rapidly than opportunities elsewhere in the economy may be created for them (Kuznets, 1955: .24-25).

For me, it is the last part of the above paragraph which is key. If indeed there is a 'natural tendency', it must surely be one where the disruptive forces of growth create inequalities as they create new opportunities which are more easily accessed by those who have the capacity to do it in terms of physical, human or social capital. Arthur Lewis (1976) makes a similar point:

> Development must be inegalitarian because it does not start in every part of the economy at the same time...there may be one such enclave in an economy, or several; but at the start development enclaves include only a small minority of the population (Lewis, 1976: 26).

However, perhaps this is too strong a position. Initially inegalitarian development may happen sometimes or even a large number of times, but it must surely depend on the initial conditions, and the conclusion cannot be independent of policy. If policy can make the process less disruptive, and perhaps redistribute after the event to mitigate the effects of greater inequality, then there is no necessary reason for inequality to increase. Ahluwalia (1976b) makes the following perceptive observation:

> But if we cannot deny that certain types of high growth processes lead to greater inequality than can be structurally expected, we can at least assert that the cross section evidence does not suggest that *all fast growers* systematically display this pattern. If there are countries in which this is true, there are others which display the opposite pattern, so that no systematic pattern emerges across countries. Such time series evidence as is available tends to support this point of view. The experience of Brazil, where the high growth was accompanied by worsening relative inequality, can be contrasted with the experience of Taiwan, where substantial growth has taken place with an actual reduction in income inequality... Recognising this diversity of country experience is perhaps the most important lesson to be learned from the data. At the very least, it shifts attention from an unquestioning suspicion of high growth rates as such towards an examination of the particular nature of growth in different countries and the implications of different types of growth for inequality. A systematic investigation along these lines can only be conducted in the context of an in-depth analysis of the historical experience of particular countries (Ahluwalia, 1976b: 337).

What then, does the recent experience of developing countries tell us? I have addressed this question in Kanbur (2010). The basic stylised facts of the past quarter century can be summarised as follows. Where there has been no growth, there has been no poverty reduction. However, the tendency for increasing inequality in growing economies has been present, unless actively counteracted by policy. The increasing inequality has been seen for example in India (Deaton and Dreze, 2002), in China (Kanbur and Zhang, 2005), in South Africa (Bhorat and Kanbur, 2006), in Ghana (Aryeetey and McKay, 2007), in Bangladesh (Deb *et al.*, 2008), and in Latin

America before 2000 (see Birdsall and Szekely, 2003 for Chile and Mexico). The causes of this increasing inequality are being debated, but the opening up of opportunities as a result of globalisation, which only a few can access initially, has been stressed by some contributors. For example, the surging ahead of regions close to markets, and regions with good infrastructure in place, has been identified as a major cause of rising spatial inequality within countries (Kanbur and Venables, 2007).

The Latin American case is very interesting, because there has been a turnaround in the trend of rising inequality. This has been documented by Lustig *et al.* (2011):

> Between 2000 and 2009, the Gini coefficient declined in 13 of 17 Latin American countries for which comparable data exist. The decline was statistically significant and robust to changes in the time interval, inequality measures and data sources. In depth country studies for Argentina, Brazil, Mexico and Peru suggest that there are two phenomena which underlie this trend: (i) a fall in the premium to skilled labor (as measured by returns to education); and (ii) higher and more progressive government transfers. The fall in the premium to skills results from a combination of supply and demand factors and, in Argentina—and to a lesser extent in Brazil—, from more active labor market policies as well (Lustig *et al.*, 2011: 1).

This phenomenon and the explanations are of great interest because they highlight the key importance of policy. The 'natural tendency' of skill premia to rise as growth processes based on trade and market openness take hold can be counteracted by vigorous promotion of the spread of education. As Lustig *et al.* (2011) note for Latin America in the first decade of the new millennium:

> The fall in the skill premium seems to be associated with a push in the coverage of basic education which made low skilled labor relatively less abundant and changes in labor demand. Through both quantity and price effects, the expansion of education has been equalizing. The distribution of human capital became more equal and the gap in returns to schooling by level narrowed. Using Tinbergen's language, in the race between education and technology, the former took the lead (Lustig *et al.*, 2011: 13).

What about broad sectoral and spatial forces in the evolution of inequality? Recall again the Kuznets (1955) simulations and Ahluwalia's

(1976b) estimations. These showed that a narrowing income gap between the agricultural and non-agricultural sectors would be a powerful force in mitigating inequality. A narrowing of this gap could occur for two reasons. First, policy interventions, through investments in physical, human and social capital in the lagging sector, could pull up the income of that sector. Second, the movement of labour from the lagging sector would eventually create labour shortage and start raising incomes and wages there. This latter tendency was pointed out by Lewis (1954). Both of these factors seem to have been present in China during the last decade. Kanbur and Zhang (2005) documented rising spatial income disparity in China in the 20 years prior to 2000. However, Zhang *et al.* (2010) have argued that China has now reached the 'Lewis turning point', and Fan *et al.* (2011) discuss various policy interventions to support the lagging regions in China. We will have to wait for the consequences of these to unfold over the coming decade.

The final element in the evolution of inequality is of course direct government intervention to redistribute through taxation and transfers. As Lustig *et al.* (2011) note, these have been central in the turnaround in Latin American inequality, through transfers programmes such as Oportunidades in Mexico and Bolsa Familia in Brazil. In India the incoming government after the 2004 elections introduced the National Rural Employment Guarantee Act, an intervention that was confirmed and strengthened by the re-election of the same government in 2009. Montek is of course a member of this government. As for Latin America, the implications of such interventions will only become clear in the coming decade, but if experience in other countries is anything to go by, they will have helped to mitigate inequality.

Conclusion

So, does Kuznets still matter? Thanks to the seminal work of Montek Ahluwalia (1976b), discussion and debate on inequality and development in the last 35 years has been structured around the Kuznets (1955) 'inverse-U' hypothesis. As I have argued, even if the inverse-U is not to be found in the cross-section data, the broad forces in the dynamics of development identified by Kuznets and Ahluwalia continue to be present in the actual experience of individual countries, and are being confirmed by the time series evidence that has accumulated since the work of these two pioneers.

It is these forces, and the policy interventions that shape them, which are central to the evolution of inequality during the course of development. It is only fitting that having started the post-Kuznets literature on inequality and development, Montek is now at the heart of Indian policymaking, addressing the distributional consequences of India's growth path. Thanks in large measure to his work, Kuznets still matters.

References

Adelman, I. and C.T. Morris (1973). *Economic Growth and Social Equity in Developing Countries*. Stanford, CA: Stanford University Press.

Ahluwalia, Montek S. (1974). "Income Inequality: Some Dimensions of the Problem", in H.B. Chenery *et al.* (eds.), *Redistribution with Growth*. London: Oxford University Press.

———. (1976a). "Income Distribution and Development: Some Stylized Facts", *American Economic Review, Papers and Proceedings* 66(2): 128-35.

———. (1976b). "Inequality, Poverty and Development", *Journal of Development Economics* 3: 307-342.

Ahluwalia, Montek S., Nicholas G. Carter and Hollis B. Chenery (1979). "Growth and Poverty in Developing Countries", *Journal of Development Economics* 6: 299-341.

Anand, Sudhir and R. Kanbur (1984). "Inequality and Development: A Reconsideration", H.P. Nissen (ed.), *Towards Income Distribution Policies* (EADI Book Series 3 Tilburg, Netherlands). pp.131-67.

Anand, Sudhir and R. Kanbur (1985). "Poverty under the Kuznets Process", *Economic Journal* 95: 42-50. Supplement, January.

———. (1993a). "Inequality and Development: A Critique", *Journal of Development Economics* 40: 25-52, June.

———. (1993b). "Inequality and Development: A Critique", *Journal of Development Economics* 41: 19-43, June.

Aryeetey, Ernest and Andrew McKay (2007). "Growth with Poverty Reduction, But Increased Spatial Inequality: Ghana over the 1990s", Chapter 3 of M. Grimm, S. Klasen and A. McKay (eds.), *Determinants of Pro Poor Growth: Analytical Issues and Findings from Country Cases.* Palgrave-Macmillan.

Bhorat, Haroon and Ravi Kanbur (eds.) (2006). *Poverty and Policy in Post-Apartheid South Africa*. Pretoria: HSRC Press.

Birdsall, Nancy and Miguel Szekely (2003). "Bootstraps, not Band-aids: Poverty, Equity and Social Policy", *Center for Global Development Working Paper* Number 24, *http://www.cgdev.org/content/publications/detail/2766.* Accessed 25 September, 2011.

Chenery, Hollis B. *et al.* (1974). *Redistribution with Growth.* London: Oxford University Press.

Deaton, Angus and Jean Dreze (2002). "Poverty and Inequality in India: A Reexamination", *Economic and Political Weekly:* 3729-48, September 7.

Deb, Uttam, Zobdul Hoque, Nafisa Khaled and Subir Kanti Bairagi (2008). *Growth, Income Inequality and Poverty Trends in Bangladesh. http://www.undp.org.bd/report/reports/growth..pdf* Accessed 25 September 2011.

Deininger, K. and L. Squire (1998). "New Ways of Looking at Old Issues: Inequality and Growth", *Journal of Development Economics* 57(2): 259–87.

Fan, Shenggen, Ravi Kanbur and Xiaobo Zhang (2011). "China's Regional Disparities: Experience and Policy", *Review of Development Finance* 1(1): 47-56.

Fields, G. (2001). *Distribution and Development, A New Look at the Developing World.* New York: Russell Sage Foundation and Cambridge, Massachusetts and London: The MIT Press.

Kanbur, Ravi (2010). "Globalization, Growth and Distribution: Framing the Questions", in Ravi Kanbur and A. Michael Spence (eds.), *Equity in a Globalizing World.* The World Bank for the Commission on Growth and Development. pp.41-70.

Kanbur, Ravi and A.J. Venables (2007). "Spatial Disparities and Economic Development", in D. Held and A. Kaya (eds.), *Global Inequality.* Polity Press. pp.204-215.

Kanbur, Ravi and Xiaobo Zhang (2005). "Fifty Years of Regional Inequality in China: A Journey Through Revolution, Reform and Openness", *Review of Development Economics* 9(1): 87-106.

Kuznets, Simon (1955). "Economic Gowth and Income Inequality", *American Economic Review* 45 (1): 1-28, March.

Lewis, W. Arthur (1954). "Economic Development with Unlimited Supplies of Labor", *Manchester School of Economic and Social Studies* 22: 139-91.

———. (1976). "Development and Distribution", in Alec Cairncross and Mohinder Puri (eds.), *Employment, Income Distribution and Development Strategy: Problems of the Developing Countries (Essays in honour of H.W. Singer).* New York: Holmes & Meier Publisheres, Inc. pp.26-42.

Lustig, Nora, Luis-Felipe Lopez-Calva and Eduardo Ortiz-Suarez (2011). *The Decline in Inequality in Latin America: How Much, Since When and Why?. https://greenspace.tulane.edu/nlustig/Lustig%20et%20al_decline_ineqLA_april2011.pdf.* Accessed 25 September, 2011.

Paukert, Felix (1973). "Income Distribution at Different Levels of Development", *International Labour Review*, August-September.

Piketty, T. (2006). "The Kuznets' Curve, Yesterday and Tomorrow", in A. Banerjee, R. Benabou and D. Mookherjee (eds.), *Understanding Poverty.* Oxford: Oxford University Press. p.21.

Robinson, Sherman (1976). "A Note on the U-hypothesis relating Income Inequality and Economic Development", *American Economic Review* 66(3): 437-40, June.

Zhang, Xiaobo, Jin Yang and Shengling Wang (2010). "China has Reached the Lewis Turning Point", *IFPRI Discussion Paper* No. 000977. *http://www.ifpri.org/sites/default/files/publications/ifpridp00977.pdf.* Accessed 25 September, 2011.

7 Poverty in India

Facts and Interpretation

SURJIT S. BHALLA

Introduction

Poverty and inclusive growth are both in the news and in a 'big time' way. Montek S. Ahluwalia has been associated with these issues for decades. He did some pioneering research on poverty and income distribution in the 1970s, and as Deputy Chairman of the Planning Commission since July 2004, he has pioneered the concept of inclusive growth. In this paper in honor of Montek I will primarily deal with the controversial, and now hot, issue of poverty in India. It is a privilege to write a paper for this volume, and to write on these issues circa November 2011.

Only in a country like India. You can add 'India, the incomparable or India, the unique.' It is important to do so. Because the nature of discussion about poverty in India, is, analytically, nothing short of bizarre. India has had a poverty line for decades, was a pioneer in the development of the poverty line, has revised this poverty line via various committees, and yet the criticism is that Indian policymakers know nothing about poverty. The ire is directed at the government, and specifically Montek. If one were to look at some of the comments in discussion today, they are as follows. In an open letter to Montek, signed by more than 50 important (poverty) dignitaries, Ms Aruna Roy, member of Ms Sonia Gandhi's National Advisory Council (NAC), declared that the Government of India/ Planning Commission urban poverty line of Rs 32 per capita per day was absurd; and that Mr Ahluwalia should try living on it. Another distinguished member of the NAC, Mr N. Saxena, declared that this Rs 32

I am thankful to Manoj Agrawal for excellent assistance in the preparation of this paper.

level of consumption was not fit for cats and dogs, let alone human beings. It is not even okay to write such absurdities in free speech journalism and certainly not in the context of a policy debate. Nevertheless, this just happened in a country like India.

It is important that the policy debate on such an important subject as absolute poverty take place in the context of some facts. Each one of us has a version of what standard of living constitutes the poor. Public policy should not be personalised. It is nobody's argument (or should be nobody's argument) that the only way a poverty line can be defined is by living according to that line.

The plan of the paper is as follows. Section II describes the data and definitions used in this study. Section III documents the facts about economic growth in India. Often in the polemical debate about poverty and policy, and the poverty of policy, the facts (unfortunately) become irrelevant. Section IV documents the level and changes in absolute poverty. Regarding poverty, one striking finding is that as of 2009/10, the Millennium Development Goals of halving poverty levels relative to 1990 for 2015 have been achieved by India at very close to a decade earlier than 'scheduled'. Section V concludes.

Data and Definitions

In the main, this study uses the large sample, National Sample Surveys (NSS) for the years 1983, 1993/94, 1999/2000, 2004/05 and 2009/2010. There are two surveys that the NSS conducts in each of the large sample years—a consumption and expenditure (CE) survey and an employment and unemployment (EU) survey. Until 1993, the households surveyed by the CE and EU surveys were identical. In addition to the 10 surveys mentioned above, the recently released small sample (half of large sample) CE and EU surveys for 2007/08 are also used. These NSS surveys provide a rich, and exhaustive, basis for examining trends in poverty in India.

Economic Growth: Some Facts

It is important to establish the background of growth, before attempting to probe its impact on poverty alleviation. There are three major phases of Indian growth. Post independence and till 1980, GDP growth in India averaged around 3.5 per cent. The story really begins in 1980 when growth started to exceed 5 per cent per annum on a consistent basis. Major economic reforms were initiated in 1991 but for a decade, there was no acceleration in GDP growth—it stayed constant at 5.5 per cent per annum. Starting 2003, however, there has been a marked acceleration in GDP growth to more than 8 per cent per annum.

The facts about GDP growth as reported are clear, but controversy and puzzles persist. There are three questions and puzzles, and hence the controversies. First, what caused India's growth to accelerate in the 1980s; second, what prevented India's growth from accelerating in the 1990s as would have been forecast by the magnitude of the 1991 economic reforms; and third, what caused the growth rate to sharply accelerate in 2003/04 without the benefit of any new policy initiatives, major or minor.

There are several determinants of the pace of economic growth—capacity to catch up (the poorer you are, the faster you can grow, *ceteris paribus*—this happens because you can borrow technology from abroad); the presence of 'good' institutions; openness to foreign trade; good fiscal policy; etc. Two of the more important determinants of growth, besides 'catch-up', are competitive interest rates and competitive exchange rates. [See Bhalla (2007; 2011) and the references cited there for a detailed exposition of this hypothesis]. It is not a coincidence, therefore, that the two growth spurts in the Indian economy were preceded with, or accompanied by, changes towards such competitive policies. A large element of the 1990s reforms was the opening of the Indian economy to foreign trade and by the devaluation of the rupee towards competitive levels. In the three years after these reforms (1993/94 to 1996/97) the Indian economy grew by over 7 per cent per annum. The next spurt happened post 2002.

An attribute of the first puzzle is that the above 5 per cent growth rate of the 1980s did not represent a significant departure from the growth rate that should have been expected. One reason this conclusion might have been missed by most analysts is that there was a global slowdown in the 1970s, a period when Indian growth collapsed to an average of only 2.9 per cent per annum. In addition to the quadrupling of price of oil in 1973 and its doubling in 1978, India was also buffeted with a war (1971 involving

Pakistan) and droughts. Hence, the acceleration or break with trend seemed to be large, when in reality there was only a gradual, and minor, acceleration to above trend growth in the 1980s. Second, the 1991 reforms did lead to a sharp acceleration to 7.5 per cent GDP growth but this growth rate was not sustained. Real long-term interest rates rose to double-digit levels in the mid-1990s and growth collapsed. This fact helps explain two puzzles—the non-acceleration in the 1990s and the 'miracle' high growth since 2003/04 or 2003.[1] The revival in 'high' growth around 2003 was preceded by a decline in real interest rates of around 600 basis points (reversal of the mid-1990s increase) in a matter of four years (1999 to 2002).

Table 7.1 provides a perspective on the comparative nature of India's GDP growth. The table presents both 5 and 20-year averages of GDP growth. No matter what the time period, India's GDP growth has shown a steady upward march. In 1980, a five-year moving average of India's growth placed it around the 60th position in the world. In 2010, it had the 11th position with average five-year GDP growth of 8.2 per cent and average 20-year growth of 6.7 per cent.

Given that growth has accelerated, a legitimate question is whether the pace of poverty reduction has also accelerated. It has not according to official data; the solution to this poverty puzzle is offered below.

Measurement of Poverty

This section examines the various dimensions of Indian poverty—the Indian poverty line, its origins, and what kind of living standards it encompasses. Does the poverty line signify bare survival, or more? Do the poor have access to education and health care? Only by looking at the consumption standards of the poor themselves can one attempt to define what the poverty line should be.

---

1. The Indian fiscal year runs from April to March and fiscal years will either be referenced as 2003/04 or 2003.

Table 7.1

Indian Growth Performance, 1980-2011

Year	*Average (5 Years)*		*Average (20 Years)*	
	Growth	*Rank*	*Growth*	*Rank*
1980	3.2	56	3.7	60
1985	5.4	19	4.1	35
1990	6.0	12	4.3	27
1995	5.2	28	4.9	17
2000	6.3	11	5.7	11
2005	7.0	7	6.1	6
2010	8.2	11	6.7	7

Source: World Bank, *World Development Indicators.*

The origins of the Indian poverty line go back to the late 1950s, according to Rath (2011). He credits Ram Manohar Lohia with the first poverty line; in a speech to the Lok Sabha in the late 1950s, he 'drew attention to the large percentage of the population living with a daily expenditure of less than three and a half annas a day' (p.40). Rath also documents that Nehru set up a committee of experts to arrive at a poverty line and report to the Planning Commission; in July 1962, this committee arrived at a figure of Rs 20 per capita per month 'as the minimum expenditure for an average Indian to stay above the poverty line. There is, however, no record of how the committee came to this figure' (p.40).

In July 1962, the Lohia line was about 4 annas or Rs 7.5 a month. In contrast, Nehru's line was three times this level. A decade later, Dandekar and Rath (1971) established the very first detailed poverty line for India. Their estimate: close to the Nehru-Planning Commission (Nehru-PC) estimate. The authors arrived at a figure of Rs 15 for rural areas, and Rs 22.50 for urban areas, 1960-61 prices. Given an urbanisation rate of 18 per cent in 1960-61, the Dandekar-Rath all-India line was a monthly expenditure level of Rs 16.4 per person per month.

During the 1960s and 1970s, more than 70 per cent of the population was absolutely poor (Tendulkar poverty line). How was the poverty line determined? By looking at what was the necessary level of food intake consistent with lack of hunger. The bare minimum of food and the bare minimum was defined in terms of calorie intake.

Unlike the 25 per cent higher Nehru-PC line, the authors defined their poverty line in terms of an implicit calorie criteria. Food consumption, actually prevention of hunger, was an important criterion. An average consumption level of 2,250 calories a day was deemed necessary for minimum survival. The poverty line corresponded to the aggregate expenditure level which yielded this consumption of calories.

In the last 40 years, food consumption patterns have changed. As development proceeds, in the first stage, the movement is from calorie rich foods (cereals) to calorie poor foods (fruits and vegetables). Urbanisation also dictates less need for calories; and being better off means eating, out of choice, more expensive calories e.g. meat. So the poverty line is not and should not keep constant calorie consumption. The Indian poverty line is updated, like in the US and every other country in the world, on the basis of overall consumer price indices, and *not* food or calorie price indices.

Calorie Consumption: Pointers towards Poverty?

Economic development means a movement out of agriculture into non-agricultural pursuits. In the early 1960s, agriculture accounted for more than 50 per cent of GDP; today, it accounts for less than 18 per cent. In 1960-61, income from agricultural pursuits was the dominant source of income for more than 65 per cent of India's population. In 2009/10, agricultural income is the dominant (more than 50 per cent) source for less than 40 per cent of the population. What does this mean for calorie consumption, and poverty? It means that calorie needs are less for the population, and especially for those who have migrated either out of, or reduced their participation in, agricultural pursuits. In other words, for a large number of people, the movement towards a more sedentary lifestyle means a lower consumption of calories. How much lower is subject to debate and estimation but a 10 per cent lower average requirement, between the needs of an average Indian in 1960 and an average Indian in 2011, is a reasonable estimate.

If calorie consumption is the criteria, then with development, and declining levels of caloric 'needs' there is an opposite force: the average price of calorie consumption is likely to increase. This is the movement from potatoes to meat. For the dominantly vegetarian Indian society, there is much less of this movement. Relative prices of food grains have stayed relatively constant in the last three decades. Since the poverty line has risen with the average price level, and since food grain prices have risen *pari passu* with the poverty line, and since the need for calories has declined, it is the case that the real value of caloric purchases have not increased for the average Indian, and certainly not for the poor Indian. The latter conclusion follows from the simple observation that the maximum movement towards a less active work life is among the rural poor.

There have been several objections to the Indian poverty line, and poverty estimates based on the official poverty lines. All of these objections have centred on caloric consumption levels remaining the same as in 1960s and 1970s. Some have even estimated caloric consumption needs to be as high as 2,450 calories per person. Clearly, at constant prices, the higher the estimate of needs, the higher the poverty line, and the higher the fraction of the poor. Arjun Sengupta (2009) assumed a 2,400 calorie requirement in 2004 and came up with an estimate that 77 per cent of the population was poor. The 1979 Nutrition Expert group to the Planning Commission had estimated caloric needs as 2,400 and 2,100 kcal in urban and rural areas respectively. Their report was published in 1981. Two years later, the large sample NSS survey for 1983 showed that the average caloric consumption was 2,240 and 2,070, rural and urban. Rath (2011), one of the pioneers in estimation of poverty, estimates that caloric norms today should be 1,970 for rural areas and 2,025 for urban areas; 'the rural norms are lower than the urban because the percentage of children in the rural population is higher than in the urban' (Rath, 2011: 43). This yields an average need level of calorie consumption of 2,000 calories per capita per day (the exact number is 1,987).

Table 7.2 documents the caloric, fat and protein consumption in India for the last 30 years. Never in these last 30 years has caloric consumption in India been even close to 2,400 calories in the rural areas; the maximum was 2,240 in 1983. Both rural and urban areas have witnessed a decline in average caloric intake of 10 to 15 per cent, with the larger decline in rural areas.

Table 7.2

Mean Per Capita Consumption of Calories, Protein and Fats (Per Day)

		1983	*1987-88*	*1993-94*	*1999-2000*	*2004-05*	*2009-10*
Calorie (Kcal)	All-India	2200	2199	2132	2150	2040	1894
	Rural	2240	2233	2153	2148	2047	1908
	Urban	2070	2095	2073	2155	2021	1860
Protein (gm)	All-India	62.2	62.1	59.6	58.9	55.7	50.4
	Rural	63.5	63.2	60.3	59.1	55.8	51.4
	Urban	58.1	58.6	57.7	58.4	55.4	48.2
Fat (gm)	All-India	29.5	31.0	33.9	39.7	38.8	37.0
	Rural	27.1	28.3	31.1	36	35.4	35.3
	Urban	37.1	39.3	41.9	49.6	47.4	40.9

Source: 2009-10 data from author's calculation from NSS survey. Other years' data from NSS-National Nutritional Survey & Centrum Research.

Thus, all the evidence suggests that, on average, caloric 'needs' and caloric consumption, have both declined in India over the last 30 years. It, therefore, is surprising that analysts and poverty experts should go back to norms that are no longer realistic. If the norms are no longer realistic, and lower, then it does mean that official poverty lines are not flawed in this respect. Indeed, to yield the same level of caloric need intake, the poverty line needs to be about 10 to 20 per cent lower.

Poverty Lines: 1960-61–2011

Given that there is no conceptual flaw in the official poverty line estimates, one can proceed to examine whether over the last 50 odd years the 'real' poverty line has been raised or not. In other words, as real incomes have increased, has the absolute poverty line also increased? It should; because the transition to development is reflected in the transition from an absolute poverty line to a relative poverty line. In Bhalla (2010a) I argue that absolute poverty lines should rise with development; that each 10 per cent rise in per capita consumption should lead to approximately a 5 per cent rise in the poverty line. Between 1960-61 and 2004/05, real per capita consumption approximately doubled (actually 113 per cent); the expectation would therefore be that the poverty line should be raised by 56 per cent.

Table 7.3 puts the various poverty lines in perspective. The data reported for each poverty line are in current prices.

Table 7.3

Evolution of Poverty Lines in India

	Dandekar and Rath			*Planning Commission*			*Tendulkar*		
	All-India	*Rural*	*Urban*	*All-India*	*Rural*	*Urban*	*All-India*	*Rural*	*Urban*
1960-61	**16.4***	**15***	**22.5***						
1973-74	43	39.5	56.2	**51***	**50***	**57***			
1983-84	78	71	101	93	89	106			
1993-94	182	164	233	226*	206*	281*	264*	253*	295*
2004-05	318	284	404	407	357	532	**484***	**447***	**579***
2009-10	474	421	599	606	529	787	720	663	857
May 2011	530	471	670	677	591	877	805	741	955

Notes: *: Data for these years as given by respective committees/institutions. Data for all other years extrapolated by author based on CPI(AL) and CPI(IW) for different years.

Several important conclusions follow:

1) The Lohia poverty line was indeed very low and according to it, less than 3 per cent of the Indian population was absolutely poor in 1983. This suggests that Lohia's line was more political than economic.

2) In their 1971 study, Dandekar-Rath poverty line increased the real rural poverty line by approximately 16 per cent over the prevailing Rs 15 per capita per month poverty line (all increases are reported for the rural poverty line, though data are presented for all three lines—rural, urban and all-India).

3) The rural poverty line was raised further by the Tendulkar committee in 2008 for the year 2004/05—by 25.2 per cent i.e., an increase from Rs 357 per capita per month to Rs 447.

4) From the original Dandekar-Rath formulation, the rural, urban, and all-India poverty lines have increased by the following percentages: rural (57 per cent), urban (42 per cent), and all-India (52 per cent).

5) This means that if India had been following the Dandekar-Rath formulation of the poverty line, in current 2011 prices, Rs 26 a day would be Rs 17 a day and Rs 32 a day would be Rs 22 per day.

What the above documentation of the poverty lines suggests is that among the many possible flaws in the formulation of the poverty line, the government cannot be accused of not raising the poverty line in a healthy manner. It is also noteworthy that for the rural poor, the poverty line has been raised substantially more than for the urban poor.

Poverty in India: 1983-2010

There are two estimates of average per capita consumption in India, or any other country. The first is that obtained from household surveys (S) such as the NSS and the second is that obtained from national accounts (NA). Until the late 1960s, the two estimates were near identical and this was a reflection of the fact that the national account estimates of consumption were derived from NSSO survey estimates. The survey to national accounts ratio (S/NA) was close to a 100 per cent in the 1960s.

There are natural differences between the two sources because of differences in definition, coverage (e.g. institutions are part of NA but not of surveys[2]), measurement (survey consumption is measured directly while NA consumption is often a residual) and prices. These differences fail to account for more than a small fraction of the two means, say about 5 per cent or so. Indeed, differences in population estimates (between NSS and NA) alone suggest a discrepancy larger than 5 per cent. The differences in growth of survey or NA consumption are even smaller (since the differences in levels are likely to persist). Hence, while one can expect divergences in levels of NA and survey consumption, there is very little reason to believe that there should be divergences in NA and survey growth rates. And it is the latter divergence that is all too critically important for understanding trends in poverty.

2. It has been speculated (see Ravallion, 2000) that the non-government organisation (NGO) population in India maybe causing a significant part of the divergence between survey and NA means, and growth rates. As pointed out in Bhalla (2003) the contribution of this factor to overall divergence in survey and NA means is very, very small.

Several explanations are possible for explaining the residual 'true' difference between surveys and national accounts. First, it could be the case that the national account estimates have a systematic upward bias, and an increasing error proportion i.e., the detailed NSS surveys (with questions even on salt consumption!) are broadly 'correct' and the NA estimates are in error. Scholars have pointed to the FINSIM category (banking services like use of cheques and insurance services) as a major source of missing consumption in surveys. But FINSIM accounted for less than 2 per cent of total consumption in 2004/05, and less than 1 per cent in 1993/94.

An alternate possibility is that the NSS data are underestimating 'true' consumption. The declining trend in S/NA ratios is indicative of this possibility, as is the fact that this decline in S/NA ratios has been observed in most countries, especially during the globalisation period post 1980.[3] A discussion of the causes behind this decline is beyond the scope of this paper. But if the assumption is made that survey data are broadly incorrect, then there is a problem of interpretation of data on both the level and trend in poverty in India.

Growth and poverty calculations, and therefore conclusions about inclusive growth, are intimately related to knowledge of which estimate of mean consumption is 'accurate'. Tables 7.4a, 7.4b and 7.4c document the unusual trend of the S/NA ratio in India. (The tables also contain 'adjusted' consumption levels, a topic pursued in detail below). The effect the declining S/NA ratio has on growth and poverty calculations can be illustrated as follows. Assume for a moment that the S/NA ratio observed in 1983 is broadly correct. This means that about 19 per cent of national accounts consumption is missed and does not accrue to anybody, rich and poor alike. It is an unrealistic assumption, but it does illustrate the underestimate of growth, and therefore, the level of income, at anytime subsequent to the 'normal' year 1983. Between this base year and 2009/10 (both large sample surveys), the S/NA ratio declined from 80.7 to 46.5 per cent. Real NSS consumption during these years grew at a rate of 1.6 per cent a year; national accounts data real consumption grew at more than twice that rate, 3.3 per cent per annum. So approximately, 1.7 per cent per year, or a cumulative 57 per cent, was no longer accruing to individuals

3. See Bhalla (2002b; 2010a) for a detailed discussion of these issues.

according to NSS data. Again, the emphasis is on growth being missed, not the level. None of the arguments in favour of using NSS data as more reliable have to do with growth being missed, and not certainly of this magnitude.

If the mean of the NA estimate of consumption is broadly accurate, and if such consumption is missed for all households almost proportionally,[4] then it is the case that mean consumption levels for the population are at least double for the poor and rich alike—double of what appears in the 2009/10 survey. Which implies that those assumed to be spending only Rs 32 per capita in urban areas, the urban poor, are most likely spending Rs 64 per capita per day, or Rs 10,000 per month for a family of five. Or Rs 1.2 lakh a year.

How high or low is this figure of Rs 1.2 lakh a year? One perspective can be obtained from what the government believes is an adequate minimum level for income taxation. For the fiscal year 2011-12, if a person earns more than Rs 1.8 lakh a year, she/he is eligible to pay tax. So at least according to the taxation authorities, Rs 1.2 lakh of consumption for a single-earner family of five is absolutely poor, and Rs 1.8 lakh deserving of taxation. Many of the people arguing that Rs 32 per person per day is a very low poverty line are the same as those arguing that our tax rates are too low. Certainly the two positions are not logically consistent.

But the argument can be made—has been made—that the missing consumption in the national accounts mostly accrues to the non-poor. So, the adjustment made above that the consumption of the urban poor is actually close to Rs 64 per person per day may be grossly incorrect. However, Bhalla (2002b) showed that such an assumption was off by no more than a few percentage points; the rich do understate their consumption more than the poor, but only by about 10 per cent or so.

Is there a method to extract information about the missing consumption of the poor? There is. A heretofore unexploited nature of the NSS data is that the households are surveyed in each large sample year for both their consumption expenditure and their work and income generation

4. An assumption supported by the simulation conducted in Bhalla (2002b).

Table 7.4a

Average Consumption from National Accounts and NSS Surveys: Adjustments to Survey Estimates

Year	National Accounts	NSSO Surveys		Real Rural Casual Wage per Day (A)	Adjustment to NSS	
	Nominal Consumption	Nominal Consumption (1)	Real Consumption (2)		Consumption Adjusted (2')	Method A Adjusted (1')=(1)*(2')/(2)
1983	153	123	486	26.5	486	123
1993-94	540	334	538	35.7	655	406
1999-2000	1058	587	540	43.3	794	863
2004-05	1472	729	624	48.5	889	1039
2007-08	2069	977	636	57	1045	1605
2009-10	2693	1253	699	63	1155	2071
CAGR	10.8%	8.7%	1.4%	3.3%	3.3%	10.6%

Notes: 1) Real wage and consumption calculated using 2004-05 rural price index as deflator; note that 1983 was a full calendar year survey, and all other surveys were conducted between July and June. So the number of years between the 1983 and the 2009-10 survey is 26.5.

2) Adjustment (2') to Survey Real Consumption (2) was done as follows: Take 1983 survey real consumption figure 486 as the correct base estimate. Then apply growth rate of real wages of rural casual labourers to this base figure for subsequent years.

Table 7.4b

Average Consumption from National Accounts and NSS Surveys and Adjustments to Survey Estimates

Year	National Accounts	NSSO Surveys		Real Per Capita Monthly Income of Bottom 50% (B)	Adjustment to NSS	
	Nominal Consumption	Nominal Consumption (1)	Real Consumption (2)		Consumption Adjusted (2')	Method B Adjusted (1')=(1)*(2')/(2)
1983	153	123	486	234	486	123
1993-94	540	334	538	313	650	403
1999-2000	1058	587	540	360	748	813
2004-05	1472	729	624	384	798	931
2007-08	2069	977	636	458	951	1461
2009-10	2693	1253	699	530	1101	1973
CAGR	10.8%	8.7%	1.4%	3.1%	3.1%	10.5%

Notes: 1) Real wage and consumption calculated using 2004-05 rural price index as deflator; note that 1983 was a full calendar year survey, and all other surveys were conducted between July and June. So the number of years between the 1983 and the 2009-10 survey is 26.5.

2) Adjustment (2') to Survey Real Consumption (2) was done as follows: Take 1983 survey real consumption figure 486 as the correct base estimate. Then apply growth rate of real per capita income of the bottom 50 per cent of the population to this base figure for subsequent years.

(EU survey). For the survey years 1983 and 1993/94, the households surveyed in the two surveys were identical.

Table 7.4c

Survey to National Accounts Ratio

(in per cent)

Year	*Actual*	*NSS Adjusted by Rural Wages (A)*	*NSS Adjusted by Income, Bottom 50 Per cent (B)*
1983	80.7	80.7	80.7
1993-94	61.8	75.2	74.7
1999-2000	55.5	81.6	76.8
2004-05	49.5	70.6	63.3
2007-08	47.2	77.6	70.6
2009-10	46.5	76.9	73.3

Notes: (A) refers to adjustment by real casual wages; (B) refers to adjustment by real per capita income of bottom half of the population; Real consumption and wages calculated using 2004-2005 rural price index as deflator.

The EU surveys contain information on the earnings of the poor (and the rest of the population). The wages of casual unskilled rural wage workers can be considered as representative of the income growth of the poor; and since the absolutely poor are unlikely to have any savings on an average basis, then income growth of these poor workers is likely to equal to their consumption growth.

What is being attempted is an adjustment to the NSS consumption data, a data which severely underestimates the true average consumption in India. Nevertheless, a search for a more accurate adjustment continues. In this paper, two new methods are offered. The first method (method A) states/assumes the following. The poor in consumption are also the poor in income i.e., the absolutely poor in India, are, almost definitionally, the ones who have zero long-term savings. While each poor household will go through savings in some years and deficits in others, in the aggregate, at any point in time, the savings of the poor are likely to be close to zero. Which earners are the poorest in India? The unskilled workers in rural areas—the agricultural workers, people with close to zero education etc. The earnings growth of such workers should match their consumption growth. If the assumption is made that the 1983 NSS consumption survey accurately measured all-India consumption (the survey to national accounts ratio in that year was 81 per cent meaning that 19 per cent of NA consumption does not accrue to anyone, rich or poor) then the consumption level in any subsequent year is increased by the growth in nominal wages of the rural poor. A second method (method B) is to increase the 1983 consumption level by the growth in per capita incomes of the bottom 50 per cent of the population. The wage and income data are from the NSS employment and unemployment surveys conducted in the same years as the consumption survey.

The results of these imputations are presented in Tables 7.4a and 7.4b. Both methods suggest that income growth has grown between 57 and 65 per cent higher than consumption growth. Even if some of the income growth goes into savings, the result is robust and emphatic—NSS consumption data severely understate the consumption of the population, and especially that of the poor.

How much Difference do the Adjustments make?

A lot. Table 7.5 documents the headcount ratio of poverty according to the Tendulkar poverty line. The original data show that, on average, the pace of decline of the headcount ratio of poverty has stayed broadly the same for the period when India was growing at 5.5 per cent per annum, 1983-2004/05, and approximately the same for the high growth period, 2004/05 to 2009/10. Is this a new Hindu constant i.e., that regardless of growth, poverty decline is only 1 per cent per annum?

Nevertheless, the steady decline in official poverty estimate is from close to 60 per cent in 1983, to less than 30 per cent in 2009/10. The official poverty ratio is very close to being half the 1993/94 level in 2009/ 2010 i.e., the Millennium Development Goal (MDG) of halving poverty by 2015 has been met in India.

The data on adjusted poverty estimates are striking. The poverty ratio in 2009/10 is in single digits. This is to be expected. Without adjustments, the poverty ratio in 2009/10 is 28 per cent. If now a 60 per cent consumption increase is imposed on the distribution, then a 20 to 25 percentage point decline in poverty is expected, if the distribution of consumption does not change by much. Which means that a 28 per cent population poor (unadjusted NSS data for 2009/10) is actually very close to 5 per cent really poor.

Table 7.5

Poverty Ratio: Actual and Adjusted NSS Consumption Data

Year	*Headcount Ratio: Poverty (in %)*		
	Actual	*Adjusted: Method A*	*Adjusted: Method B*
1983	58.5	58.5	58.5
1993/94	47.7	30.3	30.8
1999/2000	42.7	12.7	16.3
2004/05	37.1	10.8	17.4
2007/08	27.9	2.5	4.4
2009/10	28.1	3.1	4.1

Notes: (A) refers to adjustment by taking 1983 consumption figure as base and applying growth rates of real rural casual wage per day for other years; (B) refers to adjustment by real per capita monthly income of bottom half of population. See Tables 7.4a to 7.4c.

Conclusions

This paper has attempted to investigate several aspects of poverty in India. The high growth phase started in India in the 1980s and appropriately the reference or benchmark year of investigation is 1983. The last year for which household level data exists, and is examined, is the 66th round of the NSS, the survey period being from July of 2009 to June of 2010.

The major result emerging from the analysis is that the story of poverty reduction (and therefore inclusive growth) in India is very impressive. By our own reference poverty lines, absolute poverty in India afflicts less than 5 per cent of the population. The fact that there is such a large controversy in India about the efficacy of the existing Tendulkar poverty line (now enshrined as Rs 32 per person per day) poverty line says more about the content and conduct of the debate rather than the reality of poverty in India.

The ongoing controversy over the poverty line is severely 'out of line' and misses both the forest and the trees. The rapid growth that has been witnessed in India over the last 30 years has had an effect on the living standards of the entire population. The poor have become better off, as well as the rich. Unfortunately, the NSS data, by missing 55 per cent of actual expenditure, conveys a picture of stagnant progress in consumption. Adjustments based on earnings of the poor, suggest that real consumption is actually about 60 per cent higher than that indicated by the NSS data.

The construction of the poverty line, in India or elsewhere, reflects purchasing power at the poverty line. But what happens when this purchasing power is underestimated as appears to be the case with NSS data. Evidence was offered, based on earnings of the poor themselves, that the consumption of the poor was about 60 per cent higher in 2009/10 than that revealed by the NSS data for the same year. An alternate and symmetric manner of viewing the same phenomenon is to state that the purchasing power of Rs 32 is 60 per cent higher. Or that Rs 32 NSS consumption units is 32*1.6 = Rs 51.2 'real' consumption units. (Recall that if mean survey consumption was assumed equal to mean national accounts consumption, then the adjusted survey consumption would be 115 per cent higher than NSS survey consumption.) In other words, when discussion is about Rs 32 per person per day poverty line, that discussion is really about Rs 51 per person per day poverty line. And Rs 51 per person per day is Rs 92,000 per family of five in 2011.

Whether Rs 92,000 per family of five is the appropriate poverty line is for the policymakers to decide. Is this a destitute, near starvation level? If not, is it a minimum needs level? A perspective on this can be obtained from the fact that income taxation starts at twice this consumption or income level. Maybe the taxation level is too low; maybe the poverty line is just right? These are questions for a rational debate, in the context of facts about incomes, income distribution, tax rates, etc.

References

Ahluwalia, Montek S., N. Carter and H. Chenery (1979). "Growth and Poverty in Developing Countries", *Journal of Development Economics* 6: 399-341.

Ahluwalia, S. Montek (2002). "Economic Reforms in India Since 1991: Has Gradualism Worked?", *Journal of Economic Perspectives* 16(3): 67-88.

Bhalla, Surjit S. (2002a). "Growth and Poverty in India–Myth and Reality", in G. Rao (ed.), *Development Poverty and Fiscal Policy: Decentalization of Institutions*. Oxford: Oxford University Press.

———. (2002b). *Imagine there's no Country: Poverty, Inequality and Growth in the Era of Globalization*. Institute of International Economics.

———. (2003). "Crying Wolf on Poverty: Or How the Millennium Development Goals of Poverty Reduction have already been Reached", *Economic & Political Weekly* 38 (27): 2843-2856. July 5.

———. (2007). *Second Among Equals: The Middle Class Kingdoms of India and China*. Prepared for the Peterson Institute of International Economics. Available at *www.oxusinvestments.com*

———. (2010a). "Raising the Standard–The War on Global Poverty", in Sudhir Anand, Paul Segal and Joseph Stiglitz (eds.), *Debates on the Measurement of Global Poverty*. Oxford: Oxford University Press.

———. (2010b). "Indian Economic Growth, 1950-2008", in Shankar Acharya and Rakesh Mohan, (eds.), *Indian Economy: Performance and Challenges, Essays in Honour of Montek Singh Ahluwalia*. New Delhi: Oxford University Press.

———. (2011), "Devaluing to Prosperity: Misaligned Currencies and Their Global Consequences", Peterson Institute of International Economics, Washington, D.C. (Forthcoming).

Chenery, H., M.S. Ahluwalia, C.L.G. Bell, J.H. Duloy and R. Jolly (1974). *Redistribution with Growth*. Oxford: Oxford University Press.

Dandekar, V.M. and N. Rath (1971). "Poverty in India: Dimensions and Trends", *Economic and Political Weekly:* 25 and 106, January 2 and 9.

Deininger, Klaus and Lyn Squire (1996). "A New Data Set Measuring Income Inequality", *World Bank Economic Review* 10 (3): 565-592.

Planning Commission (2009). *(Tendulkar) Report of the Expert Group to Review the Methodology for Estimation of Poverty*. New Delhi.

Ravallion, M. (2000) "Should Poverty Measures be Anchored to the National Accounts?", *Economic and Political Weekly*: 3245-52, August 26.

Rath, Nilakantha (2011). "Measurement of Poverty: In Retrospect and Prospect", *Economic and Political Weekly* XLVI(42), October 15-21.

Sengupta, Arjun (2009). *Report of the National Commission for Enterprises in the Unorganised Sector*. Government of India. New Delhi: Academic Foundation.

8 Innovation and Public Information Infrastructure

SAM PITRODA

I have known Montek personally for over 25 years. We had an opportunity to work closely during Mr Rajiv Gandhi's era in the PMO over various issues of national importance. This included the first visit of GE Chairman, Mr Jack Welch, where we jointly made an effort to sell GE Indian Software capabilities, which laid the foundation for Indian software export industry. I have always found Montek to be exceptionally bright, insightful, supportive and helpful, especially on new ideas and initiatives. He also has a tremendous insight into the plan process, government procedures, of international interaction, and social and economic developments. He's been a personal friend, well wisher and an ardent colleague, with whom I've cherished working on a spectrum of national initiatives.

Introduction

'Innovation is something that people at the bottom of the pyramid have little time to think about', is a perception that we in the middle or at the top of the ladder have often sought to perpetuate. But as the telecom revolution of the 1980s showed us, give them an opportunity and their ability to innovate, create sustainable solutions, comes out on top. Innovation is not a one-off project; it is a process that goes beyond the confines of formal Research and Development (R&D). Today, India has significant challenges in health, education, agriculture, energy, urbanisation and so on where conventional approaches of solving them have been inadequate. Innovative solutions will be critical for addressing some of our most pressing challenges and creating an inclusive model of development. An innovation economy can only thrive in an ecosystem that gives birth to

and sustains new ideas. This innovation ecosystem requires enablers in the form of human capital and skills, financial support for entrepreneurs, new models of enterprise development, facilitating policies, focus on micro, small and medium enterprises (MSMEs) and collaboration with private industry and many more stakeholders.

The Global Context

The relative importance of various drivers of economic growth and prosperity has evolved over time, and now, for a growing number of countries, innovation is emerging as the foremost factor.[1] Traditional sources of power and influence, such as territory, resources, manpower and military might which have been the chief determinants of nations' prosperity, for centuries, are far less important today. They've given way to a world in which successful development is increasingly linked to sound policies, good governance, effective management of scarce financial resources, and, most important, to the extent to which societies are able to harness the latent creative capacities of their population. Successful countries today are not necessarily large, geographically; neither should they be richly endowed with natural resources, nor able to project military power beyond their borders. The mould of a flourishing society, comprising these quondam requisites, is now shattered. Increasingly, the countries to look up to are those who have managed to expand opportunities for their populace by fully exploiting the opportunities afforded by a thriving world economy, through international trade, foreign investment, adoption of new technologies, macroeconomic stability and high rates of saving.[2]

There are various forms of nationwide information infrastructures in countries around the world. Singapore is pursuing the 'Intelligent Island', Japan the 'Info-communications for the 21st Century' and the European Union (EU) the 'European Information Society' (GICC Asia Regional Meeting and International Conference, November 1995). These various government-led initiatives have become an interwoven lacing of technologies, economics, politics and potentialities. New corporate alliances across the globe are making traditional geographical boundaries

1. *http://www.innovationfordevelopmentreport.org/index.html*
2. WEF (2010-11).

(as well as those between companies and technologies) irrelevant.[3] In his State of the Union Address this year, President Barack Obama underscored the importance of a renewed US imperative to out-innovate other economies if America is to fully recover from the present crisis. Cordeiro and Al-Hawamdeh (2001), have also identified that one of the key roles in which governments of the various countries can play is to promote electronic links between national and Union administrations within the administrative geography, with a common goal of accelerating the execution of common policies and the single market; this is what the Central planning agencies of the Indian Union's administration intend to achieve through the Public Information Infrastructure (PII).

The *Innovation for Development Report,* collated by the European Business School, drafts the Innovation Capacity Index (ICI) which ranks various countries based on their innovation potential. It draws upon a sound theoretical framework and the best available data to correlate the wide-ranging set of relevant factors, policies and institutional characteristics which play a central role in boosting a nation's capacity for innovation. The ICI covers 131 countries and identifies over 60 factors that are seen to have a bearing on a country's ability to create an environment that encourages innovation, such as a nation's institutional environment, human capital endowment, the presence of social inclusion, the regulatory and legal framework, the infrastructure for research and development, and the adoption and use of information and communication technologies, etc. India ranks 88th, alongside Morocco and Paraguay, in a ranking of 130 countries in the Innovation Capacity Index, for 2010-11, below neighbouring countries like Sri Lanka and Mauritius, and lesser-developed countries like Jamaica, Ghana, Botswana, Trinidad and Tobago, Vietnam and Azerbaijan. The Global Innovation Index which is a collaborative effort between S&P and Business Week and studies 132 countries based on their innovation potential, also ranks India at 82. It's, therefore, clear that although India may possess small pockets where potentially high-value research is conducted, collectively and as a nation India is lacking in an innovation system that would provide infrastructure for fostering research and form the backbone of R&D activity in the country.

---

3. Cordeiro and Al-Hawamdeh (2001).

The World Economic Forum's recently released *Global Competitiveness Report*, ranks 142 economies based on productivity across a dozen interrelated 'pillars of competitiveness', including innovation, infrastructure, higher education and training, and the macroeconomic environment.[4] According to the report, competitive economies are those that have in place factors driving the productivity enhancements on which their present and future prosperity is built. Innovation is particularly important for economies as they approach the frontiers of knowledge; countries must design and develop cutting-edge products and processes to maintain a competitive edge. This would necessitate the provision of an environment that is conducive to the enhancement of innovation activity, as a requisite for countries to burnish their innovation capabilities. The present economic uncertainty and environment of financial volatility mandates resistance to pressures obliging cutting back on R&D spending, both at the private and public levels and it will be critical for sustainable growth, going into the future. Key to innovation-driven economies, like the US, will be continued innovation and 'business sophistication'—conducive to higher efficiency in the production of goods and services—which leads to improved productivity and greater competitiveness. Given the importance of public investment in the competitiveness-enhancing areas such as education or innovation for future competitiveness, policymakers must very carefully measure the effects of reducing such investments, as this may endanger future growth and prosperity. This would have the undesired effect of capitalising over short-term financial difficulties, at the cost of engendering longer-term competitive weakness. Policymakers should therefore focus on measures to enhance competitiveness that would strengthen their countries' growth potential and thus improve the budgetary situation. In particular, it means sufficient investment in R&D, especially by the private sector, the presence of high-quality scientific research institutions, extensive collaboration in research between universities and industry, and enhancing intellectual property (IP) protection.

4. *Global Competitiveness Report 2011-12*, released by the World Economic Forum in September 2011.

India's Case

The Need for a Paradigm Change

The advancement in the realm of connectivity has accelerated while India progressed along the path of economic liberalisation. The sea change in information, communication and technology (ICT) adoption and penetration that we are witnessing today connotes a monumental shift in the very foundation of what we, in my generation, knew as India. It is, however, also true that some decisions have caused distress but the rewards have, in time, outweighed these sacrifices and borne fruits to a larger number of the hitherto marginalised sections of our populace. So, while there are some of us who repeatedly criticise such changes and want the status quo to cement, stagnating progress, it must also be recognised that the time for gradual change is over. There is a primal requisite to create a whole new paradigm—one that is innovative, opens up new doors and challenges our traditional, hierarchical structures, by combining multiple layers of technology to access connectivity and information systems.

This strengthening imperative for effectuating a radical shift that is heightened by a sense of urgency must be absorbed in our decision-making and policy implementation. India requires innovation in government, innovation in education, innovation in health services and innovation in agriculture. The innovation paradigm will be India's key differentiator, in an integrated and increasingly globalised world economy, in the same way it has been the catalyst for prosperity and affluence in many western economies.

India *vs.* China

Increasing R&D spending can improve the absorptive capacity for the adoption of new technologies. Both China and India have increased their R&D expenditure significantly in recent years, with China's growing at almost 20 per cent per year. However, the number of researchers has grown much more slowly and in the case of India, their absolute numbers appear to have actually fallen! On the other hand, R&D wages have risen, as the premium on skills has increased. While relatively low R&D expenditure is not necessarily a problem in a developing economy, the stagnation of India's R&D intensity at about 1 per cent of GDP is a concern, particularly as China's has recently risen to over 1.4 per cent.[5] It's also noteworthy to take into account the proportionate ratio of the GDP of the two countries. While the valuation of these intangible investments is far from clear due to quality differences, the divergence in inputs is reflected in research outputs as well. In particular, the number of articles published by China's scientific community has grown at a furious pace, but India's have remained comparatively static. This is ironic, as India's legal system appears to offer better intellectual property rights protection than China's, and, therefore should promote more research activity.[6]

The 'Indian' Innovation

India, today commands an enviable position in world economy, with a crucial vantage due to the burgeoning proportion of its knowledge economy. The budding contingent of knowledge workers, with diverse skill-sets and purpose-driven ambitions, and the intensifying share of foreign investments, when combined with the teeming domestic market have led to a mushrooming of innovative products and services, inspired by the specific Indian context. It is noteworthy that while most of the developed world has been in the throes of a shrinking economic outlook, for the last couple of years, due to contracting domestic demand for credit and products, India's economy has continued to thrive because of prospering demand in the home market and a pullulating middle class. This has sketched a dynamic panorama across the landscape of the Indian economy that is abuzz with novel business models, service-delivery mechanisms, services and products. The pulse of this evolving, plasma-like economy is quickened by 'frugal' or 'reverse' innovation which is at the very core of the entire bustle.

India is uniquely poised to reap the advantages provided by a nation of a billion connected people, and the country's strength and global leadership in IT and software. This connectivity as well as IT talent is changing the nature of processes, business, industry, delivery systems: and our innovative thinking has to leverage the unprecedented advantages provided by this changing landscape of technology and collaboration. India has

5. OECD (2008).
6. Dougherty (2007-08).

continuing challenges arising from unmet needs in critical areas like health, education, employment, and economic and social wellbeing. Its complex challenges cannot be addressed through incremental approaches. Instead it calls for radical change—in fact, tectonic shifts that only innovation can enable. Our efforts have been underscored by a need to develop an inclusive innovation strategy geared towards creating 'more from less for more'. India needs more 'frugal, distributed, affordable' innovation that produces more 'frugal cost' products and services that are affordable by people at low levels of incomes without compromising the safety, efficiency, and utility of such products. The appeal of such a strategy, essential for developing economies, is increasingly becoming relevant to the developed world that is also now keen on driving down costs. The core idea is to innovate, to produce affordable and qualitative solutions that address the needs of people at the bottom of the pyramid (BoP), eliminate disparity and focus on an inclusive growth model. While conceptualising these initiatives, the key drivers will be parameters of sustainability, affordability, durability, quality, global competitiveness and local needs.

The Immediate Context

India is increasingly becoming a global innovation hub for high-tech products and services, with numerous multinationals locating their R&D facilities in the country and the enhanced capacity of existing research centres. There is no doubt that, in recent years, progress in the dissemination of knowledge and the use of ICT have become increasingly widespread, and have resulted in productivity improvements. The number of patent applications have more than doubled over the four-year period from 2004-05 till 2008-09, while the number of patents granted have actually multiplied eight-fold.[7] This not only indicates an escalation in the R&D efforts, but also signifies the quality improvements in the same. The egressing trend has been that of innovations in designing low-cost products, of agreeable efficiency standards and intuitive utility that are scalable and have positive social benefits. However, the country is still understood to be underperforming, and is said to have an 'innovation deficit' which has direct implications for long-term industrial competitiveness and economic growth.

7. Ministry of Finance Statistics, Government of India, 2011.

There are a multitude of problems as well, that hinder progress. The Indian economy employs about 90 per cent of the workforce in the informal sector which is often characterised by underemployment, as well as low-productivity and low-skill livelihood opportunities. Although India has the benefit of a dynamic young population—with more than half of the country's population under 25 years old—only 17 per cent of people in their mid-20s and older have a secondary education. In order to sustain rapid growth and accelerate poverty alleviation, India needs to aggressively harness its innovation potential, relying on innovation-led inclusive growth to achieve economic and social transformation.[8] India spends a mere one per cent of her GDP on R&D and most of it through national laboratories which are hardly the cradles of innovation-led enterprises. The need of the hour is to promote an innovation culture backed by large investments in knowledge based enterprises through agencies such as the Knowledge Commission, National Innovation Foundation and various Science and Technology departments, as well as the implementation of a National Innovation Legislation.[9]

The Changing Landscape

A cross-cutting, multipronged strategy is needed to make India's innovation system better in meeting needs of the common people. Most discussions on India's innovation system focus on formal R&D efforts and the formal part of the economy. However, India is an extremely heterogeneous economy, and most of its population operates in the informal sector, as has been sufficiently evidenced in the 66th round of NSS. Given the rising divergence between productivity in agriculture and in knowledge-intensive professional sectors, such as ICT and finance, coupled with the economy's inability to sufficiently absorb migrants from the agricultural sector (not to mention the swelling labour force), income inequality will likely increase. This has been the trend in most other economies—especially fast growing ones. Inequality is also likely to worsen unless special efforts are made to address the needs of the poor. Much of the knowledge and technology needed to achieve the Millennium

8. Dutz (2007).
9. Nair (2011).

Development Goals (MDGs) already exists. Much is known about basic nutrition, sanitation, preventive medicine, environmentally friendly technologies, cheap mobile phones, and the like. But poor people's needs are broader than the few listed and monitored as part of the MDGs, and further innovation is required to improve delivery of a wide range of public services. The recent strides in this sphere, enabled by the infrastructure facilitated by Aadhaar, smart cards and the Business Correspondent (BC) model, all build upon ICT deployment. Concurring with these projects, the ICT Committee of the Twelfth FYP has recommended deepening of the country's ICT roots, by means of various interventions, including the creation of public information infrastructure (PII) for distribution of government services, as a national resource, and publishing government information in the public domain with the aim of encouraging evaluation of government programmes. But far more needs to be done, by means of innovation in preventive medicine, clean water, education and other public services that can benefit from harnessing collaboration for formal creation efforts focussed on the marginalised. The creation of sustainable livelihoods for the poor is elemental in inclusion efforts and should be prioritised over cost-cutting and increasing access to goods and services, needed by the poor.[10] These twin goals of employment generation and providing basic services can be achieved by innovation, in product design and service delivery, and commercialisation through entrepreneurship.

Innovation is already contributing significantly to the growth of Indian economy and dynamism of the industrial sector. Indian entrepreneurs and enterprises are simultaneously developing novel solutions for the needs of Indian consumers that provide access to products and services at a fraction of the cost of the solutions available from advanced economies. Examples of such innovations are the delivery models of mobile communication services that have expanded the reach of telephony with the cheapest call services in the world, extremely low-cost eye surgeries which do not compromise on surgical standards at US $50 (compared to US $1,650 in the US), Hepatitis-B vaccine for a thirtieth of the cost of earlier products, a people's car for less than US $2,500, an innovative refrigerator using thermoelectric cooling at a price less than US $75, a water purifier

10. Dutz (2007: 105).

combining nanotechnology and rice husks to provide safe drinking water for a family of five at US $0.02 per day, a solar lighting system for rural houses at US $200 and a solar powered ATM machine that has just 4 per cent of the total energy requirement of conventional ATMs. This array of revolutionary products and service delivery models is radically altering the Indian economic landscape, by fostering inclusion, deepening social benefits and distribution of rewards to a wider, in most parts marginalised, audience.

The role of innovation in spurring growth, overcoming natural resource constraints and unleashing Indian energies and synergies is widely recognised all over the world.[11] Recognising the importance of innovation, the President of India has declared the 2010 decade as the 'decade of innovation', with a focus on inclusive growth. The first approach to promoting inclusive innovation is for India to harness, increase and redirect formal creation efforts to better meet the needs of the economically weaker sections of Indian society. The 'Unleashing India's Innovation' report, by the World Bank, recommends creating incentives for pro-poor early-stage technology development (ESTD) and commercialisation by the formal sector, possibly by providing more preferential matching grants to collaborations among public R&D entities, industry, universities, NGOs and global poverty alleviation networks.[12]

Innovation in India

India possesses a massive science and technology (S&T) infrastructure spread across the country and is in an enviable position with regard to the S&T manpower, as is witnessed in the expansive network of over 200 universities, 1,500 research institutions and 5,000 PhDs being turned out every year. Scientific institutions have been set up and nurtured in many diverse sectors. These have included agriculture, atomic energy, electronics, environment, ocean, space, biotechnology, non-conventional energy sources, defence, health, etc. The chain of national laboratories, which was set up after Independence, has built several core competencies in a diverse assortment of fields. All this gives India a reinforced launching pad, on

11. Approach Paper to the Twelfth FYP, Planning Commission of India.
12. Dutz (2007: 106).

which it can cultivate an ambitious growth agenda. India's achievements in science and technology, in the post-independence period, are something to be proud of. Thanks to the 'green revolution,' India is able not only to feed its masses but has enough to spare and export, while the 'white revolution' has made India the largest milk producer in the world. With a comprehensive defence research and development infrastructure, India is among the few countries of the world, which makes the most sophisticated weapons and defence systems, including missiles of various descriptions and multi-barrel rocket systems. It has developed low-level tracking radar, night vision devices and sophisticated ship sonar systems, while an indigeneous light combat vehicle and a remotely piloted vehicle are at an advanced stage of development. Today, India ranks among the few nations of the world that have a credible capability in space science and technology, including design and construction of satellites and launch vehicles. India's capability in nuclear technology, including nuclear fast breeder reactors, has been the result of indigeneous efforts.[13]

Three distinctions of the emerging Indian approach to innovation are worth noting. First, it focusses on finding affordable solutions for the needs of people—for health, water, transport, etc.—without compromising on quality. Second, in the Indian approach to innovation, desired outcomes are produced by innovations in organisational and process frameworks which deliver the fruits of innovation, to the people that may otherwise have to be developed in scientific laboratories. Third, there are innovations in the process of innovating which greatly reduce the cost of research and development. The open source drug discovery process being applied by the Council of Scientific and Industrial Research (CSIR), to develop drugs for treatment of tuberculosis, serves as an excellent example of these characteristics. This innovative approach to R&D is founded in a semantic search enabled, web based platform for collaboration that has been developed by Infosys; it has cut down costs and reduced the time for drug development. This new paradigm of innovation, in which India may be emerging as a global leader, contrasts sharply with the conventional approach, mostly focussed on increasing the inputs of S&T, and R&D. It

13. *The Indian Innovation System*, Ragunath A. Mashelkar, CSIR Bhatnagar Fellow at NCL, Pune. p.2. Published by United Nations Public Administration Network (UNPAN).

considers measurement of the number of papers and patents produced, as the fundamental metric to gauge innovation capacity. 'Frugal innovation' is focussed on the efficiency of innovation and on outcomes that benefit people, especially the poor. Industrially advanced countries too are examining their innovation policies to incorporate this broader concept of innovation. For instance, Sweden, ranked as the second most innovative nation in the world in terms of traditional inputs of S&T and R&D per capita, is formulating a National Innovation Strategy that is focussed on using innovation not only for enhancing growth and competitiveness of its industries, but also for addressing global challenges of inclusion, and for improving the delivery of its public services. Its national strategy broadens the scope of innovation to go beyond products to processes, services and new business models. Similarly, UK has also placed all types of innovation at the heart of its strategy to drive future growth and the country's vision. Its strategy also highlights the need for Government policy to recognise the changing face of innovation. Thus, the metrics of 'innovation' are shifting from an input oriented paradigm focussed on R&D investments and patents, towards an output oriented system that looks at impact in terms of benefits for people.[14]

National Innovation Council

As adviser to prime minister on innovations, I have been entrusted with the mandate of creating a roadmap for innovations for this decade. To spearhead this effort, the PM has constituted a National Innovation Council (NIC) with distinguished members from various fields. The NIC will seek to create a strategy for fostering innovations at the national, state and sectoral levels by focussing on five key parameters: platform, inclusion, ecosystem, drivers and discourse. The aim will be to re-define innovations to go beyond formal R&D parameters, facilitate innovative solutions that lead to inclusive growth for the people and by the people, foster an innovation ecosystem across domains and sectors to strengthen entrepreneurship, focus on key drivers to ensure sustainability, durability and quality, and lastly, to expand the space for dialogue and discourse on innovation. NIC will also be involved in facilitating state level and sectoral

14. *Approach Paper to the Twelfth Five Year Plan*, Planning Commission of India.

innovations. This will create an ecosystem to boost innovation performance in the country.[15] The agency is facilitating the setting up of State Innovation Councils (SICs) in each state, 18 of which are already operational. These councils would enlist non-government expertise and are expected to drive the innovation agenda at the state level. They will aid in harnessing core competencies, local talent, resources and capabilities, in order to create new opportunities. NIC is also encouraging the setting up of SICs aligned to Central government ministries to promote innovation ecosystems across sectors and domains; so far 19 ministries have instituted these councils.

Innovations require not just inputs and capacity but also a political economy of reform and a mindset shift. The initiatives at NIC will aim to foster this paradigm change. This will involve creating a constituency for innovation where government, academia, industry and the citizenry, are all participants in the innovation movement. This will also involve creating an innovation ecosystem not only concerned with creating high-tech products, but with enhancing the quality of life for everybody, by creating sustainable solutions, evolving processes and changing mindsets. The effort will be to institutionalise and foster a culture of innovation in the country. While we are increasingly witnessing innovative sparks in the system, as a nation we still lack an organisational culture of innovation. The time is right for India to blaze its own trail by creating a model of inclusive innovation specific to the country's needs and development goals.[16]

NIC will also undertake outreach activities to cultivate and promote a culture of innovation. It has attempted this through multiple initiatives that include the 'India Innovation Portal' for knowledge sharing on innovation, promotion of innovation by Members of Parliament through awards at constituency level and action through the public broadcasting media and collaboration with media in general. The India Innovation Portal has already become operational and acts as a gateway for innovation resources and a platform for idea exchange.

---

15. Sam Pitroda in the Foreword to National Innovation Council booklet "Towards a More Inclusive and Innovative India".

16. Pitroda (2011).

India Inclusive Innovation Fund

The National Innovation Council is working on conceptualising the India Inclusive Innovation Fund which is founded in the principle that innovative enterprise can profitably and competitively engage citizens at the bottom of the economic pyramid, through scalable entrepreneurial models, and in doing so, provide goods and services that will transform their lives for the better. The Fund proposes to invest in a new generation of Indian entrepreneurs who will build world class enterprises that focus on problems of the poor, without compromising on economic success. In doing so, the fund will help create a new Indian model of innovation: one that bridges growth and equitability. The fund will focus on providing risk capital funding to enterprises that create and deliver technologies and solutions aimed at enhancing the quality of life at the bottom of the pyramid, and—subject to applicable law—work with other funds with objectives similar to its own. The fund seeks to promote enterprises engaged in developing solutions in key areas such as health, education, agriculture, handloom, handicrafts and other small business enterprises. The fund will support investment at different stages of the enterprise development cycle, from early stages, through later phases of scaling-up of potentially successful solutions and business models.

The fund will combine commercial and social returns and proposes to seek capital from a range of sources, including seed fund contributions from the government and its agencies, contributions from various Indian public sector undertakings, and contributions from private investors, corporate and investment firms. It will, therefore, operate as a for-profit entity with a social investment focus and seek to provide its investors with reasonable financial returns. The fund is proposed to reach an eventual target size of Rs 5,000 crore, with the first close to occur at a very modest size and to be scaled up gradually. The fund has been proposed to have a lifespan of 10 years, extendable by up to three years. It will be structured as an autonomous and professionally-managed entity. The fund will seek to invest not just in enterprises focussed on inclusive innovation, but also in other funds that currently back such enterprises. This will allow the fund to maximise impact, by leveraging existing investments made by private and philanthropic investors in BoP enterprises, across a wider base of investees.

The fund will also explore the possibility of establishing a 'soft' incubation capacity and corollary resources—expertise and programmes—that will mentor and support individual investee entrepreneurs and companies, in successful enterprise development, scaling and efficiency enhancement. This effort will address social impact objectives, by kick-starting an ecosystem of capacity-building around BoP-focussed enterprises and their economic returns objectives, by providing entrepreneurial teams with the resources and institutional support required to successfully deliver on their ideas. Hitherto, the best entrepreneurial and technological talent across the world has tended to focus on the problems of the resourceful members of the international community, while marginalising the poor. The Inclusive Innovation Fund will break this convention by investing in a new generation of Indian entrepreneurial talent, capable of innovating in products, processes and business models: successfully combining profitability and business excellence, with transformational socioeconomic impact.[17]

The Public Information Infrastructure

The two underlying motives for the massive investments in national information infrastructures which are currently under way are: 1) the fear that failure to do so will result in an inability to maintain communications, social, intellectual, and even business links with those countries which do invest, and 2) the belief that investments will not only be repaid by economic growth, but will boost economies measurably—the so-called 'information payoff'.[18]

The Twelfth FYP is being developed with a focus on ICT, in the same manner that the Eleventh FYP had a singular concentration on education. The Twelfth plan is being drafted with the objective of developing Public Information Infrastructure (PII) that would create digital highways for facilitating a thoroughfare of information throughout the country. It would democratise information and provide information accessibility to the populace. This network of information highways will satiate the

17. *http://iii.gov.in/index.php/innovations/ninc-initiatives/india-inclusive-innovation-fund*

18. Harindranath and Liebenau (1998).

multifaceted requirements of spurring innovation in the country, and of providing connectivity for public administration, communication, education, governance and furthering business enterprises. This PII is being developed with the view to make it the fourth virtual pillar of the government, in addition to the existing judiciary, legislative and executive. It will integrate geographical boundaries and applications into a single secure National Information Space.

The technology necessitated for facilitating a digital information highway that would engulf the entire country, providing connectivity and access to information in every nook and cranny, has been available for over a decade now; but this technology hadn't been accessible for deployment at such a large scale, during a large part of the last decade. Since scalability has a linear relation to affordability, the erosion of price-points has made these technologies accessible for large scale employment, in the public domain. The ontogenesis of such a network on a national scale has also been impeded in the past by various other factors, such as the lack of a support ecosystem of applications, inadequate opportunities for employment, insufficient awareness among civil society members and the lack of successful implementation models. But due to the proliferation of a potpourri of widely successful pilot projects, the increasing realisation of the benefits of ICT among the populace, the exponential pace of ICT adoption and the mushrooming of successful applications developed by private as well as public state actors, have induced a favourable climate to choreograph an endeavour of providing cross-country PII. The general environment of a substantive sustained economic growth rate of over 8 per cent, a burgeoning IT sector, dilating support-infrastructure carpeting and the availability of underutilised IT infrastructure, all carve out the versatile backdrop for a fruitful orchestration of a nationwide PII deployment. There is a fabric of ICT infrastructure, comprising a million kilometres of underutilised optical fibre, operating below capacity, dispersed throughout the country. The combination of these capabilities creates the right set of conditions for bacciferous policy frameworks to capitalise on their individual capacities and bear fruits in the public domain, building upon the drive for digital and financial inclusion of the marginalised sections of the populace, and fostering social cohesion. Following in the footsteps of the Finnish, Swedish and Singapore governments, the cultivation of a pan-

India PII would undoubtedly be the largest undertaking to provide public ICT infrastructure, in a country having diversity in the likeliness of India.

The assays in this direction should commence with broadening the ambit of connectivity in the country, by providing reliable and high-bandwidth connection through a national data bus that would append to the compass of information and training services. This would form the substructure which would be leveraged to facilitate governance and administrative services alongside variegated services by private actors. The 2009 World Bank Report[19] on 'Information and Communication for Development' notes that a 10 per cent augmentation in broadband penetration leads to a 1.38 per cent increase in per capita GDP in developing economies. Moreover, the broadband penetration in India is just 0.74 per cent compared with a tele-density of around 60 per cent and hence, a growth in broadband deployment can unleash a significant wave of growth in the country, as was the case with voice telephony.[20] There are two fundamental constituent components of the PII: the National Knowledge Network (NKN) and the broadband network connecting *panchayats*. The NKN is a high-speed multi-gigabyte network that will primarily connect all Indian universities, research institutions, R&D centres and, eventually schools. This project was approved by the Cabinet and is being initiated, with 405 nodes already functioning and around 1,500 yet to be connected to a universal 40 GB bandwidth optical-fibre network. The NKN will not only connect educational and research institutes in India, but will be interwoven into global research networks to enable real time collaboration and research. Some of these international institutions include the Trans-Eurasia Information Network (TEIN3), Council for Nuclear Research (CERN) and Global Ring Network for Advanced Applications Development (GLORIAD). Thereby, this would facilitate collaboration and knowledge sharing, by connecting all clusters of innovation and learning which will buttress the tangible and intangible innovation infrastructure. The tentative timeframe for setting up of the NKN is one year, with a cost of around $2 billion.

---

19. World Bank (2009).
20. Office of Adviser to the Prime Minister on Public Information Infrastructure & Innovations (2010).

The ITC Committee of the Twelfth FYP has bespoken of prioritising the imperative for a nation of a billion connected people, as part of the Planning Commission's ICT strategy. In keeping with this, the second objective of the PII would be to connect 250,000 *panchayats* through a web of optic fibre network. These 250,000 *panchayats* form the core of the governance structure in rural India and are the foundational nodes of information collection and dissemination, and service delivery points for Government administration. The successful implementation of the various social sector schemes and programmes of the Central and state governments at the grassroot level is inextricably tied to the *panchayats*.[21] The government has only recently approved the implementation of this proposal to connect all *panchayats* through optic fibre and a rural broadband plan. NIC has begun work on applications through a pilot in Ajmer district in Rajasthan and proposes to enlarge this to one district in each state. To leverage the real benefits of broadband connectivity, it is essential to develop appropriate applications platform for government services, education, health, agriculture, employment, etc. Towards this, the NIC will also work on applications for the rural broadband, in collaboration with ministries of Rural Development, Panchayati Raj, HRD, Health and the Prime Minister's National Council on Skill Development (NCSD), so as to facilitate a comprehensive platform for communication and service delivery. The cost for the entire outlay is $5 billion and the tentative time for implementation is around two years. The *panchayats'* network would have to be supplemented with relevant applications for providing information and services. The participation of private sector in this endeavour of software development would be crucial and would serve to advance efforts of the state actors. This enterprise of germinating a PII may be better understood as comprising the stages, as shown in Figure 8.1.

The PII would also have to be aided with supporting platforms, such as the UID and GIS, for broadening the premise of public services and rendering digital service delivery to promote efficiency and standardisation. This would greatly profit the beneficiary through direct delivery, and taking out the intermediary. The government is developing seven service delivery platforms simultaneously; these are shown in Figure 8.2. These seven

21. Office of Adviser to the Prime Minister on Public Information Infrastructure & Innovations (2010).

platforms would coordinate and work in tandem with each other through application development for service delivery, under the aegis of the PII which is being developed centrally by the government. The Planning Commission is orchestrating this exercise by acting as a central body for coordination and cooperation, through planning.

Figure 8.1

Public Information Infrastructure Development Process

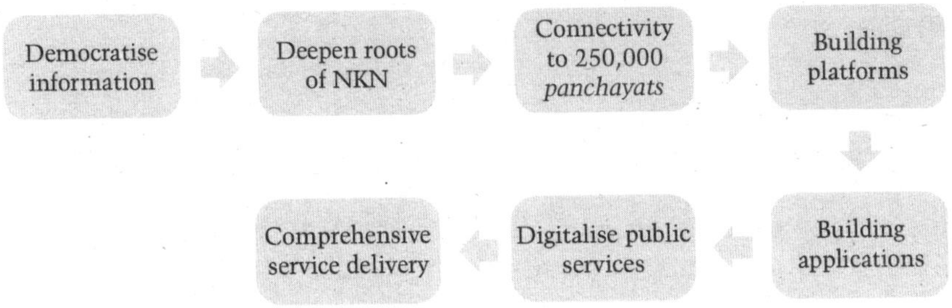

This endeavour would engage the Centre and state actors in different, but complementary roles. The Central government would be burdened with facilitating the infrastructure, while the state actors would be employed in a more localised and contextual role of providing services.

The PII would also create a new paradigm for enmeshing private and public sector actors in coordinative contact. The planning and funding of the project would rest with the Central government, while private sector would be enmeshed to contribute to application and software development. The government would render this infrastructure for service delivery by private actors through pay-per-use mechanism, where a fee would be levied for its utilisation. The execution and implementation of the PII would be carried through solely by the Government of India; private enterprises would be invited to deliver value addition services that further the impetus for financial and digital inclusion. This PII would be a national asset and is being developed along the lines of open-source systems in the realm of application development. The central planning agencies are also exploring the panorama of existing infrastructure for the possibility of operating them on a sharing basis.

Figure 8.2

Seven Platforms being Developed as Part of the PII

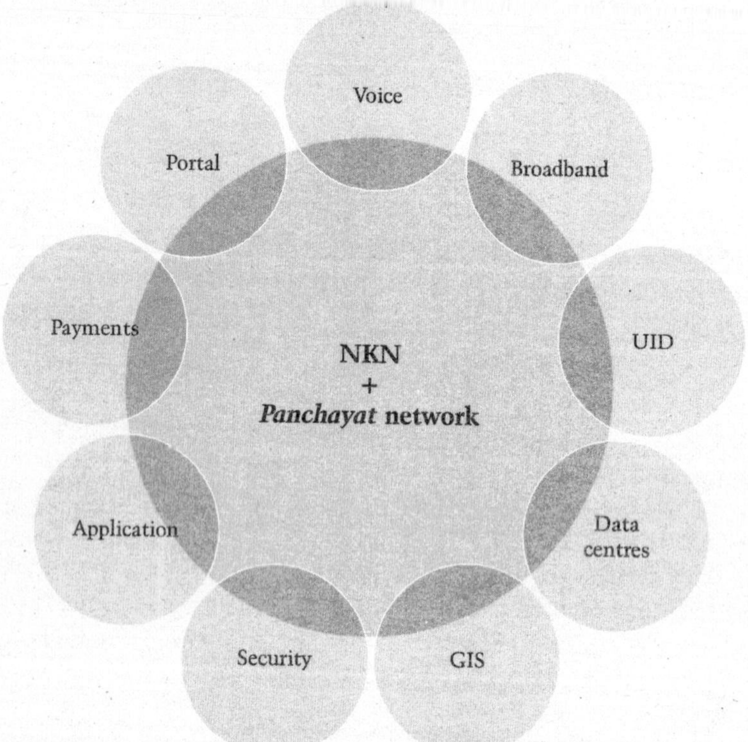

Innovations have long been part of Indian heritage and tradition—from the discovery of zero and the decimal system to being the cradle of an ancient civilisation and major world religions, from being home to the first global universities such as Nalanda and Takshila to architectural and engineering marvels. Moving forward, India also made successful strides in agriculture, milk productivity, space, atomic energy and telecom. However, this spirit of innovation has somehow been lost or subsumed in the development discourse of our nation. More than ever, there is a need to re-discover and re-trigger an innovation culture in the country to respond to our unique needs and challenges in the globally competitive marketplace. India can only rise above her innovation deficit by creating a national infrastructure that would act as a catalyst for cultivating innovation clusters and facilitate collaboration in science and research.

References

Cordeiro, Cheryl Marie and Suliman Al-Hawamdeh (2001). "National Information Infrastructure and the Realization of Singapore IT2000 Initiative", *Information Research* 6(2): 1-2, Division of Information Studies, Singapore: School of Computer Engineering, Nanyang Technological University, January.

Dougherty, Sean (2008) "China and India: Making Sense of Innovation and Growth", *The OECD Observer* No. 264/265, December 2007-January 2008, OECD Economics Department, pp.2-3.

Dutz, Mark A. (2007). *Unleashing India's Innovation: Toward Sustainable and Inclusive Growth*. World Bank.

Harindranath, G. and Jonathan Liebenau (1998). *National Information Infrastructure Policies in International Perspective*. London School of Economics, University of London. pp.2-3.

Nair, M.D. (2011). "Innovation deficit hurts India Inc", *The Hindu Business Line*, 27th April.

OECD (2008). *OECD Reviews of Innovation Policy: China 2008*. OECD Publishing.

Office of Adviser to the Prime Minister on Public Information Infrastructure & Innovations (2010). "Broadband to Panchayats: Empowering Panchayats & Rural India by 'Democratising Information through Broadband", *White Paper*, August, pp.3.

Pitroda, Sam (2011). "Towards a More Innovative and Inclusive India: Creating a Roadmap for a 'Decade of Innovation'", *Strategy Paper*, March, New Delhi: Office of Adviser to the Prime Minister on Public Information Infrastructure & Innovations. pp.47.

World Bank (2009). *Information and Communication for Development: Extending Reach and Increasing Impact*.

World Economic Forum (2010-11). *The Innovation for Development Report*.

Table 8.1

*Innovation Capacity Index Rankings 2010–11**

Sweden	1	80.3	Mauritius	46	54.7	Belize	91
Switzerland	2	78.1	Malta	47	54.6	Honduras	92
Singapore	3	76.7	Tunisia	48	54.1	Rwanda	93
Finland	4	76.1	Saudi Arabia	48	54.1	Zambia	94
United States	5	74.8	Azerbaijan, Republic of	50	53.8	Algeria	94
Denmark	6	74.3	Jordan	51	53.7	Madagascar	96
Canada	7	73.6	South Africa	52	53.2	Syrian Arab Republic	97
Netherlands	8	72.8	Croatia, Republic of	52	53.2	Tanzania	98
Taiwan	9	72.5	Kazakhstan, Republic of	54	53.1	Bolivia	98
Luxembourg	10	72.2	Romania	55	53.0	Nicaragua	100
Korea, Republic of	11	72.1	Uruguay	56	52.8	Kenya	101
Norway	12	72.0	Russian Federation	56	52.8	Nepal	102
Hong Kong SAR	13	71.4	Oman	58	51.8	Pakistan	102
New Zealand	14	71.3	Kuwait	59	51.3	Venezuela	104
United Kingdom	14	71.3	Costa Rica	59	51.3	Mozambique, Republic of	105
Japan	16	70.2	Ukraine	61	50.4	Uganda	106
Australia	17	69.4	Turkey	62	50.2	Papua New Guinea	107
Ireland	18	69.1	Mexico	62	50.2	Ethiopia	108
Iceland	19	69.0	China, People's Republic of	64	49.9	Malawi	109
Germany	20	68.9	Greece	64	49.9	Senegal	110
Israel	21	67.5	Panama	66	49.4	Bangladesh	110
Austria	22	66.7	Colombia	66	49.4	Suriname	112
Belgium	23	66.1	Argentina	68	49.3	Cambodia	113
France	24	65.3	Botswana	69	48.9	Lao PDR	114
Estonia, Republic of	25	60.5	Peru	70	48.7	Cameroon	115
Lithuania, Republic of	26	59.6	El Salvador	71	48.0	Nigeria	116
Slovenia, Republic of	27	59.1	Trinidad and Tobago	72	47.7	Yemen, Republic of	117
United Arab Emirates	28	58.9	Bosnia and Herzegovina	73	47.5	Congo, Republic of	118
Spain	29	58.8	Vietnam	74	47.1	Mauritania	118
Latvia, Republic of	30	58.7	Egypt, Arab Republic of	75	46.6	Sudan	120
Chile	31	58.3	Ghana	76	46.4	Mali	121
Czech Republic	32	57.8	Indonesia	77	46.0	Côte d'Ivoire	122
Bulgaria	33	57.4	Namibia	77	46.0	Iraq	123
Bahrain, Kingdom of	34	57.0	Dominican Republic	79	45.5	Guinea	124
Hungary	35	56.8	Jamaica	79	45.5	Angola	125
Slovak Republic	36	56.7	Philippines	81	45.3	Togo	126
Portugal	36	56.7	Brazil	81	45.3	Niger	127
Italy	36	56.7	Guatemala	83	44.7	Zimbabwe	128
Malaysia	39	56.4	Ecuador	84	44.6	Haiti	129
Poland	40	56.3	Iran, Islamic Republic of	85	44.5	Afghanistan, Islamic Republic of	130
Qatar	41	55.9	Sri Lanka	86	44.4	Chad	130
Macedonia, FYR	42	55.3	Lebanon	87	44.3		
Cyprus	43	55.2	Morocco	88	44.2		
Georgia	44	55.0	India	88	44.2		
Thailand	45	54.8	Paraguay	88	44.2		

Note: *All rankings and scores are after rounding.

Source: Innovation for Development Report 2010-11, EBS.

9 Urbanisation and Employment

The Double Headed Janus

HARI SANKARAN

One of the biggest challenges facing the country is that of urbanisation. Handled correctly, it could pay India huge dividends in accelerating growth to the double digits, addressing issues of inequity, and comprehensively dealing with the scourge of poverty through massive employment generation. Handled poorly, it will result in an urban nightmare of vicious proportions (largely on the back of underinvestment and poor employment opportunities) with unimaginable consequences. Fundamental to the success of our response to this challenge is to view infrastructure development as a means to capturing the massive externalities linked to urbanisation primarily in the form of employment generation. Capturing these externalities forms the crux of the argument. Montek S. Ahluwalia is no stranger to challenges but he will need to bring all his intellect and experience to bear, if indeed the challenge of urbanisation is to be effectively dealt with. The thesis of this paper is that urbanisation and employment are similar to a Janus. It is the failure of planning and design to see them as such that frustrates efforts to internalise the massive positive externalities associated with this phenomenon.

Introduction

The ties between urbanisation and employment have been debated for long. It has been argued that the conditions or terms of employment are essentially and integrally linked to urban life and urban sustenance. In the Indian context, however, this linkage assumes a new dimension: we have reached or, as many will argue, touched a level of urbanisation where existing cities and towns can no longer bear the burden of being able to generate growth, both economically and socially. Although, India has experienced rapid strides in socioeconomic improvement and growth of urban centres during the last several decades, her urban infrastructure has not kept pace with these advances. Urban infrastructure development has been uneven and incapable of serving all sections of our populace. This has been the case, even though it has all along been accepted that the 'pull' for migration of people from the country's villages has been influenced by the employment opportunities, as also by the choice of improving one's living standards that a country's urban centres offer.

India's towns and cities make a major contribution to the country's economy. Populated by just under one-third of its people, India's urban areas today generate over two-thirds of the country's GDP and account for 90 per cent of government revenues. In fact, it has led to a situation where more and more people are migrating from the countryside to find employment in urban centres that have little space to grow. India's urban population reaching close to 600 million, by 2031, is not merely a shift of demographics; it places cities and towns at the centre of the development trajectory. Moreover, this will, in effect also place a lot of burden on the existing urban habitations. These challenges need to be tackled if the urban sector has to play a critical role in the structural transformation of the Indian economy and in sustaining the high rates of economic growth, in the coming decades.

Constraints and Ambiguities

The provision of high quality public services for one and all, across the length and breadth of India's cities and towns is an end in itself, but it will also facilitate a full realisation of India's economic potential.[1] However, slums that account for one-fourth of all urban housing make this end a difficult endeavour. In Mumbai, for instance, more than half of the population lives in slums.[2] Again, while urbanisation is emerging as the driving force for growth, concerns are mounting about the effects of expanding cities, especially when it comes to health, water, shelter and sanitation, environment, and more importantly about generating employment. Moreover, today, more than 95 per cent of India's exports

1. *http://niua.org/projects/hpec/FinalReport-hpec.pdf*
2. *http://www.indiaenews.com/pdf/39263.pdf*

originate from the nine Tier-I cities whose infrastructure is heavily constrained. In addition, the recommended move to Tier-II and Tier-III cities has not gathered momentum given poor access, local infrastructure and talent issues.[3] This exemplifies the issue of urban sprawl and the ensuing problems that follow centred urbanisation, while making a case for spreading out urbanisation and, hence, productive employment opportunities.

The data released by the National Sample Survey Organisation (NSSO)[4] shows that only two million jobs were generated between 2004 and 2009, even as the economy grew at an average rate of 8.43 per cent. This is the lowest employment growth recorded ever since NSSO started collecting employment and unemployment data four decades ago. The concern of 'jobless growth' is thus likely to be back on the agenda, since the period 2004-05 to 2007-08 was also the best ever in terms of real GDP growth—9.4 per cent per annum. This is particularly important given that employment creation has been claimed to be an important component of 'inclusive growth'.[5] The employment numbers present a stark contrast to the Planning Commission's target of 58 million jobs in the five years between 2007 and 2012. However, if the growth in population is factored out, there has been a decline in employment in absolute terms.[6] The latest government data shows that over half the country's workforce is self-employed and women receive less pay than men for similar jobs. While 51 per cent of the country's total workforce is self-employed, only 15.5 per cent are regular wagers or salaried employees and 33.5 per cent are casual labourers.[7] It may not be far-fetched to propound that a large number of the so-called 'self-employed' are in that category not by choice but for want of some job opportunity. In fact, a large chunk of the poor in the country

3. *Perspective 2020: Transform Business, Transform India*, NASSCOM Report, April 2009.

4. The NSS 66th Round carried out during July 2009–June 2010 was the eighth quinquennial round in the series covering subjects of: (i) household consumer expenditure and (ii) employment and unemployment. NSSO, 66th Round Report, Ministry of Statistics and Programme Implementation, June 2011.

5. *http://epw.in/epw/uploads/articles/16530.pdf*

6. *http://www.transparentchennai.com/2011/08/24/nsso%E2%80%99s-66th-round-survey-reveals-shocking-data/*

7. *http://articles.economictimes.indiatimes.com/2011-06-25/news/29747818_1_rural-areas-casual-labourers-urban-areas*

belong to this category, engaging themselves in some petty part-time occupations because the mainstream economic activities have not absorbed them.

The rapid economic growth has also entailed a significant structural transformation in the economy such that the share of agriculture in the GDP has declined from 34 per cent in 1983-84 to about 15 per cent in 2009-10. There has been a sharp increase in the share of services in the GDP from 40 per cent to 57 per cent, and some increase in the share of construction as well, while the share of the secondary sector has remained relatively constant at 20 per cent. This structural transformation can be associated with the trend of reducing dependence of the population on agriculture and increasing migration from low-productivity livelihoods to high-productivity sectors such as industry and services. Since these sectors are based in urban areas, rapid economic growth is normally associated with urbanisation.[8] The rapid shift of the epicentre of economic activity coupled with trends of an accelerating proportion of knowledge-workers in the economy, rising levels of enrollment across the domain of primary, secondary and tertiary education and increasing employment opportunities for females and the rapid urban sprawl, is bringing about the migration of rural people to urban centres, in search of better pay and high productivity employment opportunities. This migration too has two facets, the in-migration i.e., the migration from smaller cities, and the migration from the rural back-country. Generation of wealth is also becoming increasingly dependent on the knowledge industry, with more and more cities becoming repositories of knowledge and technology; they have embossed over the Indian economy as centres of growth. But for this growth to be inclusive, opportunities need to be spread to other parts of the country.

The cities of India have been growing in population, which has also brought an increase in urban density, along with a horizontal sprawl, placing great pressure on scarce resources. The distance between habitations and work places has also increased, leading to increase in travel times which is further amplified by the strain over transportation infrastructure due to swelling urban populations. Then, the question that arises here is whether

8. *Report on Indian Urban Infrastructure and Services* by the High Powered Expert Committee (HPEC) for Estimating the Investment Requirements for Urban Infrastructure Services, March 2011.

the existing urban infrastructure and the pace of its melioration can sustain the burgeoning population and, also bear the burden of accelerating migration.

The Changing Urban Landscape

The plinths of industrialisation, liberalisation, globalisation and the ensuing urbanisation, that have propelled India to the fore of global economy, have created disparate opportunities in varied corners of the country. This disparity has countenanced the established cities to become centres of all productive economic activity, while stagnating progress in others. This heterogeneous urbanisation in India has isolated the majority, who live in villages, while established urban centres have become centres of wealth and affluence. In 1951, there were only five metropolitan cities (with population of over one million), i.e., Kolkata, Mumbai, Chennai, Hyderabad and Delhi. Their number increased to 12 in 1981 and 35 in 2001, while their share in urban population increased from 18.9 per cent in 1951 to 27.7 per cent in 1981 and 37.8 per cent in 2001. By 2001, all the original five metropolitan cities had grown to population of over five million, and Bangalore had joined their ranks. The number of urban centres having a population between one million and five million had dilated to encompass 29 new cities, by 2001. Projections for 2011 show an increase in the number of such cities to 50 and their population to 42.3 per cent of the total urban population, with Ahmedabad and Pune joining the rank of cities having population over five million.[9]

The issue of urban planning is rapidly making inroads in the public sphere, with migration to cities accelerating and increasing infrastructure problems in metros, compounding the issue. There is a strong view worldwide, that cities that are planned and developed by private enterprises are the solution to these problems.[10] The CEO of the Delhi Mumbai Industrial Corridor Development Corporation Ltd. (DMICDC) has concurred, succinctly condensing the issue in his statement, 'There is a very strong case for planned cities. India is going to experience rapid urbanisation involving around 300 million people within the next two to

9. Source: Census of India and High-Powered Committee estimates (March 2011).

10. *http://business.in.com/article/resolution/the-new-cities-of-india/19662/1#ixzz1ajQsTPgh*

three decades. This means that they will either drift to existing cities, thus congesting them further, or move into new cities. If it is new cities, then they will have to be either cities that are planned, or cities that evolve, more or less in an unplanned manner. The former is better.' The concept of private cities is gradually gaining acceptance in India. If all goes well, India should have at least 30 private cities across the country by the end of this decade. The number could be even greater, depending on the policy environment that might foster such developments.

Urban Melioration

It is well established that Indian cities will be the locus and engines of economic growth, over the next two decades, but the realisation of an ambitious goal of near 10 per cent growth in GDP depends fundamentally on making Indian cities much more liveable, inclusive, bankable and competitive.[11] The extent and magnitude of the urban population requires focussed efforts by city planners and developers to cope with the ever-growing strain on the urban infrastructure. Special attention is needed for management and governance of urban areas which are at present fragmented between different state level agencies and urban local bodies (ULBs), with no coordination between them.[12] There is an emerging need to set boundaries and explicate urban governance, dividing the responsibility between various agencies while ensuring cooperation and information sharing between them. Policymakers on their part need to focus on new ways to achieve these results and on different benchmarks that capture efficiency, effectiveness, quality and sustainability in governance, service delivery, intergovernmental municipal finances and social development.[13]

The cities and towns of India are manifestly deficient in the provision of basic services, even to the existing dwellers, while the quality of utilities remains poor. Public services such as drinking water, sewerage, solid waste management, roads, and street lights must be accessible to one and all, in

---

11. *www.planningcommission.nic.in/plans/mta/11th_mta/.../chap18_urban.pdf*
12. Planning Commission (2011). *Urban Infrastructure.*
13. *http://www.inclusion.in/index.php?option=com_content&view=article&id=575&Itemid=77*

order to achieve the goals of inclusion.[14] At the same time, they must meet the service norms as set out by the Ministry of Urban Development in 2008, to ensure the contribution of cities to economic growth. The achievement of both inclusion and economic growth will, however, require shifting the focus of policy from creating physical infrastructure to delivering services which would entail an increased focus on reforming governance. Without this, additional capital investments in urban infrastructure will not result in improvements in service delivery.[15]

The issue of poverty can also be addressed if the needs of the urban poor are isolated from the broader challenges of managing urbanisation. India cannot afford to get its urban strategy wrong, but it cannot get it right without bringing about a fundamental shift in the mindset which separates rural from the urban. The *Report on Indian Urban Infrastructure and Services* argues that the challenge of managing urbanisation will have to be addressed through a combination of increased investment, strengthening the framework for governance and financing, and a comprehensive capacity building programme at all levels of government.[16]

Urban Planning

In his address on World Habitat Day in 2009, Cliff Hague of the Commonwealth Association of Planners (CAP), pointed out that there can be 'no sustainable development without sustainable urbanisation and no sustainable urbanisation without effective planning.'[17] This, therefore, underscores the significance of planning in the face of the urbanisation phenomenon and the need for planners to continuously innovate. The current urban planning and management techniques are archaic and require some creative rethinking. The Master Plan concept—as is currently practised in India—is not widely used elsewhere. Besides, it is not well suited to rapidly growing cities and multi-jurisdiction urban

14. *http://www.thestatesman.net/index.php?option=com_content&view=article&id=385159&catid=36*

15. *Report on Indian Urban Infrastructure and Services* by the High Powered Expert Committee (HPEC) for Estimating the Investment Requirements for Urban Infrastructure Services, March 2011.

16. Ibid.

17. *http://www.unhabitat.org/content.asp?cid=7335&catid=588&typeid=8*

agglomerations. The Master Plan concept has also not been useful in addressing India's large and widely spread slums. By locking-in the supply of buildable land and space, the Master Plan, *inter alia*, inhibits the development of housing markets and contributes to the proliferation of slums. Therefore, there is an urgent need to develop new planning and service delivery approaches across the board.[18] There is clearly a need to shift the urban planning framework from an engineering perspective to a social one. While urban planning is crucial to opening cities to new employment and residential opportunities, most Indian cities rely on outdated master plans which underutilised available land, as they do not take into account the rapidly changing structure of city economies and the needs of the residents. While the effects cut across all income groups, they hurt the poor the most by making it very difficult for them to afford decent housing.[19]

There are various issues that need to be tackled in urban centres mostly relating to infrastructure. Metros and mega cities have to be planned beyond the municipal limits and due importance may be given to integrated transport systems, primarily because of migration. The other settlements, located in the vicinity of the mother city are to be developed as satellite magnets in order to reduce and redistribute the population and cope with the population influx. This will help in the development of metropolitan regions.[20] The government should play an active role in creating a platform for small, medium and micro enterprises, through infrastructure development, which will have a long-term benefit to the economies of such areas. It should enable the creation of environmentally sustainable cities with policies that are inclusive in their design and implementation. To this end, planning needs to redefine itself and be more pluralistic.[21]

---

18. Chapter 11, *Eleventh Five Year Plan*, Planning Commission of India, p.396.
19. *http://web.worldbank.org/WBSITE/EXTERNAL/COUNTRIES/SOUTHASIAEXT/0,,contentMDK:22952349~menuPK:158842~pagePK:64002643~piPK:64002619~theSitePK:223547,00.html*
20. *http://www.scribd.com/doc/47864305/Urban-Infra-planning-commission*
21. *http://www.afesis.org.za/Sustainable-Settlement-Publications/sustainable-urbanisation-through-effective-planning*

Employment Generation Imperative

At the centre of the development debate is the problem of creating productive employment with adequate and regular earnings. In other words, there is a challenge of creating 'decent work'.[22] While agriculture is still the main source of livelihood in many countries of Asia and Africa, the share of working population in agriculture has declined in most developing countries, with development and urbanisation penetrating deeply. Fragmentation of land, natural disasters and lack of remunerative employment on agricultural land has driven a large part of the workforce to seek work in urban areas, leading to large increase in urban population in developing economies. In the absence of structured and adequate social security, the only coping mechanism that the poor have is manual work. In the informal economy, which for many is the 'employment of the last resort', work is often distributed among more people, leading to large scale underemployment. But with recent initiatives, such as the NREGA, the government has made seasonal provisions for work for the rural poor, who benefit from guaranteed employment and standard wages. This has benefitted the rural people by providing them a source of last-resort earning and also as a source of seasonal employment that is sought in instances of crop failure or even otherwise due to the seasonal nature of agriculture, which is the mainstay of village economy. Since the NREGA scheme encompasses mostly public works and infrastructural development projects, it has also contributed towards facilitating connectivity. These initiatives should be included in an inclusive strategy for creating equitable opportunities in the interior regions of the country. The private sector has made commendable inroads in this regard with initiatives such as ITC's e-Choupal and Unilever's MART's Project Shakti.

In fact, as Montek Singh Ahluwalia himself noted in his paper—'Prospects and Policy Challenges in the Twelfth Plan'—a key challenge in the Twelfth Plan is how to ensure creation of a sufficient number of productive jobs in the non-agriculture sector, in order to absorb the expected increase in the labour force and also absorb surplus labour that must be shifted out of agriculture.[23] The agricultural sector is not expected

22. *http://www.india-seminar.com/2003/531/531%20sukti%20dasgupta.htm*
23. *http://planningcommission.nic.in/aboutus/speech/spemsa/spe_21052011.pdf*

to grow at more than four per cent, and the only way labour productivity in agriculture can rise at a rate higher than four per cent is for employment in agriculture to shrink. This is actually necessary to reduce the present underemployment in agriculture and a steady improvement in real wages in this sector. Needless to say, the proposed shift out of agriculture should not take place as distress migration, but as a gradual shift towards more productive employment which could be located in rural areas itself. Agricultural development will itself give rise to new demands for non-agricultural services and generate employment in agriculture related sectors such as modernised marketing and agro-processing activity.[24]

A National Skill Development policy has been put in place to address the urgent issue of creating 92 million new jobs, as identified by the Eleventh Plan. The Planning Commission's working group on skill development and training reports that 8 per cent growth can create employment opportunities for about 30 million people and special employment generation programmes can add another 20 million job opportunities.[25] This employment generation needs to be tailored to the needs of the country, by curbing congestion in existing cities which creates a multitude of problems. Therefore, I wish to forward a proposition for deliberation towards the development of 100 new habitations dispersed throughout the country, each of which would generate 100,000 employment opportunities. This project would entail creation of productive and sustainable livelihoods and, at the same time, avoid the various problems associated with the burgeoning urban population.

Manufacturing and Housing

The National Manufacturing Policy discussion paper, explicates various policy interventions and economic reforms that have made the country one of the fastest growing economies. However, at just over 15 per cent of GDP, the country's manufacturing sector is not representative of its potential.[26] The situation of the manufacturing sector in India is a cause of

24. *http://www.scribd.com/doc/63558073/ProspectsAndPolicyChallengesInTheTwelfthPlan-spe-21052011*
25. *http://economictimes.indiatimes.com/opinion/view-point/job-creation-and-skill-development/articleshow/4742299.cms*
26. *http://dipp.nic.in/NMP_DiscussionPaper/NMP_DiscussionPaper_2010.pdf*

concern especially when seen in the context of the transformation registered in this sector by other Asian countries in similar stages of development. While the dramatic shifts in global manufacturing bases over the last four decades have brought these economies in focus, India has not been able to fully leverage the opportunities provided by the dynamics of the world economy.[27] The *Global Manufacturing Competitiveness Index 2010*, compiled by Deloitte Touche Tohmatsu and the US Council on Competitiveness, ranked India 2nd in terms of manufacturing competence. Additionally, in light of the pullulating figures of the percentage of population in the working age-group which is indicated to reach over 64 per cent by 2021, the Planning Commission has placed a great imperative on employment generation in the Twelfth Five Year Plan. This plan aims to increase the share of manufacturing in the GDP to 25 per cent and is anticipated to create 100 million jobs by 2022. The industrial sector was targetted to grow at an average rate of 10 to 11 per cent per year in the Eleventh Five Year Plan, but the actual achievement is unlikely to exceed 8 per cent. The industrial sector must not only grow faster than it has thus far, it must also be able to absorb more labour with relatively simple skills which migrants from rural areas can easily access and acquire.

The Department of Industrial Policy & Promotion (DIPP), through its National Manufacturing Policy intervention, has proposed the creation of National Manufacturing and Investment Zones. These zones, mini-cities in themselves, will act as the key enabler in driving the growth of the manufacturing sector. Good physical infrastructure, a progressive exit policy, structures to support clean and green technologies, appropriate investment incentives, and business-friendly approval mechanisms will be the cornerstones of this new initiative. Along the same lines, the Delhi Mumbai Industrial Corridor (DMIC) project aims to create a strong economic base with globally competitive environment and state-of-the-art infrastructure. The DMIC is being conceived as a model project that is intended to be replicated in the future, with great emphasis on expanding the manufacturing and services base.[28] The DMIC is planning to create six

27. *http://smetimes.tradeindia.com/smetimes/face-to-face/2011/Jul/12/mfg-policy-will-give-a-broader-view-to-sector-arun-maira.html*

28. *http://dipp.nic.in/English/Schemes/DMIC/DMIC-Concept%20Paper%20%28English%29.pdf*

new cities along the corridor which would house industries and create employment opportunities. The developmental planning for DMIC aims to achieve certain end results with implementation that would ensure realisation of envisaged vision for the project and lead to economic development. Accordingly the project goals for DMIC are double employment potential in five years; triple industrial output in five years; and quadruple exports from the region in five years. The policy seeks to identify high-impact/market-driven nodes along the corridor to provide transparent and investment-friendly policy/facility regimes under which integrated investment regions and industrial areas would be set up. These regions are proposed to be self-sustained industrial townships with world class infrastructure, road and rail connectivity for freight movement to and from ports and logistics hubs, served by domestic/ international air connectivity, reliable power, quality social infrastructure, and provide a globally competitive environment conducive for setting up businesses.[29]

In the context of employment generation, in addition to manufacturing, we also need to truly appreciate the role of housing. Housing, besides being a very basic requirement for the urban settlers, also holds the key to accelerate the pace of development. Investments in housing, like any other industry, have a multiplier effect on income and employment. A study at IIM-Ahmedabad, in 2005, estimated that the overall employment generation in the economy due to additional investment in the construction sector is eight times of the direct employment. Construction sector employment is growing at the rate of 7 per cent per annum. Housing also has a direct impact on the allied industries of steel and cement, stone, ceramic, electrical, fitting, etc., which make a significant contribution to the national economy. In order to improve the quality of life in urban areas, it is of critical significance that the housing stock is improved through urban renewal, *in situ* slum improvement, and development of new housing stock in existing cities as well as new townships.[30]

---

29. Ibid.
30. *http://www.scribd.com/doc/47864305/Urban-Infra-planning-commission*

The Way Forward

The McKinsey Report (2010) on India's urbanisation prospects estimates that over the period 2010-2030, urban India will create 70 per cent new jobs and these would be twice as productive as equivalent jobs in the rural sector. Although this was largely anticipated because of the accelerating pace of urbanisation and growth in the knowledge economy, this is a welcome sign, a positive development due to the greater significance of more productive sustainable employment generation. But this also throws two challenges at us: one of moving development away from large metros by dispersing job creation, and second of sustaining the rural economy by increasing agricultural productivity and creating new growth opportunities. These issues can be leveraged as opportunities for homogenising urbanisation across the expanse of India, while creating public policy frameworks to tackle them more comprehensively.

The High Powered Committee for Estimating the Investment Requirements for Urban Infrastructure Services under the chairmanship of Isher Judge Ahluwalia concluded that India's economic growth momentum cannot be sustained if urbanisation is not actively facilitated. This is in direct concurrence with the observation of the teeming real estate, and (more broadly) the infrastructure and utilities sectors, in India. The Indian context is typical of that of a developing country where infrastructure development is a key driver of growth. There is also a clear need for developing the infrastructure and utilities in the rural hinterland. The Public Information Infrastructure (PII), being developed by the Office of Adviser to the Prime Minister on Public Information Infrastructure & Innovations, would take us one step closer to realising fair opportunities for the rural people but an information highway can only append the physical infrastructure of roads and bridges and utilities; ICT infrastructure can't substitute the physical infrastructure.

In western economies, employment generation that followed in the aftermath of industrialisation was only possible due to a robust network of physical infrastructure. A classic example would be the revolutionary economic galvanisation caused by the invention of the steam engine and the subsequent laying down of railroads, connecting mines and other production sites to markets in Britain. Later, in the first half of the 20th

century, the recovery of the US economy from the Great Depression, which is largely attributed to the economic momentum generated in the wake of the World War II, could only be sustained due to the unprecedented investment in the construction of roads, bridges and other public works. The existence of a robust physical infrastructure is widely recognised in policy circles as a requisite for inclusive economic development. Taking cue from this, the Government of India should create a comprehensive vision that would encompass an environment of synergetic policies, dovetailing the efforts of each other, for the creation of a countrywide network of physical infrastructure. The need of the hour is to develop the rural areas to an equitable level of infrastructure, utilities and services, since they are lacking in these amenities and are largely alienated from peripheral development. This physical infrastructure would be elemental in the creation of new habitations and transplanting seeds of urbanisation in the back-country. The government has tried to make special provision for the development of rural areas as is clearly evident in the allocation of resources for the development of the rural areas (Rs 2,810 billion) which exceeded more than 10 times than those allocated to the urban areas (Rs 230 billion), as part of the Eleventh Five Year Plan.[31]

The creation of 100 new habitations that will spur employment generation and invigorate an equitable growth in economic activity, would have to be selected from motley of Tier-II and Tier-III cities, *panchayat* clusters and the new cities proposed under schemes such as the DMIC. This should also encompass the new cities being developed by private actors, to create an overarching prospicience of development and employment creation, in the country. The momentum of this project can later be leveraged to urbanise and modernise, spurring industrial expansion and employment creation in more than 6,000 MSME clusters that exist in our country. The various legislative and planning agencies of the Central government should consider the creation of a framework for building new habitations which would encompass these MSME clusters.

31. *http://web.worldbank.org/WBSITE/EXTERNAL/COUNTRIES/SOUTHASIAEXT/0,,contentMDK:22952349~menuPK:158842~pagePK: 64002643~piPK:64002619~theSitePK:223547,00.html*

The Provision of Urban Amenities in Rural Areas (PURA) Scheme of the Ministry of Rural Development has referred to the development of infrastructure for clusters of villages/*panchayats*. The PURA project spans several *panchayats*, in a cluster, and aims to develop sub-projects proposed by the private partner(s) with the fundamental elements of PURA remaining intact, at the village level. This scheme proposes to identify clusters of geographically contiguous *gram panchayats*, having a population of about 25,000-40,000, and develop them collectively. This would entail strengthening connectivity between these *gram panchayats*, which would create new opportunities by cementing collaborative efforts. These clusters, in India, have a distinct cultural and traditional flavour, comprising artisans, craftsmen, nomads and peasants, producing same or similar types of products and facing common opportunities and threats.

Clusters have been in existence in India for centuries and are known for their products at the national and international level. India has more than 6,400 clusters. Clusters represent the socioeconomic heritage of the country where some of the towns or contiguous group of villages are known for specific products.[32] In these clusters, the livelihoods pertain to traditional heritage and skills. The preservation of these skills has been identified as crucial to their advancement, and can be furthered by skill identification and cataloguing, as noted by the Ministry of Human Resources Development (HRD). Although there are two dozen schemes for the development of these clusters, as identified by the Foundation for MSME Clusters, but a coordinated and concerted effort is required for each of them to complement the efforts of others. Also, these schemes should be contained in an overarching central guiding vision and an actionable framework that would comprise infrastructure development as a mainstay of the vision. There is a pressing need for cohesive action for the melioration of India's rural hinterland and the planning efforts should consider provisions to proliferate the main tenets of urbanisation to these clusters.

With two-thirds of India's GDP coming from the urban areas, cities are the driving force of the country's economy. This trend is set to increase

32. Foundation for MSME Clusters, Article No. 58 *http://www.msmefoundation.org/folder/Article/58.pdf*

as the country undergoes a massive urban transformation where, within a span of 30 years, its urban population is expected to double—from 288 million in 2000 to 590 million by 2030—making up some 40 per cent of India's people. How India manages this urbanisation will go a long way in determining the shape of the future for its more than a billion people.

10

SEWA: Towards Self-Reliance and Empowerment[1]

SAMEER KOCHHAR and
GURSHARAN DHANJAL

Introduction

India has since the beginning of new millennium registered an impressive record of economic growth. But still the benefits of economic growth have not adequately reached the poor, marginalised and minorities. Gender empowerment still continues to seek more attention from policymakers. A decisive reduction in poverty and expansion in economic opportunities for all sections of the population has become a crucial element in all policy planning. The ability to generate an adequate number of productive employment opportunities is a major factor on which inclusiveness of growth will be judged. This is what we call 'demographic dividend' and 'demographic transition'. Montek Singh Ahluwalia has been instrumental in bringing the focus of all policy planning around these areas wherein he has insisted that inclusiveness must go beyond the traditional objective of poverty alleviation to encompass equality of opportunity as well as economic and social mobility for all sections of society, with affirmative action for SCs, STs, OBCs, minorities and women. He firmly believes that the degree of empowerment leads to participation, which is so necessary in a democratic polity. The empowerment of third layer of democracy at the

1. Sameer Kochhar and Gursharan Dhanjal recently visited SEWA in Gujarat and interacted with Elaben Bhatt, the co-founder of SEWA. They also toured number of villages, as far as Patan in Surendranagar district, and held detailed sessions with members and beneficiaries. Majority of inputs have come from field visits and primary research. Narendra Kaushik, Resident Editor, *Inclusion*, and Rohan Kochhar, pursuing graduation in Economics at Delhi University, assisted them in field research. A detailed account of SEWA activities was also published in "SEWA: Last of the Gandhian Economics?", *Inclusion* 2(3), July-September 2011. It also carries an exclusive interview with Elaben Bhatt.

Panchayati Raj Institution (PRI) level and providing opportunities for empowerment and participation of disadvantaged and hitherto marginalised groups therefore forms all policy initiatives that have been steered by him during the Eleventh Five Year Plan and will continue during the Twelfth Plan.

Self Employed Women's Association or SEWA is a shining example of empowerment of women and marginalised and enabling them with a voice and participation. Ahluwalia's conviction that the growth should not remain centralised and trickle down but also should be coupled with several centres of localised growth to positively impact numerous pockets, resonates well with all that SEWA has done in last three decades.

Prologue

'We sometimes talk and write as though only one or two individuals were really doing useful work and the rest only vegetating. It is, however, a mistake to think so. A nation's true greatness depends upon its average man and woman,' said Gopal Krishna Gokhale, freedom fighter and once president of Indian National Congress whom Mahatma Gandhi regarded as Guru.

Gokhale said this about a century ago and over six decades before SEWA, the largest women organisation in the country, which provides opportunity to average woman to increase her income and break free of the poverty stranglehold, came into being. The trade association, which supports 103 cooperatives on employment, health, nutrition, child care, education, housing and banking insurance, helps the poorest of the poor woman in the country to own productive assets, take part in decision-making and be a catalyst in changing the fate of her family and the society. The organisation, which spans over eight states and 1.3 million members (2010), builds capacity of its cadre and allows the women to be the leaders. It forges links between poor women, government departments and markets.

'Average' Greatness

The organisation believes in inculcating leadership qualities in every other woman, who as a member has a stake in SEWA, rather than trailing one or two individuals. A half of SEWA's urban members live in households where per capita income is below $1 and more than one-third live in households where per capita income does not exceed $2. The rest (around 15% or so) are only slightly better off (Chen and Snodgrass, 2001).

Figure 10.1

Concentric Circles of SEWA Membership

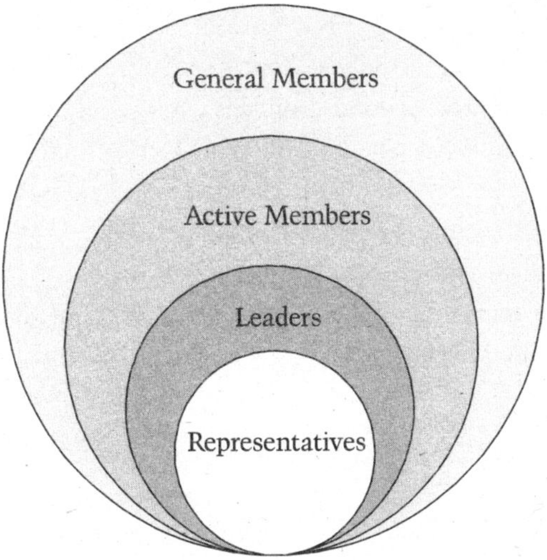

Right from its inception in 1972 when it organised head loaders, cart pullers, garment makers, vegetable vendors against the oppression of police and civic authorities in Ahmedabad to 1988 when it first time intervened in rapidly desertifying Banaskantha district to generate employment for farmers who suffered the most due to inadequacy of irrigation and market linkages, the women employed in the informal sector have been at the core of SEWA. Be it salt pan workers, health workers, fish vendors, artisans, nursery planters, midwives, it has been the sole endeavour of SEWA to bring about collective self-reliance (not individual self-reliance) of its women members.

The primary objectives of SEWA—spelt out in a set of 11 points (employment, income, ownership, nutrition, health care, housing, childcare, organised strength, leadership, self-reliance and education)[2]— are designed to generate enough regular remuneration for its poor members so that they and their families can live with dignity and security. The organisation knows very well that sustainability of its programmes hinges on how well they are implemented and how many of its members benefit from them.

SEWA Catalogue

The organisation largely comprises home based workers, street vendors, small scale traders and producers, and workers who offer manual labour and services. While the home based workers mainly consist of *beedi* rollers, incense stick rollers, and producers of garments, cloth, small furniture, footwear, food products and handicrafts, the street vendors include sellers of vegetables, fish, fruits, paper, eggs etc. The third category encompasses providers of contract labour and construction labour and workers who sell services such as cooking, cleaning, laundering and transporting goods.[3]

For home based workers, their living space is also their workplace. And invariably this space is very small, congested and dimly lit. The trader or middleman gives a card every month to the home based workers, on which the number of *beedis* or incense sticks rolled by them, is recorded. The name of the worker is written on the card, but the trader's name is not written. There is no proof of an employer-employee relationship. The trader pays the worker a specified amount for a thousand sticks/*beedis* rolled. In case, he is not satisfied with the quality of the finished good, he reduces the amount he has to pay to the worker. The worker hardly has a say in it. More often than not, the home based work is performed by all members of the household including women, children and elderly. The trader/middleman has no responsibility towards the workers and is not obliged to pay them insurance, pension and benefits for other eventualities. Their working hours are not defined as the idea is to assemble as many pieces as possible. The story of street vendors, manual labourers and workers who provide services is no less exploitative. In the case of vendors,

2. Channa (2004).
3. Jhabvala and Bali (1993).

the police and civic agencies are the oppressors. Since the illiterate and semi-literate vendors are hardly aware of their rights, the police and the administration extort money from them and do not let them operate in peace. Though the workers inherited the vending business from their parents and grandparents, law did not recognise their right to trade. The policemen would take advantage of this, harass them for bribes and fling their produce on the ground in case they refused to pay. The situation was worse before 1972 when SEWA finally came into being.

Organised Strength

In Ahmedabad, the largest city of Gujarat, things came to a boil in late 1960s as head loaders, cart pullers and vegetable vendors, organised by SEWA, took on the police and the administration. A large number of vegetable vendors were evicted from a market on the pretext of attack on a cyclist though the incident had nothing to do with women. The market was closed. When it opened again, the police did not allow the vendors to resume trade saying that the women were a nuisance and blocked pedestrian traffic and traded without official permission.[4]

Manual labourers and service providers too suffered due to lack of legal protection for them. Take for instance the case of construction workers. Till 1996, there was no Act to govern their work. In the case of Gujarat, there was no law till 2004 to protect them. Each worker was an island unto herself.

Unlike the organised workers who generally have unions to take up issues like wage hike and welfare of the workers with the employer, the mobile, irregular and often illiterate characteristics of the informal workforce, a large proportion of which are women, make organising such workers a real challenge. While the Trade Union Act in India is very liberal in its definition of a union (any seven workers can get together and form a union), the actual registration of a union lies with individual state Labour departments, which often complain about absence of employer-employee relation in the informal sector, diversity of workers and their wide dispersal.[5]

---

4. Crowell (2003).
5. Dasgupta (2002).

The first thing SEWA did was to organise these informal sector workers who hitherto suffered their fate individually. In fact, their organisation laid the foundation of SEWA when head loaders and cart pullers of Ahmedabad approached Ela Bhatt, a lawyer and head of women wing of Textile Labour Association (TLA), a labour union, which had its genesis in the plague epidemic of 1920 and where Mahatma Gandhi experimented with his ideas on industrial relations and model labour union.

Bhatt's role was to organise sewing, typing and other classes for wives and daughters of textile workers. When Bhatt visited the head loaders and cart pullers, she realised the women were hugely underpaid and did not even own the carts they pulled. She took the initiative of bringing them together. Their organisation kicked off a chain reaction as word about the initiative spread to other women in the informal sector. The collective action soon brought about victories for the cart pullers and vegetable vendors, forced the police to beat a retreat and paved the way for registration of SEWA as a trade union in Gujarat under the Trade Union Act of India.

Collective Self-Reliance

SEWA's organising strategy can be split into five steps. While the first step involves recruiting and mobilising members to build awareness and solidarity: to identify needs, constraints, opportunities and to undertake activities; the second step entails organising members into one or more local organisations (trade group, cooperative, producer group, savings and credit group, campaign committee). The third step requires promoting and building leadership that emerges out of the local organisations while the fourth implies training and deploying leaders to help implement SEWA activities through decentralised management systems: as members of local spearhead teams (which implement projects or undertake campaigns) or as paraprofessionals who provide technical services. The fifth step involves convening elections of representatives from among the leaders to serve in the various structural tiers of the SEWA Union and SEWA Cooperative Federation.

Figure 10.2[6]

Organising Strategy of SEWA

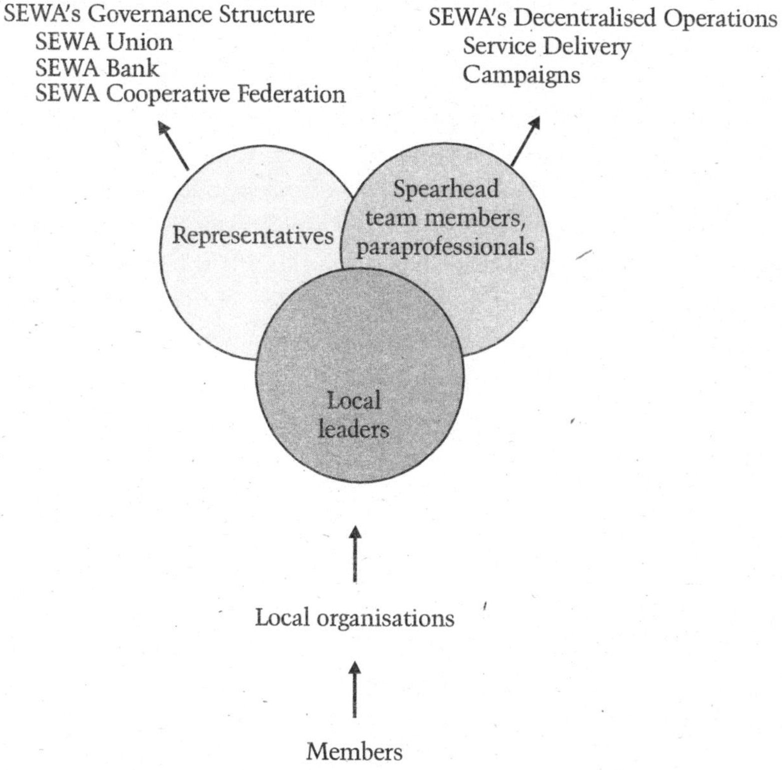

SEWA's organising strategies are aimed at pushing for structural changes in the wider environment through organised strength. In other words, it organises to be strong, to cut middlemen, eliminate harassment of workers in the informal sector by getting them recognition, create employment, leadership, self-reliance and improve on income, assets, nutrition, health, housing, child care and education. The focus obviously is on achieving collective self-reliance rather than individual self-reliance and improving the lot of households through its self-employed women members.

The Gandhian principle of self-sufficiency of local economy—whatever is made or produced or earned in a village must be used first and

6. Chen (2005): Figure 1 and 2.

foremost by the members of the same village—is at the core of its movement against the middlemen.

SEWA sells the packaged products to the same clientele from which it buys the raw material from. In fact, the model of creating local ecosystems applies to almost every other of its over 100 ventures the association has promoted. Be it project for salt pan workers, *vanlakshmis* (women who work to promote forests), *beedi* workers, Rudi (rural distribution) products, ecotourism, sale of medicines or SEWA Trade Facilitation Centre it has set up for women embroiders, the idea is to add value to the existing structures, hone skills, make women aware about their rights and talent, build capability and train a selected few to market the produce in the same ecosystem. Gandhi's entire concept of self-rule and village economies is being replicated in the cooperatives promoted by the SEWA.

The biggest example of this is Rudi Multi Trading Company Limited, which was started from Sabarkantha district on a pilot basis and has since been expanded to 14 districts and into multiple processing centres. The company procures directly from the farmers, processes, packages and markets products through a network of rural self-help groups (SHGs) of women called Rudiben in Gujarati parlance. The unique rural distribution network of Rudibens reduces incidental expenses, makes available good quality products to rural consumers, and eliminates middlemen and thus brings about socioeconomic development of underprivileged rural people.

Standing for small, beautiful and nice in the local dialect, Rudi bazaar is built on the smallest consumer with a purchasing power of only Rs 50 to Rs 100 a month but multiplies into 5,30,000 members of SEWA resulting into an annual turnover of over Rs 160 million. Hindustan Lever Limited (HLL) and the Grassroots Trading Network (GTN) have provided the technical and capacity building inputs in setting up the Rudi bazaar. Incidentally, Rudi was also the name of the first rural member of SEWA.

Both the authors recently got a first-hand experience of the Rudi when they along with a team of researchers spent two days in a packaging centre in Surendranagar district. The team got to see how Rudi provides employment and an opportunity to add to their wealth to rural women.

Move over Moneylender and Middleman

Having realised that a major impediment for women workers to have gainful employment and achieve collective self-reliance is the middleman or the commission agent, SEWA has systematically gone about eliminating his role. From vegetable vending, fish selling, salt farming, street vending, *beedi* rolling to embroidery etc., the organisation has replaced the middleman to an extent by providing transport and easy credit to the women workers. Since the middleman would procure fish from Saurashtra (Gujarat) and supply it to vendors in Ahmedabad and extract an overblown margin resulting in less profit for the vendors and high price for the customer, SEWA decided to have its own trucks for transporting fish to its member-vendors. Similarly, it uses its own transport to fetch vegetables from the farmer.

The elimination of middleman has brought about huge benefits for the fish vendors. While earlier a fish vendor would earn a profit of Rs 50 at the end of the day, now the daily profit is in the range of Rs 200 to Rs 300. A number of fish sellers vouched for this when the team Inclusion visited them.

Since the women workers were dependent on local moneylenders for capital and consumption loans, the latter exploited them in more ways than one. Not only would they charge heavy interest on credit but would also force them to sell their yield at a low price. Due to this, salt farmers would be compelled to sell their produce to the moneylenders at a price much lower than the market. The women workers would pay heavy interest to the moneylenders for credit they would need for construction of their houses or setting up small trades.

The elimination of middleman is what has made SEWA Vegetable Cooperative in Agricultural Produce Marketing Committee (APMC), Ahmedabad, popular among the women farmers and vendors. The commission agent kiosk number 40 owned by Gujarat Rajya Mahila Sewa Sehkari Sangh (GRMSSS) Limited in APMC is always buzzing with activity during working hours even as the agents placed next to it have less work. When team Inclusion visited the kiosks, it could witness Bina and Usha of the GRMSSS selling sacks of gourd, ridge gourd, bitter gourd, cumin etc., after weighing them on an electronic platform scale at early hours in the morning (3.30 am).

Like the fish market under Chamunda Bridge in ChamanPura (Ahmedabad) where Shri Matsyagandha Women's SEWA Co-operative Ltd. (SMWSCL) collects minimum margin from the fish sellers for procuring and delivering produce, the GRMSSS charges minimum possible commission from the vegetable suppliers i.e., farmers. While the other shops charge 10 per cent (2 per cent higher than the government rate) from them, the GRMSSS charges 6 per cent. Besides, SEWA agricultural consultant K.G. Mehta gives free advice to farmers on what to grow and when to grow. He also advises them to use natural manure instead of urea and pesticides.

Like the GRMSSS and SMWSCL (fish vendors), Shri Lok Swasthya SEWA Mandali, a health cooperative, also runs a medical store in Ahmedabad on the pattern of 'no profit, no loss' basis. The 24x7 store, located in front of a government hospital provides 10 to 17 per cent discount on medicines to all its customers. Run by 15 members, headed by manager, Harshida, the medical store not only sells branded medicines but also vends 15 products of SEWA. On injections etc., the store at times offers even 50 per cent discount.

Vertical Growth

Though initially SEWA's membership grew at a steady pace, in 1990s it witnessed a dramatic growth due to the expansion of its rural activities. The 21st century has further brought about a stupendous increase in its membership. So much so that between 2000 and 2002 its organisational strength more than doubled (318,527 in 2000 to 694, 551 in 2002). A major contribution to this came from 2001 earthquake and a membership drive. In 2009, it had 1,256,944 members with Gujarat alone clocking 631,345. It is estimated to be more than 1.3 million-strong currently.

What has boosted the growth of SEWA is the fact that any self-employed woman in India can become its member by paying Rs 5 (annual subscription fee). Though not all members need all the services from SEWA equally. A major chunk of SEWA's current membership joined SEWA few years back and may not participate in its various activities and services, membership has definitely helped them gain confidence and feel less insecure due to SEWA's protective umbrella. The organisation adds to their prestige in the community and prepares them to deal with police and other government officials.

Table 10.1

Impact of SEWA on Leaders and General Members

(in per cent)

	Leaders	*General Members*
Increased prestige in the community	75	38
Increased courage to speak out	85	47
Argued case in *panchayat* (local council)	58	16
Dealings with municipality	23	20
Dealings with police	66	37
Dealings with other govt. officials	73	27

Source: Jhabvala and Bali (1993).

Towards Economic Freedom: The Impact of SEWA

SEWA breeds members to grow from within the organisation as leaders from regular local meetings, periodic campaigns and sometimes special leadership training and exposure opportunities (travel within India and outside). It has one local leader (local manager) for every 100 members and one representative for every 300 members who represents her trade in SEWA Council, in the Government and elsewhere. The elected representatives form the Trade Council and elect the 25-member executive committee of the SEWA Union. The elected members of the executive committee take care of overall governance while elected representatives bring about decentralised management.

SEWA Proliferation

Since like Gujarat, self-employed women in other states also face similar disadvantages *vis-à-vis* men and women employed in the formal sector, it was but natural for SEWA to extend its footprints beyond Mahatma Gandhi's native state. In 1982, the association set up SEWA Bharat, an All India Federation of Self Employed Women's Association, to facilitate formation of new membership based organisations across the country. And within next few years, it reached Uttar Pradesh, Madhya Pradesh and Bihar by raising SEWA Bhagalpur (1983), SEWA Indore (1985) and Lucknow Mahila SEWA Trust (1988) and other branches under the aegis of either SEWA Bharat or SEWA Ahmedabad. Over the years, the association has registered footfalls in Rajasthan, Kerala, Assam, Delhi, West Bengal and Uttarakhand too.

Today the Madhya Pradesh chapter has the second largest membership (over half a million) after Gujarat comprising *beedi* workers, incense stick workers, *tendu patta workers*, agriculturalists, brick kiln workers, tailors, fruit and vegetable vendors and construction workers. Besides SEWA Indore, SEWA Chattarpur in Madhya Pradessh has united a good number of women workers. Lucknow Mahila SEWA Trust has organised *chikan* and *zardozi* workers, *beedi* rollers, *papad* makers and hawkers in Barabanki while SEWA Bareilly has brought together home based women workers in a few villages of the district.

In Bihar, SEWA Bhagalpur has been joined by SEWA Katihar and SEWA Munger. In Rajasthan, SEWA Bikaner, SEWA Jaipur and SEWA Jodhpur have sprouted as offshoots of SEWA Bharat while Uttarakhand has SEWA Dehradun and SEWA Almora working for unorganised women workers. SEWA Kerala, on the other hand, formed in order to help the women of marginalised communities in the state, has members from both inland and coastal areas of Thiruvananthapuram district. Likewise SEWA Delhi has united tens of thousands of women who are working in lower middle class settlements like Jehangirpuri of the national capital.

In Assam, SEWA has founded Indian School of Microfinance for Women in collaboration with Citi India and Friends of Women's World Banking (FWWB) to empower women economically and spread financial literacy among the women workers. The association has keenly been working on getting into the backward northeast and has, for this purpose, established links with various groups and NGOs working there. It has organised at least a few exchange visits with these NGOs.

SEWA Joins SAARC

In the last few years, SEWA has travelled to different parts of the world to share its experience of training self-employed women workers. At the same time, it has volunteered to train the home based workers in South Asian countries like Afghanistan to bring about their empowerment through financial inclusion. The association has trained Afghan women in tailoring, handicrafts, embroidery, food processing and eco-regeneration activities to make them financially independent. Till February 2010, it had trained over 1,000 Afghan women in different trades and over 65 per cent of them had started their own business in Bagh-e-Zanana, a place in Kabul, and were earning good profits. A group of SEWA trainers helped the Afghan women launched their brand 'Sabah' for selling garments and processed food with a monthly turnover of 2 to 3 lakh Afghani.[7]

In November 2009, SEWA entered into Pakistan when Urdu version of SEWA Co-founder Ela Bhatt's book *We are Poor, But So Many* was released in the country and the Pakistan chapter of SAARC Business Association of Home Based Workers (Sabah-Pakistan) was launched in Islamabad. It also registered presence in Nepal, Bangladesh, Sri Lanka, Bhutan and Maldives when SAARC initiated a project called 'SABAH' (SAARC Business Association of Home Based Workers) for strengthening the livelihoods of home based workers a few years ago. The project involves SEWA as well as HomeNet South Asia, an organisation that comprises 300 organisations from Pakistan, India, Nepal and Bangladesh and was created in 2007. Modelled on STFC (the Trade Facilitation Centre, SEWA has set up in Ahmedabad to facilitate trade of products made by its artisans), the SABAH, has set up Trade Facilitation Centres for equipping home based workers with modern technical facilities, design inputs, skill upgradation, production techniques and forward market linkages. Earlier SEWA organised a seminar in May 2008 in collaboration with SAARC and the Government of India to facilitate policy dialogue on issues related to home based workers. The seminar, attended by government representatives of eight SAARC countries, first time recognised HomeNet South Asia and the country HomeNets as nodal agencies to represent home based workers in South Asia. It also asked HomeNet and SEWA to submit a list of products to be included in South Asian Free Trade Agreement (SAFTA). In short, it paved the way for setting up of SABAHs in SAARC countries except India which already has a full-fledged similar network of SEWA.

7. *http://www.indianexpress.com/news/undeterred-by-fridays-blast-sewa-vows-to-continue-activities-in-kabul/585301/0*

Trade Union First

Despite having further organised into cooperatives, district associations, and banking, SEWA has not relinquished functions it set out to perform originally. The 15,000 *beedi* rollers who are their members in Ahmedabad would vouch for this as not only they got for themselves identity cards from Government and opened a medical clinic for them under the Bidi Workers Welfare Act (1976) but also made sure that their children get scholarship till college. The organisation has also been responsible for launch of a housing scheme for them and a multi-fold increase in their daily wages. It has also got them insurance against natural (Rs 2,000) as well accidental (Rs 25,000) deaths.

SEWA has fought long and hard for legal status and official recognition of its members under labour law, labour statistics and international labour movement. Its representatives have been members of Prime Minister Office's Committee on Microfinance, RBI's Rural Credit Committee, National Housing Bank's Task Force on 'Housing Finance for the Poor', Planning Commission's Advisory Committee for Childcare, Social Security Taskforce of National Commission of Labour and Insurance Regulatory Development Authority's Advisory Board. Globally, it has been on board of various committees in International Union of Food (IUF), International Federation of Workers' Education Associations (IFWEA) and International Textile, Garment & Leather Workers' Federation (ITGLWF) .

Today most of the informal trades aligned with SEWA have licences or are recognised by Central and state governments. When SEWA registered as a trade union in Gujarat under the Trade Unions Act of 1926, it was first time that workers in 'informal sector' were formally recognised by the government as workers. Even now the union initiates campaigns from time to time to demand higher wages and better prices and to negotiate more favourable commercial and employment relationships.

Building Institutions

In around 39 years of its existence, SEWA has built over 100 institutions to provide a leg up to rural and urban development through growth of informal (synonymous with unorganised in India) sector there. It has raised cooperatives to boost organised strength, leadership, self-reliance, employment, income, assets, child care, education, health, nutrition and housing the 11 point-motto it aims to further for growth of self-employed women in informal sector.

Besides organising vegetable vendors, fish sellers, tree growers, head loaders, cart pullers, *beedi* rollers, incense stick rollers and artisans, it has brought together garment workers, *chindi* workers, paper pickers, construction workers, salt farmers, tobacco workers, kite makers and milk cooperatives. When it comes to providing services to its members it has set up cooperatives for child care, housing, health, insurance, financial services, water, land, marketing, video, education, research, relief and rehabilitation, land, marketing and infrastructure services.

Broadly, the SEWA institutions can be listed as SEWA Union, SEWA Cooperatives, SEWA District Associations, SEWA Bank, SEWA Marketing Groups, SEWA Housing Trust, SEWA Academy and SEWA Health. Shree Dev Dholera Milk Production SEWA Cooperative, Shree Vanalaxmi Tree Growers Women's SEWA Cooperative limited and Shree Trupti Snacks Women's SEWA Cooperative Limited are a few of the cooperatives it has floated. Kutch Craft Association and Surendranagar District Women and Children Development Mandal are two of the district associations it has formed.

Great Campaigner

The organisation has not only helped the women engaged in informal employment to be a force to reckon with but also helped SEWA run many a campaigns for improvement in condition of the self-employed women. Its campaigns for rights of street vendors, home based workers, construction workers etc., have brought about many policy changes. Earlier this year, it notched up another success when Ahmedabad Municipal Corporation (AMC) allotted space to fish vendors who would sell from pavements in Chamanpura, blocking the pedestrian movement. The corporation has provided them cubicles in about half a dozen enclosures under Chamunda Bridge in Chamanpura itself. Each vendor will have to pay Rs 500 to the AMC for 18 months to own the cubicle.

As a result of SEWA's street vendors' campaign, the AMC has granted licences to the vendors and entitled them to receive bonus from contractors.

Table 10.2

Impacts of the Earthquake and Drought on Domestic Water Supply (%)[8]

		Wells	*Ponds*	*Standposts*	*Bore Wells*
% of villages with water sources		60	100	88	40
Earthquake	Not affected	7	31	33	32
	Temporarilly affected	21	13	38	16
	Affected	66	52	24	47
	Missing values[a]	7	4	5	5
Drought	Not affected	0	0	31	68
	Temporarilly affected	0	2	62	16
	Affected	90	90		5
	Missing values	10	8	7	11

Note: a: The high percentage of missing values is explained by the difficult circumstances in which the data had to be collected that where prevalent during the period shortly after the earthquake.

Its campaign for water in Banaskantha district along with increased economic opportunities and a supportive environment has led to women empowerment. Two successive draughts and the subsequent earthquake in 2001, had drastically cut down the water table in the district.

The piped water supply has not only conserved the long hours women spent in collecting drinking water for their households but also encouraged them to get into income generating activities. A joint research by International Water and Sanitation Centre, SEWA and Foundation of Public Interest (FPI) reveals that the time released by an improved water supply enables women enterprise members to make a substantial contribution to the household income, especially at times when other income generating activities are absent. The combination of water supply and embroidery skills in Radhanpur and Santalpur blocks of Patan district has not only led to overall prosperity (*pucca* houses, toilets, sanitation etc.) of households but also put a stop to migration that would take place every year. This has also made women, who were not even allowed to venture out of their village earlier, equal partners in growth and decision-making process.

8. Francis (2004).

Thanks to SEWA's campaign for better conditions for construction workers, the Central government enacted Construction Workers Act in 2004 and has decided to set up a national level school for skills training. On street vendors, the organisation successfully persuaded the government to adopt a national policy under which the vendors will get legal status, social security, credit and legitimate hawking zones.

Partnering in Governance for Policy Changes

The building of powerful self-sustained institutions has helped SEWA to seize representation in various government bodies in the country and outside and influence policy changes. From time to time it has partnered with Central government, Government of Gujarat and international institutions to bring about changes in policies on informal workers, home based workers and their welfare. Right from 1987 when SEWA co-founder Ela Bhatt chaired a National Commission on Self-Employed Women to produce a Shramshakti report with policy recommendations paving the way for introduction of women's credit fund and child care crèche to June 2002 when SEWA represented India on the drafting committee of the Workers' Group in an International Labour Conference and thus pushed for a resolution on informal economy, SEWA has persuaded many a policy changes.

In 2004, when Government of India decided to set up a National Commission on Enterprises in the Unorganised/Informal Sector (NCEUS), it invited SEWA to be on its board. A year before this, the government had invited SEWA to be a member of the Second National Commission on Labour to draft the first ever umbrella legislation for unorganised sector workers.

SEWA has been a pioneer when it comes to introduction of welfare schemes for the informal sector employees. For instance in 1992 it launched first ever integrated insurance scheme for informal workers which led to recognition and promotion of microinsurance for the poor in India. Similarly, when it registered SEWA Trade Facilitation Centre (STFC) in 2003 to provide a marketing platform to women artisans from Santalpur and Radhanpur blocks in Patan district, the STFC became the first company to be formed by more than 15,000 women who are the owners and suppliers. Today the STFC has over 60,000 members and has its own brand called 'Hansiba'. Shri Mahila SEWA Sahakari Bank Limited or SEWA bank also became the first bank created for and by women workers in the informal sector when it registered as a woman workers' cooperative bank with the Reserve Bank of India.

SEWA has frequently represented women workers to the governments and brought about change in their minimum wages and welfare. Be it *beedi* rollers, incense stick rollers, street vendors, paper pickers, construction workers and even kite makers, SEWA has been on board in various committees to bring about a change for better. Almost all the informal trades where its women members are engaged have been recognised either by the Central government or the state governments. Government of Gujarat, for instance, included garment workers in minimum wages schedule for the first time in 1987-88 and fixed per piece rate for them. Similarly, the state passed a government resolution in 1987 giving waste paper from government offices to paper pickers for free.

Such is the credibility of SEWA that the governments not only readily accept most of its recommendations but also feel obliged in entering into partnership with it on developmental works. Government of Gujarat in 2002, for instance, permitted SEWA workers to do handpump repair and water management without submitting a tender. Similarly, SEWA women have been running the Group Water Supply Scheme of the Gujarat Water Supply and Sewerage Board since 2000. The association has joined a public-private partnership (PPP) scheme to provide slum infrastructure services to some of its urban members in designated project for slums.

International Catalyst

SEWA has time and again successfully lobbied for policies which would help the informal sector workers grow. Its role as a catalyst has been recognised nationally as well as internationally. SEWA pressed for increase in Integrated Child Development Services (ICDS) for several years before the Central government accepted it in 2003. World Health Organization (WHO) invited SEWA's midwives as health experts in an international best practices meeting in Mexico in 2000 and followed it up with an invitation to the organisation to implement a tuberculosis control programme in the same year. SEWA is part of the curriculum for training of Indian Administrative Service (IAS) probationers.

SEWA majorly contributed to International Labour Organization's (ILO) 177th convention (passed 1996) on needs of home based workers as it collaborated with many unions and HomeNet, an international alliance of home based workers' organisations in a campaign for the convention. Consultative Group to Assist the Poor (CGAP), the German Technical Corporation for Development (GTZ), ILO and the Asian Development Bank (ADB) supported SEWA's insurance work as a viable model and publicised the model in policy circles. The group also had a contribution when there was an International Declaration demanding policy and space for vendors in Bellagio, Italy in 1995.

Besides this, SEWA was an observer in ADB Board meeting and International Labour Conference discussion on Convention for Home Workers. SEWA was also a member of United Nations Conference on Trade and Development (UNCTAD) Task Force on women in trade.[9]

Financial Inclusion

Financial inclusion is rightly considered the bedrock of all other inclusions. SEWA realised it in the early years of inception itself when it found out that the women employed in the informal sector had no access to savings, credit, insurance or pensions. Though SEWA Bank registered as a women workers' cooperative bank in 1974, it obtained licence from the RBI and the District Cooperative Registrar to undertake banking work in Ahmedabad only in 1989. Four years later it obtained permission to operate in five districts of Gujarat.

Over the years, the bank has become the pivot around which the largest women's movement in the world orbits. The bank is the finest example of how financial inclusion should be pursued as it helps poor women to gain employment and add to their income and assets.

9. Chen (2005).

The bank has been relentlessly pushing for livelihood linkages or financial inclusion in today's parlance and providing its workers banking facilities and related savings and loan products. The bank has gone a step beyond no-frill accounts and allows the woman worker to open a zero-balance account to start with and make it operational by depositing whatever sum she can afford. Yet, the RBI has been pestering it to open a certain number of no-frill accounts.

Since account holders are also members of SEWA Union and involved in an income generating activity, the bank allows them to convert a part of their increased income into savings instead of looking for ways to splurge it on her household consumption. With seven branches in Gujarat, the SEWA Bank holds deposits worth Rs 2 billion.

Saving Patterns

Bank staff and field workers help the applicants in filling out the required applications. The review process involves oral interviews and appraisal by a loan committee and is completed in a short time. To pay her monthly installments, the borrower is required to either visit the bank branch in person or hand over the money to bank employees who visit local places in rickshaw vans to create financial literacy. The loan period in most cases is three years.

There are a few things that really stand out in the case of SEWA Bank. Foremost among these is that an overwhelming majority of its loans have gone for housing and small trades. Housing in particular consumes the largest chunk of credit. SEWA is probably the only cooperative bank which provides credit to low income groups for housing. Since many of the small trades are home based, the housing loan serves a dual purpose of entwining employment and shelter. Also, for women to have a roof over her head is the first security necessity.

Table 10.3

Saving Patterns

	Always Savers	*New Savers*	*Control Group*
Age			
Average age (years)	33.8	34.4	35.0
Marital Status (%)			
Married	87.50	80.00	83.71
Caste (%)			
Upper caste	17.93	10.00	23.98
Backward caste	41.30	45.00	37.10
Scheduled caste or tribe	40.76	45.00	38.91
Educational Attainment[1] (%)			
No education	39.67	40.00	41.63
Primary education	34.78	50.00	34.39
Secondary education	21.74	5.00	20.36
Higher education	3.80	5.00	3.62
Household Members			
Average no. of household members	5.70	6.30	5.90
Earning household members (average)	2.80	2.70	2.70
Observations	184	20	221

Note: These estimates refer to the status of 425 women at the time of the first survey.

Primary education refers to classes 1-7 or techinal, secondary education to classes 8-10 and higher education to classes 11-12, college or postgraduate programme.

1. Defined according to the household questionnaire.

Source: Socioeconomic Review Gujarat State 2005-06.[10]

The bank disburses small secure and majority loans as unsecured loans. The women can get a secured loan using jewellry as collateral. To obtain an unsecured loan, the applicant is either required to open an account and accumulate a certain level of savings or provide a SEWA member as guarantor. The conditional saving not only encourages the applicant to get into saving mode but also allows the microfinance institution to find out whether the applicant will be able to pay back the loan and how much.

10. Berg (2010).

Table 10.4

SEWA Bank in 2007-08

	2006-07	*2007-08*	*Increase/Decrease*
Audit Grade—A			
Shareholders (no. of women)	55,311	60,720	5,409
Share capital (Rs)	3,20,96,000	3.64,36,600	4,34,06,000
Depoistors (no. of women)	3,04,933	3,07,558	2,625
Total deposits (Rs)	65,85,78,000	73,99,70,000	8,13,92,000
Working capital (in Rs)	94,60,43,000	1,02,91,79,0000	8,31,36,000
Loan accounts (no. of women)	91,096	1,03,678	12,583
Loan (Rs)	30,29,74,000	33,45,49,000	2,15,75,000
Surplus (Rs)	53,99,000	52,41,000	-1,58,0000

Source: Annual Report SEWA 2008.

Second, considering that its members hail from variety of caste and ethnic backgrounds—weavers, tailors, blacksmiths; and pursue diverse occupations like *beedi* rolling, vegetable vending, paper picking and kite making and head loading, it brings about social inclusion along with financial inclusion. Besides since most of its members are from lower castes and religious minorities, it fosters inclusive growth in the truest sense. About one-third of SEWA's members are scheduled castes, the caste placed at the lowest rung in the Indian caste system.

Microcredits, Pensions and Insurance

Considering that to complete financial inclusion, there is always a need to introduce a bouquet of microfinance tools along with savings, SEWA has taken steps to take microcredits, insurance and pension to its poor members.

The bank also disburses pensions, insurance and microcredits for productive services. According to Jayshree A. Vyas, Managing Director, SEWA Bank, the bank has disbursed 50,000 micro-pensions to women workers in collaboration with UTI. It also offers vimoSEWA, a bouquet of microinsurance products (while the annual premium for an insurance of Rs 10,000 for a family is Rs 400 in a year, the individual accidental insurance of Rs 75,000 requires payment of Rs 150 annually) to SEWA members. SEWA puts the number of insured women at 200,000.

Table 10.5

Loans through SEWA Bank

Reason for Loan	*Total Women*	*Total Amount (Rs)*
To purchase equipment required for work	600	10,828,000
To purchase stock of raw materials for the goods	2,348	60,130,700
To purchase sheds	2,246	60,745,000
Total	5,194	1,31,703,700

Source: Annual Report SEWA 2008.

The seriousness with which SEWA treats providing security to its members can be gauged from the fact that SEWA bank launched a new Pension Scheme in October 2002 even as 5,000 accounts opened under an old scheme accounted for a corpus of more than Rs 7.5 million.

Another interesting aspect of SEWA Bank is that despite extending loans to the poorest of the poor, it manages to keep the cost down and earn profits. It manages to control the cost by keeping the salaries low and yet extracts a high level of dedication resulting in long working hours. Since the bank branches are located in high population density in the labour area, its field staff is able to contact large number of borrowers. Most of the field workers are union organisers and are paid by the trade unions rather than the bank. What further helps the bank to keep the cost down is that SEWA charges rent lower than the market rate for the building it occupies in Ahmedabad. In case when a worker defaults in loan payments, the SEWA Bank and the union staff sit together to find out the reason behind it and a possible redressal.

Building Skills

That research and training play a crucial role in success of an organisation is common knowledge. In SEWA too, the twin factors have made a huge contribution to the burgeoning organisation. In fact, it was after an investigation of textile mill workers' impoverished housewives that Ela Bhatt, decided to form the union. The decision to form SEWA Bank crept up from realisation that the women workers and farmers were in dire need of credit either for continuation and expansion of their businesses or consumption of their households.

Research, in fact, has almost become a must in SEWA every time the organisation plans to raise a new workers' cooperative. The research helps it to devise a strategy to make the cooperative income-generating and self-sustainable. The research involves conducting surveys, field studies and designing the right kind of equipments for the women workers. The organisation also conducts surveys and studies to see whether its intervention has improved the lot of its members.

An example of this is a large scale survey, SEWA undertook in 1996 of incense stick workers. Conducted eight years after the formation of incense stick workers cooperative, the survey found that husbands of 50 per cent workers were unemployed and 14 per cent were doing casual labour or working in a factory. It found that over 90 per cent women did their work from extremely cramped space and complained of backache, pain in their hands, legs and abdomen. Close to 50 per cent of the women spent anything between Rs 50 to Rs 100 on health and medicines. They had no access to social security benefits and welfare schemes and only 3 per cent of them received a bonus.[11]

Like research, there is equal emphasis on training in SEWA. Right from salt farmers to Rudi bazaar managers, there is an effort to build skills of the women involved in trade. The organisation trains around 500 salt pan workers every month in making industrial salt which fetches more price than the edible salt. Considering that the salt pan workers who are members of SEWA cooperative number 14,000 and it has already trained 2,000 such workers, the organisation is set to complete the process in next two years.

The workers of Rudi Multi Trading Company have been trained in packaging spices and lentils etc., for sale in rural and urban pockets. The education of members on insurance and banking products is another aspect, which requires trained manpower. SEWA has trained a number of women for the purpose. The organisation also lays equal stress on training health, education and housing workers. It has trained an army of women for constructing houses and maintenance services (hand-pump repairers etc.) as well.

11. SEWA Academy (2000).

In an attempt to ensure that its literacy training is functional, SEWA delivers functional literacy training through a 'life school'.[12] Since 1988, when it added education as its eleventh point, SEWA has introduced literacy classes for its members, child care for their children; and skills training and job placement services for their teenage daughters.

Building skills in SEWA has one more facet i.e., leadership skills. The association aims to build leadership of two kinds: leadership skill in each of its member by making her self-confident, competent and responsible; and leadership among local leaders who emerge from within each organised group. It builds leadership by convening regular local meeting and giving exposure to the potential leaders at state, national and international level.

Considering that many of its members are either illiterate or semi-literate, SEWA uses pictorial training and videos to good effect. Such group based training programmes have helped many women to pick up new skills and thus add to their income.

It is no secret that child care and domestic chores leave no time for women workers for training. To understand and overcome this, SEWA initiated an Exposure Dialogue Programme (EDP) whereby a SEWA worker would stay with a family for three days and do all the tasks that the women do. The programme enabled SEWA to identify and overcome such constraints.[13]

Apart from this, SEWA Academy provides skills and knowledge training through eleven courses including conversation training, worker training, leadership training and research training. The Academy functions as a members' 'university' and provides most of the members with their first introduction to a formal learning environment.[14]

ICT in SEWA

Information & Communication Technology (ICT) serves as an important tool to create employment and bring in transparency in SEWA.

---

12. Collect and Gale (2009).
13. Ibid.
14. *www.sewacademy.org/aboutus.html*

Computer training in particular has helped the organisation to find jobs for wards of its members.

It has trained many daughters of SEWA members on MS Office, Excel and on using internet and a few of them have got jobs as data entry operators (DEOs) in their respective *gram panchayats* or opened their computer training centres. A small office of SEWA in a small hamlet in Surendranagar district, where the women members congregate once in a week to take stock of their accounts and work and package Rudi products, also houses a computer institute where eight girls are trained any time.

At the same time, the association has computerised many of its departments and embraced technology to cut down use of paper and bring in more efficiency. For instance, it is using computers for documentation in SEWA Bank and SHG records. SEWA Bank in fact, not only has software programmes for financial accounting and portfolio tracking purposes but also has developed a customised, rigorous client risk rating instrument for microloan evaluations. The bank enters daily cash collection data into databases by the back office bank staff based in the head office, once the handholders pass the scrolls filled out by bank *sathis* to them. The bank has about 10 DEOs and an exclusive IT department that takes care of data entry, troubleshooting, maintaining the hardware and tweaking software products.[15]

Invention & Innovation

The proliferation of cooperatives and the problems that emerge out of working in difficult environment has forced SEWA to invent and innovate. It has discovered new strategies, mechanisms and tools every time the old ones failed to work. There are plenty of examples of it.

For instance, having realised that the poor women workers would not be able to afford large savings, insurance or pension products, SEWA Bank has come out with schemes to suit them. Thus, one can open an account and as well as take membership of the bank with Rs 11 (Rs 10 goes into account and Re 1 is membership fee).

---

15. *http://www.sewabank.org/itandsewa.htm*

The organisation has thought of new plans whenever it has run into hurdles. An example of this is Santalpur block in Patan district where there was unofficial ban on women venturing out of the village. When village *panchayat* imposed a penalty on five women, who travelled to Delhi with Reema Nanawati, Director of Economic and Rural Development in SEWA, to exhibit their embroidery skills, SEWA decided to put in the front wives of members of village *panchayat*. And once *panchayat* members' wives were able to convince their husbands about the profitability of the business, it became a smooth ride for the SEWA. This resulted in formation of SEWA Trade Facilitation Centre (STFC) in 2003 to promote and facilitate selling of embroidered clothes. Today the woman who would earn only Rs 15 per month for the embroidery easily takes home anything between Rs 5,000 to Rs 6,000 a month.

Similarly, to overcome resistance from husbands to their wives' training, SEWA organised a three day training programme for couples to introduce the former to the organisation as well as training. This not only demonstrated women's capabilities but also convinced the husbands about the earning potential of the business projects.

Besides innovative strategies, SEWA has not lagged behind in adopting new technologies to make work faster and safer for its members. For instance, when the women workers in Shree Vanlaxmi Ganeshpura Mahila SEWA Vriksh Utpadan Sahkari Mandali Limited saw a land in Ganeshpura (village in Mehsana district of Gujarat) and wanted to grow trees and plants, but it soaked too much of water, it approached Indian Petrochemicals Corporation Limited (IPCL) for help. The IPCL advised it to cover the vacant land with agri-films. Today the 10-acre land leased by Ganeshpura village *panchayat* to the cooperative supports an ecotourism project where all kinds of flora and fauna flourish.

Another example of it is a new sickle SEWA got designed after the members complained of getting sores on their hands from the traditional sickle used for harvesting. Although the innovation failed to replace the traditional sickle due to the huge price gap between the two and other advantages of the latter, it definitely showed how much the SEWA leadership cared for its members.

Another example of innovation is solar lantern and stove, SEWA has got designed for salt pan workers who toil in farms which are located far away from habitations. Electricity and LPG are yet to reach these farms. SEWA plans to sell during a period of three years, 200,000 rechargeable off-grid solar lanterns to its member-clients in Gujarat, Bihar, Rajasthan and Uttar Pradesh. SEWA proposes to finance the lights and stoves through its 'Hariyali Bond' in three years (2011-2013). Similarly, to simplify the work of salt pan workers, it has designed a number of tools.

SEWA: The Caretaker

In SEWA, the focus is not just on creating employment, increasing income and assets and taking financial services to women workers' doorstep. It is as much on caring about the welfare of the members. There is pronounced emphasis on child care, nutrition, health, education, drinking water and housing because these impinge directly on ability to work and productivity. An effort is made to ensure that women workers' households get at least two meals a day, children are taken care of so that their mothers can concentrate on work and the workers have access to basic amenities like water, health, education and housing.

The collection of drinking water by women in arid Banaskantha district and parts of Patan district consumed most of their time and energy till SEWA decided to intervene. SEWA has not only taught villagers to harvest water but also partnered government in taking piped water supply to them. Done in conjunction with income generating activity, SEWA's watershed development programme has put a stop to migration, allowed the women to play an active role in decision-making on water related issues and brought about overall prosperity in the region. Thanks to SEWA's intervention, the villages in Santalpur block of Patan district, where people were forced to live like nomads—roaming around in search of green pastures for their cattle—no more marry off minor daughters, have better income, better literacy rate and *pucca* houses now.

Having known that illness majorly contributes to pushing a family into poverty and keeping it chronically poor, SEWA is involved in health promotion and local capacity building and operates 60 health centres that provide medical treatment, health care training and tuberculosis control programmes.

Table 10.6

Health Services provided by SEWA

Service Delivered	*Women Reached*	*Men Reached*	*Children Reached*
Health education	29,451	9,348	11,265
Curative care through health centres	42,658	14,660	15,391
Curative care through diagnostic camps	19,473	10,247	7,848
Tuberculosis care (curative)	—	—	—
Immunisation (in collaboration with govt.)	72,798	2,131	69,675
Family planning	2,297	2,230	—

Note: — Not available.
Source: SEWA Main Office, Ahmedabad.

Women Empowerment[16]

SEWA has attained success on all known parameters of women empowerment—increased participation in decision-making, more equitable status of women in the family and community, increased political power and rights, and increased self-esteem. The women own houses (SEWA Bank gives loan on a condition that the house would flaunt housewive's name!) in villages, get elected to local institutions of governance and travel out of the country to train women for self-employment. They perform bank transactions on their own. The money has brought them respect in the society and a definite say in chalking out future plans for their wards. They have overcome, to a great extent, factors like gender inequalities and discrimination against women that contribute directly to perpetuation of poverty in many nations.

To create a common identity and shared purpose among its members and ensure continuity of the movement, SEWA provides selective incentives—employment opportunities and the increased income and

16. *Empowerment Case Studies: SEWA.* Neeru has reaped rich dividends by working in the ecotourism project. For one, she is able to finance her children's education. Her daughter is in class 10. This has helped her learn lot of new things. They've put name plates on all trees for students and put up a stall in Indian Institute of Management (IIM) Ahmedabad during the food festival there every year. 'We sell off everything there,' she informs. The 30-year lease of the land is set to expire in another five years but why would a *panchayat* not prefer a green ecosystem to a barren land (See Annexure A-10.1).

assets etc. Besides, it has provided its members a sense of dignity in work. The sweepers in the organisation, for example, are provided uniforms and part of a 'Committee for Beauty and Cleanliness' which gets contracts to clean office buildings. Likewise, trash pickers are given protective gloves and aprons and are organised.[17]

SEWA Bank and the 103 cooperatives, the organisation runs are an evidence of how over 1.3 million women have been empowered through legalisation of informal sector, organised strength, self-reliance, leadership, employment, increased income, savings, credit, insurance, self-reliance, education, health and training. How a sense of common purpose, atmosphere of informality (members addresses each other by first name suffixing *ben* (sister) to it) and camaraderie pervades through the organisation in Gujarat and eight other states.

A travel to several SEWA centres—fish vendors, vegetable sellers, Rudi packaging centre, computer centres, ecotourism project—gave us a first hand experience of how SEWA women have gained a sense of empowerment. We came across hundreds of women who recounted how they had benefitted from regular employment and increased income, how the organisation and economic independence had brought them respect and allowed them a say in household as well as social matters. They talked about how health insurance and pension had given them a sense of security and wellbeing and how national and international exposure had bestowed on them confidence to face the world head on. They are more aware of their rights and entitlements and have forced the men to think in a feminine way, which, according to Ela Bhatt, is more inclusive. The women would rather work with administration to bring about a change in policies that affect the informal sector workers.

17. Schuler *et al.* (1995).

References

Berg, Gunhild (2010). *Evaluating the Impacts of Microsaving: The Case of SEWA Bank in India*. KfW Development Bank, Goethe University Frankfurt. March.

Channa, Subhadra (2004). *Encyclopedia of Women Studies: Women and Human Rights*.

Chen, Martha Alter (2005). *Towards Economic Freedom: The Impact of SEWA*. Harvard University.

Chen, Martha Alter and D. Snodgrass (2001). *Towards Economic Freedom: The Impact of SEWA*. Harvard University with Ruchi Khurana and Nidhi Mirani. SEWA Academy.

Collect, Kathleen and Chris Gale (2009). *Training for Rural Development: Agricultural and Enterprise Skills for Women Smallholders*. December.

Crowell, Daniel W. (2003). *The SEWA Movement and Rural Development*.

Dasgupta, Sukti (2002). *Organising for Socioeconomic Security in India*. Geneva: International Labour Office. October.

Francis, Jennifer (2004). *Gender and Economic Benefits from Domestic Water Supply in Semiarid Areas: A Case Study in Banaskantha District, Gujarat, Western India*. Gender and Water Alliance.

Jhabvala, Reena and Namrata Bali (1993). *My Life My Work. A Sociological Study of SEWA's Urban Members*.

SEWA Academy (2000). *The Fragrance of Hard Work: Women License Stick Rollers of Gujarat*. June.

Schuler, Sidney, Syed Hashemi and Harshida Pandit (1995). *Beyond Credit: SEWA's Approach to Women's Empowerment and Influence on Women's Reproductive Lives in Urban India*.

Annexure A-10.1

Case Study: Salt Pan Worker

Though India gained independence in 1947, for Devuben Jayantibhai Rathore, a salt pan worker from Kuda village in Surendranagar district in Gujarat, the freedom from drudgery and slavery only came about a decade ago. Till then, she was enslaved to local moneylenders. Not only would the latter charge exorbitant rate of interest on the working capital loaned to her but also would bind her into selling her produce to them at extremely low prices—often at one-third of the market price.

The pattern had continued for over a decade. Devuben and her family, despite being registered with Gujarat Government's Meetha Sehkari Namak Mandali (MSNM)—an organisation raised to protect salt workers, would slog in extreme circumstances between every October and May in the salt pans and yet live in penury. 'We would stay in the salt pans in darkness with scorpions and other insects and yet make a profit of only Rs 50 per tonne at the end of the season,' she recollects her voice betraying a sense of regret.

For eight months (the season when salt is prepared), her family would be without proper shelter and access to food and water. They would be exposed to blazing sun, salty waters and hazards like sunburns and ulcers associated with the sun and the salt. What was worse they knew to produce only edible salt, which would fetch them much less price than the industrial salt.

Devuben joined SEWA's Childcare Co-operative in 2001 and has since not looked back. Thanks to the market linkages and training for production of industrial salt, she gains almost double the price what she would get earlier. 'I get to make double on each ton now,' she beams, standing on a high pedestal as if to exhibit her exalted status.

The profit has brought about several changes in her household. For one, her daughter Kavita has topped the village school because the mother could pay for her tuitions. Devuben is already planning to get her enrolled for BBA. Now she has even started sending her other daughter and son for tuitions.

Case Study: Rudi Trader

Suryaba Vikram Singh Jadeja, mother of three grown up children from a nondescript village in Surendranagar district, joined SEWA eight years back. For two years, she was part of a savings group, associated with the trade union. Then she was transferred to Rudi Multi Trading Company Limited, another group aligned to the Union, which procures, packages and sells spices, lentils etc., to local populace. And this turned out to be the defining moment in her life.

Suryaba, whom Inclusion met in Surendranagar's packaging centre, earns Rs 3 for packaging one packet of turmeric, chilli or lentils. She does packaging work on two days out of seven days. On the rest of the days, she goes to neighbouring villages to sell the packets. She is paid Rs 5,000 per month for selling in 20 villages.

Suryaba (38) has trained 20 Rudi sisters and come to earn great respect in her family and outside. Besides, the extra income has helped her buy a plot of land and enroll her three sons in better educational institutions. Her eldest son is doing graduation in agriculture in a boarding institution in Mehsana. 'I pay a hefty fee for him every month,' she proudly declares.

Another son of Suryaba wants to join police and doing well in class 10. She sends him for tuitions.

For Suryaba, working outside the village is a thing of pride. She wants to stick to Rudi for good. 'My mother Ranjanba says I did the right thing by joining SEWA. She tells me not to leave it,' she adds with a grin on her face.

Case Study: Fish Vendor

Jyotiben Ramobai (50) is a contented person. She has a house of her own, a strategic vending cubicle in an Ahmedabad Municipal Corporation (AMC) fish market under Chamunda Bridge and well-settled three sons and two daughters. Besides, she also has her own and her family's health insured.

But this was not the scene till six months back. She would buy her stock of fish from three middlemen at very high margins and sell it from an unauthorised pavement in Chamanpura. She would face constant harassment at the hands of middlemen, municipal workers and policemen. Though she had inherited the pavement space from her mother-in-law 35 years back, this did not protect her from the oppressive government machinery.

Her fate took a turn for better when she joined Shri Matsyagandha Women's Sewa Co-operative Limited, a cooperative aligned to SEWA. After SEWA fought for nine years to get them designated places for selling their stuff, the AMC allocated 56 cubicles under the Chamunda Bridge to fish vendors six months back. Jyotiben and other cooperative members now buy from SEWA which delivers about 500 kilogram of fish from Saurashtra everyday in off season and 1,000 kilogram otherwise to their doorstep. And this is sold at lowest margins.

Jyotiben has not looked back since then. 'Earlier I would buy from the middlemen. Since their profit margins were very high, I would earn only Rs 50 per day. But since SEWA intervened, I earn anything between Rs 200 and Rs 300. Besides, I also save the money I would spend on traveling to the middlemen,' she says proudly displaying Rau, Silver and other variety of fish, placed in large bowls in front of her.

Unlike the pavement space which would have been unauthorised forever, the cubicles under the flyover would come to the vendors provided each one of them pays Rs 500 per month for 18 months to the AMC. Apart from this they would also be entitled to a health insurance after paying just Rs 50 per month. 'If I or a member of my family fall ill and get hospitalised, SEWA pays up to Rs 2,000 for our hospitalisation. Only condition is that these hospitals should be empanelled with SEWA,' Jyotiben claims weighing piece of a fish for a customer.

Jyotiben has not only paid off loan for her house, she has also bought a separate flat for her son. She proudly informs that she saves Rs 1,500 per month in SEWA bank and her youngest grandson goes to an English school now. The Fish Cooperative is 300-member strong and growing.

Case Study: Vegetable Seller

In 1999 when Bina joined Gujarat Rajya Mahila Sewa Sehkari Sangh Limited (GRMSSSL), a cooperative aligned to SEWA, as a saleswoman along with Usha, they had never imagined the kind of hostile reception they would get. Theirs was the only women cooperative in the 300-strong commission (*aadhti*) shops in Agricultural Produce Marketing Committee (APMC), Ahmedabad.

People would throw tomatoes at them. They would taunt them saying, 'this is not your job. *Ghar Jaake chapatti banao (Go home and cook food)*. They would write on their walls '*Behnon se sawdhan* (Beware of sisters)." Though their shop was next to a gate, their jealous neighbours would tell customers through gestures not to visit them.

But since then things have turned for better. Taunts and warnings have subsided. There is grudging acceptance that *behns* are here for good now. Now there is a constant stream of visitors at the GRMSSSL to buy gourd (*ghiya*), ridge gourd (*turai*), bitter gourd (*karela*), mint (*dhania*) and other vegetables because the cooperative charges less than the other commission agents. 'We charge at least Rs 10 less on 20 kilogram of vegetable. We are the cheapest of them all,' Beena proudly declares.

A big number of customers and farmers have become members of the cooperative. The customers buy vegetables from the GRMSSSL and sell on the roadside earning a handsome profit in the process. The farmers on the other hand get better prices for their produce as GRMSSSL charges 4 per cent less commission than other agents.

Visit the shop any time between 7 am and 4 pm and you can see Bina buying and selling bundles of vegetables, weighing them on the electronic weighing platform scale and disbursing receipts for the same. She has greatly benefitted from her salary of Rs 8,000 per month. Her only daughter is enrolled in engineering while the two sons are studying in good schools. In short-life is all hunky doty for her.

Case Study: Computer Operator

Beena (20 plus) had just completed graduation and was enjoying her vacations when her mother, Geetabehn, a member of SEWA, got her registered for a computer course in SEWA.

The idea was to get her trained in computers during the college holidays. The training centre was exclusively for girls with 19 others learning computer basics there. Beena learnt MS Office, Power Point, Excel for a month and internet for 10 days and this is what got her a job in a *gram panchayat* at Panva, her in-laws' village in Surendranagar district.

Beena is a Data Entry Operator and earns Rs 4,000 per month. Together with her husband Prakash who is a hardware engineer, she earns enough to lead a comfortable life. She also teaches MS office to several children at her home at a discount (she claims to charge Rs 400, Rs 900 less than the market price) to add to her income.

The computer education and subsequent jobs have helped Beena and Prakash buy every household item with their hard-earned money. 'We've a computer, a refrigerator, a television and just bought a bike,' she informs. The couple plans to settle in Dhanradaghra, an army area so that they can put their baby daughter Dhruvi into an English school.

Case Study: SHG Member

Before joining SEWA's Self-Help Group (SHG), Chandrika (42) could barely speak in public. And travelling alone was completely out of question. But now she does both with elan. A member of a saving group called Nari Sewa Sawasai Mahila Sangh in her village Gajanavav, not only has she become eloquent but also travels alone to Ahmedabad and Surendranagar every time she has to update the registers on SHGs.

Though each member of her 15-member strong SHG only saves Rs 25 a month, this has not only helped them set up small businesses but also built her reputation in the village and SEWA. 'I joined SEWA 12 years back after paying Rs 5. When they (SEWA seniors) saw we save regularly. We got good grading for it and we got a loan of Rs 40,000,' she recalls.

Some time back her village offered to make her *sarpanch* unanimously but it did not excite her much. 'I am already half Sarpanch. I got *dhobi ghat* and drinking water pool constructed. SEWA *hamare saath hai* (is with us). What else do we need?', she asks.

The SHG has helped Chandrika put her daughter in boarding and bought a computer for her son. She herself has learnt computer. 'Initially people would laugh on me. But now they respect me. Because I have grown a lot financially and stand on my feet.' In all Surendranagar has 270 SHGs.

Case Study: Artisan

Till 1990 Puriben, daughter of Hansiba had never seen a hundred rupee note. A middle-aged woman belonging to Ahir community, she along with her family would migrate to a new place every year in search of grazing grounds for her cattle.

Her handicraft skill—drawing intricate designs of embroidery on clothes—was limited to stitching for future marriage of her daughters. The most her skill would earn her in a year was Rs 500, less than four days of daily wages of an unskilled labourer.

She learnt or rather inherited the embroidery skill from her mother at the age of 10. Initially she would earn only Rs 15 in a day. Now the earnings have gone up to anything between Rs 5,000 and Rs 6,000 per month. Her three sons and daughters-in-law are all educated. Yet, the daughters-in-law are as good in stitching designs on cotton apparels as she is.

Unlike the past when Puriben and her family members would roam around the year in search of water and food after putting their farms on lease, today she lives a fairly comfortable and settled life. She has constructed a *pucca* house after taking loan from SEWA. She cultivates her farms.

Moreover, she has a toilet in her house and installed a few water tanks as well to harvest rain water. The transformation of Puriben is not stand alone. All people in Vava, her village in Patan district, have water tanks and toilets and lead an easy life. Hansiba, the brand named after her mother, has changed their lives for better.

Case Study: Tree Grower

When Neeruben Babubhai Senma joined Shree Vanlaxmi Ganeshpura Mahila Sewa Vriksh Utpadan Sahkari Mandali Limited, the ecotourism project of SEWA on a 10-acre plot in Ganeshpura village *panchayat*, much of the work was already in place. The land, which was once covered with shrubs, cactuses and wild growth and infested with snakes and other poisonous reptiles, had already been made arable. But growing saplings and crops on it was still a problem. And the doubting Thomas's still did not believe that women could cultivate and grow crops.

The women would carry water from one and a half kilometres to irrigate the plants but the sandy soil would soak all the water within minutes. It was Indian Petrochemicals Corporation Limited (IPCL) Vadodara which taught the women to blanket the ground with agri-films.

Sprinkling irrigation was also introduced. But the shepherds from the village would still push their cattle into it for grazing. To stop this, it was decided to appoint a shepherd as a watchman.

Hindustan Petroleum Corporation Limited (HPCL) gave all agricultural equipments—power tillers etc.—to the group. Another organisation taught them how to use organic compost. Today the land is not just green and grows colour cotton, cluster beans, castor, wheat and millet and trees are laden with ripening fruits, the place also has beautiful bamboo tents to accommodate the tourists.

Neeru has benefitted as much from the growth as the other 14 active members in the green heaven. 'I get paid Rs 6,000 per month. Besides, the profit gets divided among all the members. Today we have mangoes, guava, lemon, *amla* (gooseberry), *chicku* and the trees of all kinds,' she proudly declares.

Neeru has reaped rich dividends by working in the ecotourism project. For one, she is able to finance her children's education. Her daughter is in class 10. This has helped her learn lot of new things. They have put name plates on all trees for students and put up a stall in Indian Institute of Management (IIM) Ahmedabad during the food festival there every year. 'We sell off everything there,' she informs. The 30-year lease of the land is set to expire in another five years but why would a *panchayat* not prefer a green ecosystem to a barren land.

11 Central Bank Governance Issues

Some RBI Perspectives[1]

D. SUBBARAO

I have known Dr Montek Singh Ahluwalia for over 20 years now. I was just promoted as Joint Secretary in the Department of Economic Affairs in 1991 when he came in as Secretary. He had already earned a formidable reputation by then for his sharp and analytical mind. Within just a few weeks of seeing him work, it became clear to me that that reputation was eminently well deserved. Even a brief discussion with him will clearly show why he is so highly regarded. As I got to know him better, I realised that Dr Ahluwalia has several other positive attributes. He has the rare ability to pare down even the most complex issues to their essentials in a way that leads to better evaluation of policy alternatives. He thinks and speaks very clearly and his debating skills are legendary.

As a Joint Secretary working under him, I obviously had an opportunity to interact with him on a continuous basis. But I must specially mention the extraordinary competence and skill that he showed in negotiating the settlement of the rupee-rouble debt deal in 1993 in which I had the opportunity to assist him.

What is also impressive about Dr Ahluwalia is that he is one of the few people at the top levels of the Government who has avoided making his policy positions hostage to his job affiliation. No matter what job he might be in, he has always thought from a broader, whole-of-government perspective. Having held several stressful jobs myself, I have both envied and admired his equanimity under pressure, and his easy, friendly and

1. Based on comments by Dr Duvvuri Subbarao, Governor, Reserve Bank of India at the meeting of the Central Bank Governance Group in Basel on May 9, 2011.

cheerful demeanour. It has been my privilege to know Dr Ahluwalia who has made such an outstanding contribution to India's economic policy management.

As Finance Secretary, Dr Ahluwalia served on the Central Board of the Reserve Bank of India. Even as he moved on, he kept in close touch with the RBI. Over the last three years that I have been Governor of RBI, I have had the opportunity and privilege of seeking his counsel on a number of complex issues, including on issues on the agenda of the G-20 for which he has been the Prime Minister's Sherpa. I am happy to contribute this piece on 'Central Bank Governance Issues: Some RBI Perspectives' based on my comments on this topic at the meeting of the Central Bank Governance Group in Basel on May 9, 2011 for this festschrift.

RBI's Mandate

RBI has a mandate that is wider than is typical of central banks. The preamble to the RBI Act, 1934[2] describes its main functions as '...to regulate the issue of Bank Notes and keeping of reserves with a view to securing monetary stability in India and generally to operate the currency and credit system of the country to its advantage.' This preamble indicates the two core functions of the Reserve Bank: (i) issue of currency and (ii) monetary authority. The Act also entrusts other functions to the Reserve Bank such as regulation of non-bank financial institutions, management of foreign exchange reserves, management of sovereign debt—by statute in respect of Central government and by agreement in respect of state governments—and regulation of forex, money and government securities markets and their derivatives.

The legal mandate for our other key functions and responsibilities comes from specific statutes: the Banking Regulation Act, 1949 together

2. The legislation to establish a central bank for India was passed in 1934 and the Reserve Bank of India came into being a year later in 1935. The Bank was set up on the basis of the recommendations of the Hilton Young Commission. Earlier in 1913, John Maynard Keynes who served as an officer of British Administration in India, had proposed a 'State Bank' to be set up in India, which was to engage in both central banking and commercial banking functions. Keynes proposed that the Bank be run by a Central Board consisting of the Governor, the Deputy Governor, a representative of Government and three or more non-voting assessors.

with the RBI Act, gives RBI the power to regulate and supervise commercial banks and cooperative banks; the Foreign Exchange Management Act, 1999 empowers the RBI to regulate the foreign exchange market; the Payment & Settlement Systems Act, 2007 mandates RBI to regulate and supervise the payment and settlement systems.

All the statutes put together make the Reserve Bank a full service central bank. The RBI is the issuer of currency and is the monetary authority. It regulates and supervises banks, non-bank financial companies (NBFCs) and segments of the financial markets. It is the banker and debt manager to the Government. It is the gatekeeper of the external sector. It regulates and supervises the payment and settlement system. Being both the monetary authority and banking sector regulator gives RBI also the principal responsibility for financial stability.

Even as the Reserve Bank's statutory mandate is wide compared to that of other central banks, what really sets us apart is the key role the Reserve Bank has had in driving India's development agenda. Several national level programmes such as those for the flow of credit to the agriculture sector and for small and medium industries were initially designed and implemented by the Reserve Bank. The apex national institutions for agriculture credit (NABARD), industrial finance (IDBI) are offshoots of what were once departments within the Reserve Bank. The Reserve Bank has been at the forefront in nurturing institutions and developing financial markets in India—the money market, the foreign exchange market and the government securities market. Efforts in recent years have focussed on enhancing the depth, integrity, transparency and efficiency of these markets.

The Reserve Bank pioneered the Lead Bank Scheme in 1969 whereby a designated bank in each district coordinates the flow of credit from all institutions in the district in support of the district credit plan. The Reserve Bank also issues directions and monitors the priority sector lending scheme, whereby all commercial banks are required to set apart a prescribed share of their total advances to priority sector. In recent times, the Reserve Bank has been leading the effort towards financial inclusion and financial literacy with the aim of eventually providing all households in the country meaningful access to the formal financial sector.

Autonomy and Accountability

Neither the RBI Act nor any rules lay down a formal accountability mechanism. In the absence of a specific formulation, the fallback is on the general principle underlying a democracy—which is to render accountability to the parliament through the Finance Minister. The Reserve Bank assists the Finance Minister in answering parliament questions that pertain to its domain. Besides, the Standing Committee on Finance of Parliament summons the Governor for testimony on specific issues including legislations under consideration.

As regards autonomy, the Reserve Bank has not been accorded autonomy under the statute. The RBI Act lays down that the Central government may give directions to the Bank, from time to time, after consultation with the Governor, where considered necessary in public interest.

To an untutored observer, the above arrangements present a picture of a central bank with limited autonomy, and that too enjoyed at the pleasure of the Government, juxtaposed with relatively loose systems of accountability.

The reality, however, is quite different. RBI in effect functions with a functionally autonomous mandate and there has been no instance so far of the Government exercising its reserve powers to issue a directive. This is all the more remarkable since the interaction between the Government and the Reserve Bank is closer and more frequent than is typical in other countries, and this draws from the key role of the Reserve Bank in financial sector reforms and economic development. But this close relationship has not spilled over into the Government encroaching on the Reserve Bank's autonomy in making monetary policy and regulatory policy.

The systems of accountability too are not loose contrary to what the formal picture might suggest. Since RBI is not an inflation targetting central bank, there is no formal memorandum of understanding (MoU) or a 'Results Agreement' between the Government and the Reserve Bank. Nevertheless, it renders accountability for our performance on inflation. It explains the rationale for our monetary policy stance quite extensively. Importantly, the Governor addresses a press conference following each policy review in order to disseminate the specifics of the policy and the expected outcomes, and to respond to questions from the media. This is followed by structured interviews in the print and electronic media. Our latest initiative in the dissemination process is a post-policy teleconference with researchers and analysts where the Governor and the Deputy Governors respond to questions from them.

For most of the other important, non-monetary policy decisions, it has now become standard practice for the Reserve Bank to consult with stakeholders and call for feedback on the draft policy before a final decision is taken.

One of the determinants of rendering accountability is the quality of accounting standards and of financial reporting and disclosure. The RBI complies with best practices in accounting, and marks to market its holdings of domestic and foreign currency assets. However, only realised gains are recognised as income. Disclosures provided in the Annual Report of the RBI are fairly comprehensive and provide disaggregated analysis in respect of all major balance sheet heads including reserves and income and expenditure.

The sum and substance of this is that RBI renders accountability not as a matter of compliance with a specific provision of law but as a matter of self-discipline required of a responsible public institution, and this self-discipline has over time got enshrined into a code of conduct.

After these introductory comments on the mandate of the Reserve Bank, and our systems of accountability, let me turn to some specific governance issues.

Formulation of Monetary Policy

As a standard, monetary policy decisions are made by the Governor. There is no formal committee structure like the Federal Open Market Committee (FOMC) of the Fed or the Monetary Policy Committee (MPC) of the Bank of England. The Governor holds structured consultations with the four Deputy Governors and they constitute an informal MPC although a committee structure is not enjoined under the law or the rules. By its very nature there is no voting in this committee and the final call is that of the Governor.

RBI also has a Technical Advisory Committee (TAC) on Monetary Policy that acts as a proxy policy committee, but it is advisory in nature. It comprises the Governor as chairman, the Deputy Governor in charge of monetary policy as the vice-chairman and other three Deputy Governors as members. Besides, the committee has five external members, two of whom are experts from the Central Board of the Bank while the other three are drawn from a wider pool. The external members are nominated by the Governor. They give specific recommendations on policy options and these are minuted. RBI has recently started putting the minutes of the meeting in the public domain, including specific recommendations, without directly identifying members with their advice.

Ahead of each quarterly monetary policy announcement, there is also an extensive process of structured consultation by the Governor with banks, financial market representatives, trade bodies and industry associations. It convenes a meeting of economists and analysts twice a year, ahead of the annual policy in April and the second quarter policy in October.

Finally, close to the policy decision, an established practice for the Governor is to meet the Prime Minister and the Finance Minister informally, give them an assessment of the macroeconomic situation and indicate to them his proposed policy stance. This is only a matter of courtesy, and the process has not impinged on the autonomy of the Reserve Bank in monetary policymaking. The consultation with the Finance Minister, in particular, should be seen as an avenue for fiscal-monetary coordination, since on a reciprocal basis, the Finance Minister too takes the Governor into confidence on the fiscal stance ahead of presenting the budget to the Parliament.

An issue that comes up often is that even as the current system is working, whether RBI might be better served by having a formal MPC with its majority advice becoming binding. My own view is that it should be moving towards an MPC system, but in a phased manner. There are some pre-conditions to be met. First, the central bank should be given legally backed formal autonomy. Second, in a situation where inflation dynamics are more often dictated by supply-side elements, the central bank's ability to control inflation is restricted. An MPC mechanism in such a situation can weaken the coordination between the Government and the Reserve Bank. However, when our financial markets deepen further, operating procedures improve and monetary transmission becomes more efficient, shifting to an MPC system becomes a realistic option.

Inflation Targetting

Inflation targetting, by its very nature, is an issue in central bank governance. The defining features of an inflation targetting central bank are a precise mandate, a single instrument (the policy interest rate) in its armoury, a single-minded devotion to achieving this target and a principal-agent relationship with the Government.

The Reserve Bank is not an inflation targetting central bank. Nevertheless there is an influential view that our economy will be better served if the Reserve Bank becomes one. The argument is that inflation hurts much more in a country like India with hundreds of millions of poor people and that the Reserve Bank will be more effective in combating inflation if it is not burdened with other objectives.

This argument is contestable. Inflation targetting is neither feasible nor advisable in India, and for several reasons. First, in an emerging economy like ours, it is not practical for the central bank to focus exclusively on inflation oblivious of the larger development context. The Reserve Bank cannot escape from the difficult challenge of weighing the growth-inflation trade off in determining its monetary policy stance.

Second, the drivers of inflation in India often emanate from the supply side, which are normally beyond the pale of monetary policy. In particular, given the low-income levels, food items have a relatively larger weight in the consumption basket in India compared to advanced economies and even many emerging market economies (EMEs). It has three consumer price indices each covering different segments of the population with the weight for food ranging between 46-70 per cent. Monetary policy, as is well known, is an ineffective instrument for reining in inflation emanating from supply pressures. It is unrealistic, under these circumstances, to expect the Reserve Bank to deliver on an inflation target in the short-term.

An alternative that is put forward is that RBI could target core inflation rather than headline inflation. That is not a feasible solution either. An inflation index, with half the basket excluded from it, hardly reflects reality. Moreover, the exclusion of food from the core index can be justified if average food inflation is the same as the average non-food inflation. If food inflation is higher, as is typically the case in many low income countries including India, then it would be underestimating inflationary pressures on a systemic basis. That would mislead policy prescriptions.[3]

Even if, for the sake of argument, RBI settles on inflation targetting, it has a problem about which inflation index to target. The headline inflation index is the wholesale price index (WPI), and that does not, by definition, reflect the consumer price situation. However, getting a single representative inflation rate for a large economy with 1.2 billion people, fragmented markets and diverse geography is a formidable challenge. The recent introduction of CPI-Urban and CPI-Rural is welcome, but it still does not solve the problem of heterogeneity.

Finally, a necessary condition for inflation targetting to work is efficient monetary transmission. In India, monetary transmission has been improving but is still a fair bit away from best practice. There are several factors inhibiting the transmission process such as an asymmetric relationship between depositors and banks, administered interest rates on postal savings that are not adjusted in line with prevailing interest rate trends and rigidities in the financial markets. All these factors dampen the efficacy of monetary signals and complicate the adoption of an inflation targetting regime in India.

Importantly, there is a political economy argument too against the Reserve Bank becoming an inflation targetter. The intellectual basis for central bank independence draws from Rogoff's conservative central bank construct. The construct is based on the assumption that governments tend to favour growth and employment while central banks, left to themselves, would seek to lower inflation. Precise inflation targetting formalises this arrangement and dilutes the scope for interference in each other's domain. Such independent policy pursuits by the Government and

---

3. In our case, over the last six years average food inflation (8.7%) has been more than double of non-food inflation (4.0%).

the central bank, it is contended, serve the best interests of the national economy.

This assumption does not hold in the case of India because societal tolerance in India for inflation is low. Given the compulsions of democracy and the large population of poor, any government in India has always to be, and indeed has been, sensitive to price stability even if it means sacrificing output in the short-term. So, the argument of divergence of natural preferences as between the government and the central bank that underpins the inflation targetting framework does not hold in the case of India. Indeed both the Government and the Reserve Bank have to factor in the short-term growth-inflation trade off in their policy calculations.

Macroprudential Regulation and Supervision

One of the important lessons of the crisis is that a collection of healthy financial institutions does not necessary make for a healthy financial system, and consequently that microprudential regulation and supervision at the individual institution level have to be complemented by macroprudential regulation at the systemic level to guard financial stability. There are several debates that have surfaced centred around this issue including, what should be the ambit of macroprudential policies, what are the instruments to be used, should macroprudential concerns be part of the monetary policy calculus, which institution or institutions should be given the responsibilities for macroprudential supervision and what should be the arrangements for coordination. All the above questions raise several governance issues with political economy dimensions.

Consider the context. As part of the post-crisis reforms of regulatory architecture, there is an increasing trend of entrusting macroprudential supervision to central banks as an additional responsibility. Where central banks already have this responsibility, it is being more explicitly defined.

All policy decisions, as much as they are based on analytical constructs, eventually involve making judgements. But judgement plays a bigger role in formulating macroprudential policies. This is so because formalising the analytical framework for macroprudential policies, demanding as it entails defining the metrics for identifying systemic risk and identifying the appropriate instruments, is conceptually more challenging than is the case for other policies.

Possibly because of this judgement dimension, among central banks that are new to macroprudential regulation and supervision, there is an apprehension that performing this task will make them vulnerable to political interference. There is also an unstated fear that once a culture of political interference into central bank business gets a foothold, it will rapidly 'spillover' into all areas of central bank business, including monetary policy, and thus erode the much prized autonomy of the central bank.

The Indian experience does not bear out this apprehension. Macroprudential regulation and supervision have historically been a part of the Reserve Bank's mandate. Yet there have been no instances of political influence on the macro prudential policies of the Reserve Bank acting in its capacity as the regulator. In fact, the Reserve Bank enjoys as much autonomy over its regulatory decisions as it does on its monetary policy decisions, and the political system has not tried to influence the Reserve Bank's stance.

Indeed, in spite of India being a vigorous democracy with very little that remains outside the political domain, the political system has respected the Reserve Bank's autonomy over its domain. This is a testimony of the credibility and reputation that the Reserve Bank has earned for its professional integrity. The political system has an incentive in keeping it that way.

Debt Management Office

The RBI Act mandates the Reserve Bank to be the debt manager of the Central government. The Reserve Bank also manages the debt of state governments by mutual agreement as provided in law. There is now a proposal to shift this function out of the central bank, and this has generated a debate around several governance issues.

To set the context for this debate, it should be noted that the Reserve Bank has an impressive track record in debt management. Even as the Government's borrowing had gone up both in absolute and proportional terms, it has managed to complete the borrowing programme in a cost-efficient manner. With the average maturity of government debt at around 10 years, India has one of the longest maturity profiles in the world, which proved to be a source of major strength and comfort during the crisis.

It could be argued that public debt management in India has been effective because the Reserve Bank, which is the monetary authority, is also entrusted this task. Nevertheless, the progress on fiscal consolidation by the Government in the years before the crisis suggested that there could be operational efficiencies to be gained by shifting debt management to a separate Debt Management Office (DMO). The Government has accordingly set up a middle office of the DMO and is proposing to move forward with a Public Debt Management Agency of India Bill.

There is need to reconsider the content and pace of this process in view of the revised circumstances post-crisis. The case for shifting debt management function out of the central bank is made on several arguments such as resolving conflict of interest, reducing the cost of debt, facilitating debt consolidation and increasing transparency. These advantages are overstated.

The most potent of these arguments is the one relating to conflict of interest. The other arguments pertain to mechanics of debt management, which can be said to be model neutral. Let me, therefore focus on the conflict of interest issue.

The primary conflict, which is generally associated with a central bank managing sovereign debt pertains to the one between its inherent responsibility as the monetary authority, and its obligations as a debt manager. In particular, it is argued that the central bank will be biased towards a low interest regime in order to reduce the costs of sovereign debt even if it compromises its anti-inflation stance. A similar conflict may also distort the open market operations of the central bank.

The above arguments, though valid in some countries, fail to recognise that in countries such as India, given the large size of the government borrowing programme, sovereign debt management is much more than merely an exercise in resource raising. The size and dynamics of government borrowing programme has a much wider influence on interest rate movements, systemic liquidity and even credit growth through the crowding out of private sector credit demand. Management of public debt, therefore, has necessarily to be seen as part of broader macroeconomic management framework involving various tradeoffs. Once this is recognised, the centrality of central banks in this regard becomes quite evident. Only central banks have the requisite market pulse and instruments to aid in making contextual judgements, which an independent debt agency, driven by narrow objectives, will not be able to do.

Also, it is not that these conflicts would disappear merely by shifting debt management out of the central bank. In fact resolving those conflicts could become much more complicated leading to inferior outcomes. This is because even after the separation, the central bank would continue to be expected to manage the market volatility and market expectations arising out of government borrowing.

Admittedly, a few years back, the challenges of managing the above conflicts in the then prevailing context seemed to weigh in favour of separation of debt management from the central bank. The constraining factor, even then, was the high fiscal deficit. The fiscal position, which was improving in the years before the crisis, got off-track during the crisis. The Government is making attempts to get back on to a path of fiscal consolidation post-crisis. The difference as far as the Reserve Bank is concerned is that the Fiscal Responsibility and Budget Management (FRBM) Act, 2003 is in place which prohibits the Reserve Bank's participation in the primary auction for Government securities. A separate mechanism for conveying monetary stance in the form of repo and reverse repo rates under the Bank's liquidity adjustment facility (LAF) has been put in place in 2000. Furthermore, in a situation of excess capital flows requiring forex intervention from the Reserve Bank and the consequent sterilisation through issuance of Government bonds by the RBI, the coordination of debt management with monetary operations needs to continue. This makes the case for separation much weaker in the revised circumstances.

In the Indian context, there is the added complexity of managing the debt of the states. The sensitivity of the states to entrust debt management to an agency of the Central government also needs to be kept in view given the political-economy dimensions of our federal structure. This is all the more important since market borrowings have emerged as the dominant source of deficit financing at the sub-national level. Taken together, the borrowing by states has attained a critical mass *vis-à-vis* the absorptive capacity of the market. That makes it imperative to harmonise the market borrowing programmes of the Centre and the states. Separation of the Centre's debt management from the central bank will make such harmonisation difficult.

Thus, on balance, as long as there are institutionalised mechanisms to negotiate various tradeoffs in a given context within the overarching objective of achieving monetary and financial stability, separation of debt management from central bank seems to be a sub-optimal choice. Even internationally, the emerging post-crisis wisdom recognises the interdependence between the functions of monetary policy, financial stability and sovereign debt management and the need for close association of the central bank with sovereign debt management.

Responsibility for Financial Stability

The Reserve Bank's mandate for ensuring financial stability arises mainly from its mandated functions of regulator of the banking system, regulator and supervisor of the payment and settlement systems, regulator of the money, forex, government security and credit markets, banker to the banks, as also the lender-of-the last resort. This unique combination of responsibilities for macroprudential regulation and microprudential supervision, together with an implicit mandate for systemic oversight has allowed the Reserve Bank to exploit the synergies across various dimensions. The micro level information coming from supervision of individual institutions has been a valuable input for shaping the macro-perspective. On the other hand, the broad understanding from macroprudential regulation has been effective in instituting prudential safeguards at the micro-institution level.

Financial stability is explicitly entering the objective function of central banks post-crisis. The Reserve Bank though, had all along pursued financial stability as an important objective. Indeed, one of the main reasons the impact of the crisis on India has been blunted is because the Reserve Bank tightened the provisioning norms and risk weights for sub-sectors that experienced rapid credit growth in the years before the crisis such as real estate and consumer credit.

In India, there are other market regulators besides the Reserve Bank such as the Securities and Exchange Board of India (SEBI), the Insurance Regulatory and Development Authority (IRDA) and the Pension Funds Regulatory and Developmental Authority (PFRDA) who contribute to the building block for financial stability. Nevertheless the Reserve Bank has played an apex role by tradition and by the fact that it regulates banks in a financial system that is bank-dominated. The channels of interconnection between banks and other financial sector entities are within the regulatory perimeter of the Reserve Bank.

Though the Indian financial system weathered the global financial crisis relatively unscathed, there was enhanced focus on the regulation of financial system in India too in the wake of the global financial crisis. While the post-crisis debate in most countries was on the reform of the regulatory architecture, and what responsibilities to entrust to the central bank, the focus in India was on coordination amongst regulators. With a view to establishing a body to institutionalise and strengthen the mechanism for maintaining financial stability, financial sector development and inter-regulatory coordination, in December 2010, the Government constituted the Financial Stability and Development Council (FSDC) to be chaired by the Finance Minister. The FSDC is to be assisted by a sub-committee to be chaired by the Governor, RBI. This sub-committee has replaced the erstwhile High Level Coordination Committee on Financial Markets (HLCCFM) under the chairmanship of Governor, RBI. While constituting the FSDC, the Government held out a clear assurance that the setting up of the FSDC will not in any way erode the autonomy of the regulators.

In terms of governance structure, the two-tier framework of FSDC and the sub-committee presents an interesting case. The crisis has clearly demonstrated the need for explicit delineation of responsibilities for financial stability across agencies and the protocol for coordination among such agencies. The crisis has at the same time brought forth the critical stake of the sovereign in ensuring financial stability—the spillover costs in a crisis have to be borne by the governments. In the Indian context, the proposed FSDC structure attempts to strike a balance between the sovereign's objective of ensuring financial stability to reduce the probability of a crisis and the operative arrangements involving the central bank and the regulators. While the sub-committee under the Governor, RBI is expected to evolve as a more active, hands-on body for managing financial stability in normal times, the FSDC would have a broad oversight and will assume central role in crisis times.

Since the Reserve Bank has historically been a macroprudential regulator, not all the governance issues surrounding financial stability that have emerged post-crisis are new to us. Nevertheless, there are always unknown unknowns and the system should be able to respond to them. Now that the regulatory architecture of the FSDC is in place, it is important for the Government and the regulators in India to develop conventions and practices, which will serve the goal of preserving financial stability without eroding the autonomy of the regulators.

12 Future of Financial System

Emerging Issues

Y.V. REDDY

It is an honour to be invited to contribute to this volume to felicitate a distinguished economist and policymaker, Mr Montek Singh Ahluwalia, widely known as Montek. I have the privilege of knowing him personally, and working with him professionally, both within India and in multilateral bodies. He was my superior for some time, and a colleague for some time, but he always remained a close friend for well over three decades. He is razor sharp in his intellect, has mastery over economic theory and is a communicator par excellence. What he enjoys most is a policy-debate, and he spans the worlds of theory and practice; economists and political leadership; and national government and multilateral bodies. Despite impressive presence in any gathering, he is disarming in his interpersonal relations. While his contributions to policy are many, I would like to place on record, from my experience, a few of the most important ones. He was instrumental in the formal agreement between Government and Reserve Bank of India for ending automatic monetisation, which laid ground work for legislation on fiscal responsibility. He was critical to strengthening the balance sheet of Reserve Bank by establishing a framework for buildup of reserves in its balance sheet and transfer of principle based surplus to Government. He pioneered and established a credible and efficient Independent Evaluation Office in International Monetary Fund. More recently, Montek has shown interest in financial sector (he was always very much into monetary policy), especially its development and regulation. I have, therefore, chosen to contribute a paper on the future of financial sector.

The future of the financial system is being debated globally since the financial system, as it existed in the recent years, had brought about a crisis in the global economy since 2008. The crisis originated in advanced economies, with highly sophisticated financial sector, which were considered to be ideal models, both for market participants and regulators. The crisis was brought about as a result of several enabling macro-economic and other factors, but the core of the crisis has been in the financial sector. It is also recognised that the crisis is having huge repercussions on economic output, employment, prices and, overall stability. The financial crisis has resulted not only in economic crisis, but has also affected political economy significantly, particularly in Euro area, in USA, and perhaps, to some extent in Middle East. There is a potential for spillover into social cohesion across nations. There is a frustration among policymakers on dealing with the crisis in general, and financial system, in particular. There is anger among many people, particularly in advanced economies, that they are being asked to pay heavily for the faults of the financial system.

It is recognised that the dominant financial system as it existed before the crisis was flawed since the benefits from such a system appear, in retrospect questionable, while costs are patent. It is also realised that there should be a systemic approach to the reforming of the financial sector as part of economic systems. But, it is not very clear as to what could be the ideal model of such a desirable financial system. The future of finance affects the totality of the economic life and, possibly political economy, and hence it is useful to explore some fundamental issues in order to appreciate how financial sector will evolve in future.

Components of the Modern Financial System

The modern financial system consists of financial intermediaries, financial markets and financial instruments. It would be evident that different intermediaries may be operating in several markets, though there is often a predominance of certain types of intermediaries in certain types of markets. Traditionally, the financial instruments were fairly watertight, such as equity or fixed income, but the financial innovations inspired by technological advances, have brought about a variety of instruments, especially through a process of what is known as securitisation. In the process of securitisation, often the link between the original contract involving two parties with underlying exposure and the new instrument is broken. It is almost like trading in commodities by using a mirror, and not necessarily the commodities themselves. An indicator of depth in financial system is the range of financial intermediaries, the linkages between the markets, and the sophistication of the instruments. Further, improvements in technology have enabled several innovations with complexity and enormous speed in transactions in a highly interconnected financial world. As a result, the financial system has to be appreciated as a huge and complex network, simultaneously providing immense opportunities for efficiency, risks and contagion.

Infrastructure is required for the intermediaries, markets and the instruments to operate smoothly. Such an infrastructure is necessary for effective interaction within and between intermediaries, markets and instruments. The infrastructure includes the stock or security exchanges, and the payment and settlement system. It can also be extended to include credit rating agencies, accounting firms and standards, and other standards accepted by self-regulation. In a broader sense, infrastructure could be expanded to include what may be described as the ecology of financial system. The ecology consists of the existence of property rights, enforcement of contracts, the traditions of compliance with business ethics, etc. These are non-quantifiable, and represent significant qualitative aspects of the financial system.

The regulatory system governing the financial sector constitutes the most important element of the financial system. The regulatory component of the financial system can vary as between different countries in terms of its structure, philosophy, governance and policies. The regulatory institutions do interact closely with the market participants, have a stake in infrastructure, and operate in the ecology of the financial system. The global crisis has provoked a review of the regulatory system and has resulted in rebalancing of multiple considerations that guide the operations of the system as a whole.

Rebalancing of Considerations

Most of the underlying principles of regulation and supervision of financial sector are unexceptionable. However, in the light of the crisis, conflicting considerations in the actual framing of the regulations and their implementation are being explicitly reassessed and rebalanced. Financial crisis has shown that in the past, in the absence of a good balance between conflicting considerations in regulations, aggressive private interests have prevailed over public interest, resulting in a crisis not only in financial sector, but also in global economy as a whole. The crisis is, to a significant extent, attributed to excessive deregulation in recent years. It is also necessary to recall that in the not so distant past, excessive regulation and financial repression had negative consequences on growth. In this background, rebalancing of considerations may be warranted to avoid both excessive regulation and excessive deregulation. For this purpose, it is necessary to briefly recall the relevant considerations in the review of regulation in financial sector.

First, it is generally assumed that market forces and competition will have a tendency to impart efficiency. In the financial sector, however, short-term efficiency may often threaten longer-term stability. The crisis is indicative of underweight to stability accorded by regulators. Second, the interests of shareholders who have to contribute to the risk capital of the financial intermediaries should be weighed against the benefits of giving higher priority to financial stability and social goals such as development or stability. The crisis may reflect excessive importance to economic value of capital by regulators. Third, assurances of support by public policy in times of difficulties would enable the financial intermediaries to assume risks that could add to overall efficiency in normal times, but there is a moral hazard since assurance of support may be encouraging excessive risk taking. Assurances of support should be minimal and only to the extent of not creating a moral hazard, but it is very difficult in practice to say, *ex ante*, what is a minimal support. Fourth, it is well known that higher the risks (measured in terms of price), higher the returns in a risk-return frontier. The financial intermediaries are expected to assess risks in their businesses and enable risk-taking by economic agents that helps economic growth. However, the accumulation of higher risk by several financial intermediaries in the system may threaten systemic stability, especially if the risk is being taken with borrowed resources. In regard to complex instruments, the issue is whether the consumer of the product is provided with adequate information to assess risks and returns, thus ensuring market efficiency. Fifth, there is need for market participants in financial sector to be fully aware of the rules that they should follow. But, it is not possible to envisage all circumstances and lay down rigid rules in advance warranting exercise of discretion. However, giving excessive discretion to the regulators may add to uncertainty, thus adding to the cost of intermediation. It is also possible that the regulators are captured by the regulated. One approach is to depend on rules in normal times while permitting discretion under extraordinary circumstances, though it may be difficult to define extraordinary circumstances in advance.

Sixth, benefits of an intrusive regulation may not be commensurate with the costs of regulation and the costs of compliance, as was evident during the periods of financial repression. Soft regulation, especially self-regulation, may be less costly since the regulator can state principles that should be complied by the regulated, and leave details to the regulated. However, recent experience has shown that excessive reliance on self-regulation has a tendency to be a weak regulation, thus defeating the objectives of regulation. Where standards of governance in both public and private sector are high, it can be argued that self-regulation could be preferred to external regulation and hence the regulatory framework could focus on standards of governance more than external regulation. Defining appropriate governance standards and ensuring their implementation, however, is a complex task and may involve subjectivity. Seventh, the regulators have a fiduciary responsibility in as much as the banks are licensed to conduct businesses that are highly leveraged and take deposits without collaterals. Hence, adequate regulatory prescriptions are essential, though beyond a point they restrain operation of markets that are essential for promoting efficiency by constraining genuine competition. Eighth, because of the changing circumstances, particularly fast changing technologies, the regulatory framework should be dynamic and be able to cope with changes in the market's products and practices. Innovations in financial system may be good for the society or may not be good in some circumstances, and it is difficult to determine in advance their consequences. Hence, the regulatory regime may need to get full information on such innovations, assess the possible social consequences to the system and to the consumers, and design regulatory systems virtually on an ongoing basis. Ninth, consumers of financial services, in particular retail depositors, need to be protected from sale of low quality or toxic products. However, undermining basic principle that buyers should be vigilant about their products is not conducive to efficiency or choice.

Finally, the regulatory framework will have to take into consideration the relevant tradeoffs in the context of a particular country. However, to the extent, finance is increasingly globalised, these tradeoffs will have to be built into a globally applicable framework. Financial sector may be increasingly globalised, but its regulation continues to be national since the regulatory system of a country should fit into the financial system prevalent in the country and subserve the objectives set for regulations in public policy. Further, financial system and its regulation should fit into the overall economic system of the country. At the same time, regulation and supervision of cross-border financial institutions and activities are inevitable and hence some arrangements for coordination among the national level regulations would be essential. Keeping in view the lessons from the crisis, regulatory systems are being reviewed in the more seriously affected countries, and notably at the global level through Financial Stability Board.

Emerging Issues in Regulation

There are several specific issues that are being addressed in national and multilateral bodies, which reflect rebalancing of considerations described above. These relate to size of intermediaries, the scope of commercial banking; the regulation of what is described as shadow banking; the countering of procyclicality in financial sector; the prescription of leverage and capital standards and liquidity standards; ensuring systemic stability; regulation of financial innovation and incentive systems in regard to risk-taking; insuring of public deposits and taxation of financial sector; role of credit rating, accounting and governance and financial inclusion. In addition, issues relating to cross-border activities of financial intermediaries are also being considered.

Size of the Intermediaries

Some of the financial conglomerates were very big, and in managing the financial crisis, the public policy was not in a position to allow them to fail, resulting in huge bailout operations, particularly in the USA, the UK and Europe. This situation generally undermines market discipline. In order to avoid the problem of 'too big to fail' in future, several options were considered. These include statutory limit on the market share, forcible splitting of the conglomerates to reduce their size, and imposing higher regulatory rigour especially in terms of higher amount of risk capital. So far, the increase in capital requirement has been under serious consideration, while requiring them to draw-up 'living wills' that would establish modalities of their exit when warranted.

The large financial conglomerates are resisting the efforts to prescribe higher capital standards on several grounds. They argue that it creates unlevel playing field and makes them less competitive. They fear that the cost of financial intermediation will become higher, and thus will affect growth. They also argue that seeking additional capital at this stage would delay the nascent economic recovery.

An objective assessment would indicate that the problem has many dimensions. There may be cases where the large sized financial conglomerates are 'too big to save', with inevitable adverse consequences on the whole economy and society. Further, creating a separate category of 'too big to fail', will give an assurance of what may be called eternity and, thus, greater incentive to such institutions to indulge in even greater risk-taking, despite prescription of higher levels of capital. There is considerable difference between regulators and the large conglomerates in the calculations made in regard to additional costs due to additional capital required. There have also been occasions where banks of smaller size, but with a disproportionate presence in a specific activity, made even small banks important from stability point of view. Finally, the major issue in regard to large sized banks is not the size itself, but huge scope for conflicts of interests among activities undertaken and more important, their proclivity to favour cross-border activities to dilute the impact of regulation on their profitability.

The favoured approach now is to enhance the risk capital required to be held by such large conglomerates. However, there is considerable uncertainty in regard to the new capital standards for the 'too big to fail' entities in terms of operational detail, possible magnitudes and time-table for bringing them into operation. Currently, it appears that the new standards may come into force in 2019. It is interesting that large conglomerates have become larger since onset of the crisis.

Scope of Commercial Banking

Bailout of many banks and some non-banks was needed during the crisis to avoid collapse of the system and to protect the interests of a large number of depositors in the banking system. Major cause of the losses for these banks was the risky investments that were made by the banks mainly in their non-traditional banking activities, such as investment banking, merchant banking, securitisation, etc. Some of them originated loans but distributed it to others through a process of financial innovation, but the risks came back to them when the system was under distress.

The solutions suggested after the crisis include revival of Glass Steagall Act in United States, which separated commercial banking from investment banking. They also include narrow banking or confining the banks to traditional commercial banking. Another approach known as Volcker Plan, is to separate client service activities of the bank and proprietary trading in order to avoid conflict of interest, which could be the root of the problem. Yet another approach known as Vicker's Plan is to ring-fence through regulatory requirements the traditional banking activities from other activities in the entity.

All of the above suggestions are challenged by many market participants on several grounds, such as: (a) questioning the universal banking as being the cause of the failure of the system; (b) the loss of economies of scale and scope and finally (c) difficulties in implementation of such separation of traditional banking and others in the highly intertwined modern financial system.

In brief, there is considerable recognition of the special nature of traditional commercial banking functions. It is not clear how this will translate into regulatory prescriptions in different jurisdictions, especially the more sophisticated international financial centres. It is unlikely that the powerful lobby of financial conglomerates would countenance strict limits on proprietary trading or non-traditional commercial banking.

Shadow Banking and Scope of Regulation

Financial innovation included innovation of products and institutions; and deregulation enabled financial deepening and possibly efficiency. During pre-crisis period, a number of financial intermediaries other than banks started performing bank like functions, taking advantage of softer regulation or no regulation of non-banks, relative to banks. This phenomenon has been described as shadow banking. It is possible that the growth of shadow banking in pre-crisis period threatened profitability of banks which led to the pressure on regulators to reduce regulatory burden on traditional banking. There is some consensus now in favour of extending the scope of regulation beyond the banks to non-banks and applying different degrees of regulation to different type of entities, including private pools of capital.

While such an approach is endorsed in principle, several reservations are expressed by market participants. These include difficulty in categorisation of institutions, designing complicated multiple regulatory systems, inadequate skills of regulators, and possible regulatory overkill.

Despite these differences, there is an agreement in principle that regulations should extend to non-banks also in the interests of systemic stability. There are difficulties in designing regulations as appropriate to a wide spectrum of financial intermediaries and resistance to implementing regulatory prescriptions effectively is palpable. International financial centres are averse to introducing regulations that penetrate private pools of capital in view of the threat from the market participants to move their activities to other regulatory jurisdictions.

Procyclicality

The regulatory requirements for provision of capital were essentially procyclical during the pre-crisis period, and hence tended to add to the incentives for creation of asset bubbles. It is now agreed that the regulatory policy should be countercyclical.

While this approach is agreed in principle, there are discussions on several aspects of implementing this policy. These include difficulties in identifying cycles in time, agreements between the financial regulators and other associated policies related to fiscal and monetary considerations about the state of the cycle, and designing appropriate coordinated policies. There is some broad agreement at the global level in regard to a common framework for these measures.

In regard to emerging market economies, however, there are additional difficulties for assessment of cycles, since they are undergoing significant structural transformation. The structural and cyclical components are greatly intertwined in developing and emerging market economies that are growing at a significant pace.

More generally, countercyclical policies are expected to warrant greater judgement and discretion, rather than rules in deciding on the state of the cycle, the timing of measures and the magnitude of measures.

The market participants' views are yet to be tested on this. They may extend support to countercyclical policies at this stage since they stand to gain at the current phase of the cycle when liquidity is injected and interest rates are lowered. They may not support this policy at a future date when the cycle moves upwards, since such measures tend to contain their short-term profitability.

Leverage and Capital Standards

Excess leverage was one of the main reasons for the collapse of the financial institutions. Excess leverage happened through a variety of innovations and business practices whereby the amount of risk capital available as a proportion of the total borrowed capital was inadequate to meet the inherent risks associated with assets. There is awareness after the crisis that the regulatory standards will have to be changed to avoid excess leverage and ensure appropriate capital in future. One of the major developments has been the Basel III norms based on the lessons from the recent crisis.

There is general agreement that appropriate quantity of risk capital should be in the financial system for a given level of activity. Attention is now being paid to the quality of capital also. For instance, the long-term bonds were also considered risk capital in the past, but now there is effort to find mechanisms by which such bonds automatically get converted into equity in times of stress. Apart from limiting leverage through several prescriptions about the quantity and quality of capital, there is a broad agreement to prescribe an aggregate level of leverage in order to restrict manipulation of the balance sheet to avoid the rigour of regulatory prescriptions.

While there is broad agreement and some standards are being developed, there is resistance from financial conglomerates. Their arguments against the magnitudes of additional capital desired, generally relate to the consequent higher cost of capital and hence the higher cost of intermediation with consequent impact on growth, particularly in current times of incipient recovery. The assessment of additional cost of implementing the proposed capital standards by the market participants is at variance with that made by standard setting bodies. In fact, the additional cost is eight times more, according to market participants. There are also analysts who argue that there is really no requirement of additional capital, but only substitution of debt with equity to the extent of additional capital that is being sought.

Liquidity Standards

During the crisis, there was serious mismatch in the maturity profiles leading to liquidity spirals and interbank market freeze. Many financial conglomerates funded long-term assets through short-term resources like money markets. The regulatory regimes in most countries had in past ignored the issue of liquidity standards.

There is general agreement that this aspect should be covered adequately by the regulators, and regulations have been put in place when they were inadequate. The Basel III proposes introduction of global minimum liquidity standards. The effectiveness would critically depend on operational detail.

Systemic Stability

It has been realised after the crisis that the focus of much of regulation in the past was on stability of the individual institutions within the financial system. The individual institutions adopted similar models for assessment of risks, making it difficult to have different points of view in the markets that are essential for price discovery. Prescription of same regulation for similar institutions, however justifiable, may also have a tendency to impart uniformity in their practices.

There is a broad agreement now on the need to focus on systemic stability in addition to stability of individual institution and protection of customers' interests also. In this direction, the work on developing the basic elements of macroprudential policies is underway. There is also an agreement that there should be a more formal mandate to specific public institutions to ensure systemic stability. Two major issues that remain largely unanswered relate to the implications of cross-border presence on systemic stability and the scope and limits for global coordination in this regard.

Financial Innovations

A characteristic of the development of financial system before the crisis related to several innovations in financial instruments. These were complex and increased exponentially in terms of magnitudes as well as complexity. Many of these financial innovations were not in standard form, and they were traded over-the-counter.

While it is argued that financial innovations add to efficiency and dispersal of risks, there are many others who held that such innovations have no social value. In any case, as the crisis has shown, there was no genuine dispersal of risk in many cases of innovations.

There is general agreement that, as far as possible, trading of derivatives should be preferred on the exchanges in the interests of stability and transparency; and that there should be strengthened consumer protection. There is resistance from market participants to this approach on the grounds that many innovations are tailor-made to suit specific, evolving and unique needs. The policymakers observe that such resistance may also be because the innovations had been adopted often to circumvent regulations, and in particular, to take advantage of ignorance of some of the customers.

The solutions that have been partially agreed, relate to minimisation of over-the-counter trade, expanding trading in exchanges, central clearing, reporting of over-the-counter derivatives transactions to trade repositories and establishing product's safety commissions to oversee the innovations. There are signals that exemptions from the mandatory exchange trading could undermine the efficacy of these agreements.

Incentives

The remuneration for managers in many of the financial institutions was based on short-term profits shown in the books, and hence heavily tilted in favour of risk-taking behaviour. Many argue that these incentives were a major cause of the global financial crisis. This creates highly distorted incentives for risk-taking by managers. The policy circles have recognised the importance of addressing the issue of incentive framework in the regulatory regimes.

While in civil society, there is a massive and intense unhappiness over the huge bonuses and huge risks that were taken; the public policy has been constrained by significant pressure from the financial sector to avoid restrictions on remuneration on the ground that it would undermine incentives for efficiency among the institutions. In some countries, there has been some progress in regulating the incentives towards risk-taking.

Deposit Insurance and Taxation

At one stage prior to the crisis, it was believed that insurance of retail deposits would encourage the commercial banks to take excessive risks, and the depositors to be less vigilant. In managing crisis, it became evident that formal deposit insurance may have its merits in the event of the threatened collapse of confidence in banking system. Hence, such systems have been revived and expanded where needed.

In addition, there are proposals to impose a tax on the financial sector which could provide resources for bailout in future. In some jurisdictions there are proposals to tax the financial sector in order to recover a part of the cost of bailout that has occurred. More generally, a tax on financial transactions, particularly foreign currency trade, is advocated to reduce the volatility in forex markets.

Market participants question the feasibility effectiveness and implementability of many tax proposals. There has been increasing support for such taxes at national level, including in Euro zone while agreement for global level taxation has not been possible so far.

Role of Credit Rating Agencies, Accounting and Governance

The existence of acute conflicts of interests and the dominance of credit rating by two credit rating agencies in the global markets has been brought to the fore at the time of the crisis. Many instruments which were given highest rating suddenly collapsed at the time of the crisis, eroding the credibility of the credit rating system.

While there are some efforts to introduce more effective supervision of the credit rating agencies, the regulators continue to depend heavily on the credit rating. No alternative mechanisms have been designed so far. China has sponsored a new rating agency in the public sector.

The complicity of the accounting firms and the inadequacy of accounting standards in enabling the crisis have been acknowledged. While recognising the importance of achieving a single set of high quality improved global accounting standards, the International Accounting Standards Board (IASB) and the Financial Accounting Standards Board (FASB) have committed to complete their convergence project by the end of 2011. Cognisable improvements are, however, yet to be agreed upon.

Financial Inclusion

The role of subprime mortgages in USA in the global financial crisis is well recognised, and in this connection some argue that populist schemes in public policy to extend credit often demand laxity in regulation and hence result in crisis by encouraging irresponsible borrowing by those who do not have capacity to repay. Such argument is countered by those who hold that many other factors as being responsible for the crisis in general. They also argue that there was financial crisis in many other countries though their regulatory regimes did not focus on encouraging lending for housing. Further, within housing sector, they argue that there were other factors unique to USA in this regard, *viz.*, legal procedure for foreclosure, construction lobby, and financial sector's appetite for risk and expansion.

There is an increasing recognition of the need for intervention, particularly in emerging and developing economies, by public policy to enable financial inclusion, broadly designed to include financial services, especially retail banking, and not confined to credit. The role of 'for profit' microfinance sector (MFS) as an instrument of financial inclusion has become controversial. While technology and several initiatives by central banks, especially in developing countries are addressing the issue, fundamental issues remain unresolved. The issue of financial inclusion cannot be addressed in isolation from what may be termed as economic inclusion, to mean incomes to meet subsistence needs at least. A complex issue relates to the designing of institutional frameworks and incentives, which reduce rigour of regulation on instruments catering to the cause of financial inclusion but ensure that they do not pose systemic risks. These need to be done without perpetuating a dual financial system, one for the poor such as MFS, and other for non-poor, *viz.*, banks. Further, there is need to protect the interests of depositors and integrity of payment system. Yet, another issue relates to the huge unequal nature of parties to the contracts involved in programmes relating to financial inclusion in general, and microcredit in particular.

Yet, another challenge is to integrate the informal systems such as traditional moneylending, with formal or semi-formal systems. There is no evidence of sensitivity to these issues in the discussion in FSB, though the formal statements in G-20 make a mention of the importance of financial inclusion.

Cross-Border Activities

There was an exponential growth in cross-border financial activity in the years preceding the crisis, reflecting increased globalisation of financial markets enabled by both technological progress and regulatory regimes. However, the cross-border activities of large financial conglomerates have been an important source of the crisis, and significant bailout operations were conducted for the benefit of large conglomerates. Their activities are able to take advantage of differences in regulatory regimes across the countries, differences in regulation of different market segments, the tax regimes as between different countries, and above all, possible transfers of money with suspect legality by high net worth individuals.

After the crisis, there is some recognition of some of these problems, though not all of them. There is concentration on coordinated parameters of regulation of different entities across national jurisdictions. There are also efforts for exchange of information on regulatory issues, and on tax dodging. As regards the mode of presence of foreign banks, there is a distinct preference for wholly owned subsidiaries rather than foreign bank branches.

However, the large financial conglomerates with cross-border operations continue to exercise significant influence over political economies as well as the regulatory regimes. This situation may change in future, when the advanced economies have to service large public debt. Often, large public debt requires an element of financial repression or use of financial regulation for financing of public debt through domestic savings.

There is also an increasing attention to the issues arising out of excess capital flows and volatility in capital flows, and the conduits for these are large conglomerates with cross-border presence. In this connection, use of prudential regulations over financial sector for moderating the volatility has been reluctantly agreed in the policy circles.

Regulatory Structures, Philosophy and Policies

There is no clear-cut empirical evidence about the relationship between different regulatory structures and global financial crisis, but based on experience, there has been an effort to review regulatory structures in advanced economies that are most affected by the crisis. The general trend has been: (a) to give greater importance to central bank while reinforcing accountability; (b) to accord priority to coordination among monetary authority, financial sector regulators and government; (c) to formally assigning responsibility of maintaining financial stability to an institution, usually the central bank; (d) to strengthen the mechanisms for consumer protection and (e) to extend the scope of financial regulation to non-bank intermediaries and derivatives.

It is clear that the regulatory changes that have been brought about mainly in the USA, the UK and Euro area are in the nature of reaction to the crisis with a view to imparting stability to the system. These recent changes reflect an underlying assumption that the financial system will deliver efficiency and growth through market mechanisms but requires to be regulated mainly for purposes of imparting stability, and to some extent, consumer protection. Developing and emerging economies question this assumption and consider it appropriate for regulation to have both growth and stability as objectives.

In terms of regulatory philosophy, the faith in soft touch regulation, self-regulation by market participants and principle based regulation has been significantly eroded. There is some review of this philosophy in favour of tighter regulation than before, though with significant reluctance on the part of some central banks and resistance from the financial market participants.

As regards policies, the policy frameworks in different countries are currently fighting: (a) divergence in the health of financial industry and (b) ineffectiveness of policies to influence outcomes, and to bring about lasting improvements in the functioning of the financial industry.

Global, Monetary and Financial System: Issues

There are several global issues which have significant bearing on the future of financial system and are yet to be resolved. First, the dominant international reserve currency is still US dollar. It is recognised that there are severe problems with this non-system since the supply of global reserve currency is not governed either by rules set by global order or by market discipline. The policies of US government give priority to the interest of US domestic economy, as required under the law, while these policies have large impact on the global economy because US dollar is the dominant reserve currency. The national interests of USA and the global interest need not always converge. While it is recognised that this situation should be corrected, there are no signs of agreement on feasibility of the alternatives.

Second, the lender-of-last-resort function in terms of providing liquidity to countries facing liquidity problems is being performed by the IMF. Its governance is flawed; its ideology has proven to be deficient, and its resources are constrained. Reforms in this regard are considered essential, but in reality are painfully slow. This has resulted in greater activism towards strengthening the regional financial architecture. Some examples in the Asian region are the Chiang Mai Initiative and the Asian Bond Market Initiative. More recently, the IMF is closely involved in providing support to the Euro zone.

Third, there are no institutional arrangements for restructuring of sovereign debts. This situation has imparted huge uncertainties to the financial sector which holds a large part of the public debt of distressed countries. Post-crisis, these arrangements have acquired significance for some advanced economies as well with the sovereign debt crisis in Euro zone.

Fourth, the standards for regulation and regulatory coordination are being harmonised by the Bank for International Settlements (BIS) and the FSB. These are still evolving, and compliance could be stretched over an uncomfortably long period with significant variations in levels of compliance among the countries. Besides, there are some financial system issues that are unique to emerging and developing economies, and it is not certain whether international standard setting bodies are considering them adequately.

Some Unorthodox Questions

It is useful to explore some unorthodox questions that could be relevant for the future of the financial system, and these may have to go beyond the regulatory issues currently under consideration as an immediate response to crisis.

Is there an Optimal Level of Financialisation of an Economy?

Financial system is the central nervous system of a market economy, and it is expected to direct real resources to their ultimate uses. The question is whether the financial sector directed a disproportionately large amount of real resources to itself in the recent years, causing a crisis? That does seem to be the case because the growth, and more importantly profits of financial sector, relative to non-financial sector has been very high in the countries where the global financial crisis originated, and are most affected. There is some evidence pointing that the financial sector was, in recent years, innovating and expanding to benefit it more than it was trying to allocate resources efficiently in the economy. This trend is significantly more in non-retail bank operations than in traditional banking activities, and more in cross-border financial activities than predominantly domestic activity. At the same time, it is widely recognised that lack of adequate and efficient financial intermediation can hinder economic growth. Then the question is: whether there is an optimal level of financialisation of an economy? If so, what are the factors that would help identify such an optimal level?

Is there an Optimal Composition of Financial Sector?

In order to enhance savings and channelise them for investments to enable growth, public policy particularly in developing economies, gives priority to development of financial systems. In the recent past, it is found that Asia has posted significant growth, but concentrated significantly on traditional banking activity relative to other developing economies. Traditional banking may be taken to mean domestic diversified credit predominantly funded by retail deposits. There are examples of Canada and Australia where financial innovations did not dominate. Therefore, is it possible that, in addition to an optimal level financialisation, there is also an optimal composition of financial sector appropriate to the country?

Which components of financial sector are more conducive to efficient allocation of resources after taking account of the costs involved? It is difficult to demarcate clearly various components, but experience with policy in some countries shows that it is possible to do so despite complexities. For example, as is being contemplated, a distinction can be made between basic banking and financial innovation, or financial services to the customers and transactions between financial intermediaries.

Are there Intermediate Regimes to Financial Sector Regulation?

Recently, in a meeting of Institute for New Economic Thinking (INET) in Bretton Woods, Professor Summers was asked about the need to increase the rigour of regulation of financial sector in the U.S.A. after the crisis. He replied that the alternative to a deregulated financial sector of U.S.A. was the Indian banking sector before the reform of 1990 which produced a very low rate of growth. The impression given, therefore, is that there are only corner solutions in the financial sector, *viz.*, a deregulated financial sector prevalent immediately before the crisis in advanced economies and the financial repression of 1980s. In the case of exchange rate management, for example, there has been a greater realisation than before that intermediate solutions between totally fixed and entirely flexible are possible, and perhaps for many countries, inevitable. In regard to the extent of financial sector regulation also, would it be possible to visualise several intermediate systems between financial repression and soft touch regulation, with varying degrees of regulatory rigour, consistent with the institutional and market environments of individual countries?

Should Governance Structures be Redesigned?

After the global financial crisis, there is a realisation that governance mechanism in both public and private sector in the financial sector as a whole displayed serious deficits. There is also a realisation that lack of coordination between monetary policy and financial sector regulation was one of the reasons for financial instability, and that coordination is critical for macroprudential regulation and countercyclical policies. At the same time, it has been recognised that huge conflicts of interests existed in the private sector, and they were responsible for the crisis. In other words, the financial system suffered because of an effort to avoid conflicts of interests in public sector, and in not being able to control the operation of conflicts of interests in the private sector.

Hence, is it appropriate to have governance arrangements that promote coordination within public sector and create more effective firewalls or splitting of institutions in the private sector. This may involve loss of traditional independence for central banks but it would still legitimately retain its central role in arrangements for coordination.

Is Diversity a Source of Stability in Finance?

The downside risks of financial intermediaries using a common model for risk assessment have been evident with the onset of the crisis. If there were a uniform global model of regulation five or 10 years ago, a similar 'soft touch regulation' would have prevailed in all countries, including India and in China. The global economy could have, in consequence, faced worse crisis, if a wrong model was applied universally. It is not possible to be certain that after learning from the crisis, the right model of regulation has been discovered or invented. Is there merit in having diversity in regulatory regimes in different countries? Perhaps, the global effort should be to encourage diversity as well as innovation in regulation of financial sector, while focussing on common regulation of cross-border operations and institutions that operate significantly across the borders.

How Far should Non-Level Playing Field be Applied?

The principle of non-level playing field in financial markets has gained respectability when systemically important financial institutions are sought to be identified, and higher capital charge is being suggested. Once the principle of non-level playing field has been accepted, it can as well be invoked, if necessary, to design differentiated regulatory regimes for different sizes of intermediaries or identifiable categories, as long as there are reasonable grounds for such discrimination. In other words, systemically not important financial intermediaries could have less stringent capital requirements, particularly in the developing and emerging economies.

Are there Areas of Special Concern in Developing Countries?

The review of regulatory philosophy consequent upon the crisis is focussed on using state intervention to correct market failures in ensuring stability. There appears to be an implicit assumption that markets will continue to be efficient in bringing about growth, as long as stability is ensured. Is there enough empirical evidence to assume that it is so?

It is difficult to distinguish between cyclical and structural components in an economy undergoing significant structural transformation. There may be credit expansion in real estate and credit contraction in agriculture. Hence, the regulations may spillover into credit allocation in some form or the other. Is there a renewed interest in some form of selective credit controls?

Use of prudential regulation for countering volatility in capital flows has become acceptable in the mainstream policy circles, including IMF. It is recognised that major sources of volatility in forex markets are operations of financial intermediaries, as distinct from households and corporate sector in real economy, which undoubtedly, are sources of capital allocation also. How would the use of prudential tools in regard to capital flows affect the allocative efficiency of the financial sector globally? What should be the role of capital account management or capital controls to supplement prudential regulations?

Where is Burden of Proof that Financial Innovation is not Toxic?

Like all innovations, some financial innovations may be good, some may be bad and self-serving, and many susceptible to multiple uses, and thus, good as well as bad. Much depends on the magnitudes of transactions, context, use, user and rules of the game. Further, the good or bad of a financial innovation depends not only on the product but also on who are selling or buying them, and in what environment of assessment of risks in a given transparency standards. In regard to food and drugs, there is basic information asymmetry between seller and buyer, and that phenomenon should not be ruled out in regard to financial innovations. There are also externalities and systemic implications unique to financial sector, especially if the products are traded by entities with leverage or with limited liability and such products are synthetic assets. Hence, the issue is: where does the burden of proof of social value of financial innovations lie—with the market participants or the regulator?

Should we assume that only markets have monopoly over financial innovations? There may be some scope for financial innovation by regulators, and they could sponsor innovation for public good. Initiatives could be taken in introducing technologies and products to facilitate financial inclusion; and also to establish a unique clearing and settlement mechanism for money, forex and government securities markets. In developing countries there may be merit in central banks and market players playing active role in promoting financial innovations which add to social value.

How do State and Market Interact with Each Other?

Finally, the global movement towards deregulation and liberalisation of financial sector that preceded the crisis was based on the understanding that failures of state or governments exceeded the market failures in the past. The current debate on regulation of financial sector proceeds on the assumption that serious market failures can be avoided through intervention by state, after accounting for the latter's failures. However, the most important lesson from the crisis is that there were elements of failure of both state policy and market practices that reinforced each other to bring about the crisis. Hence, it is not appropriate to assume that state action will normally or automatically compensate for market failures. In a way, the problem in regulation of financial sector is not only technical but also one of political economy. The dynamics of relationship between state and market may be critical for designing a good financial system for future. How to design a structure and philosophy of regulation of financial sector that can transcend the myopia that characterises the functioning of both political and financial markets? How effectively could that be done at national level, relative to global level? How does regulation of financial sector relate to broader economic and social objectives that it is meant to serve?

13 Global Imbalances
Policies, Structure and Finance

ROBERTO ZAGHA

Introduction

Starting with the *Arthasastra* around 300 BC, economic thinking has had a long tradition in India. In more modern times, particularly in the last 50 years, Indian economists have made a mark on economic thinking and enjoy an international reputation. Montek Singh Ahluwalia has a special place among those as a researcher and as a practitioner not only because of the contributions he made to the economic literature, as an advisor to the Government of India, as an advisor to international financial institutions, or as decision-maker at critical times in the economic history of India, but also because he has persistently believed in the power of ideas and struggled to recognise the good from the bad, and pushed for the good ones. He has been one of the main architects of the country's embrace of a more market oriented economy and more modern society. The transition from a highly controlled economy to a more market based one is a complex process. It has been done in a variety of countries in Latin America, Africa, and the former communist countries in Central and Eastern Europe. In virtually all of these countries transitions were accompanied by sharp declines in growth rates, frequently negative growth rates, inflation and deterioration of social conditions. In India, there was a temporary slow-down, quickly followed by a return to historical rates of growth, and a gradual acceleration that has put India among the small group of fastest growing economies in the world. This was the result of a thoughtful and measured implementation of reforms, deep understanding of economics, and the creative manner with which old and new were combined, and the old phased out. This is not the place to go into details on how this was done but suffice it to say that Montek and his intellectual insights were central to this outcome. More recently, as a participant and a voice for India in the G-20, he has brought wisdom and depth of understanding to complex global issues at a time when the global economy is facing its most serious challenges in a generation, particularly the challenge of leadership. This paper is a tribute to him, and deal with some of the themes he has spoken about in the recent past.

Background

Often one reads or hears in conferences, academic articles, and the financial press that global imbalances are one reason behind the economic crisis facing the global economy: 'In my view...it is impossible to understand this crisis without reference to the global imbalances in trade and capital flows that began in the latter half of the 1990s.' (Bernanke, 2009). While global imbalances and the global financial crisis are clearly connected, the common inference is to conclude: the first is the cause of the latter. This typically leads to two conclusions. One is that the policies behind global imbalances, in particular the combination of China's exchange rate policies, the associated 'saving glut', and the US low interest in the last decade, are the reasons for the crisis. The other is that correction of these imbalances requires international coordination of macroeconomic policies, an issue to which meetings of the G-20 have paid considerable attention. The September 2009 G-20 Pittsburgh Summit for example, concluded that a '"Framework for Strong, Sustainable, and Balanced Growth" was needed to ensure "...more balanced global growth"'. Except for the Fall of 2008, at the height of the financial crisis, coordination has had limited success, however.

This paper seeks to bring nuances to the understanding of global imbalances and to identify deeper forces at work. First, it reviews global imbalances over the last decade and reminds us that global imbalances need not be destabilising. What matters is the underlying cause. In the process, the paper highlights structural trends in the major economies that have contributed to global imbalances. Second, it looks back to financial crises in the last three decades, how they differ, or don't, from the current one, and what we can learn from them. Third, it concludes that the global crisis may be less the result of global imbalances than of what rendered them possible—a financial system that does not adequately evaluate and manage risks, and thus enables unsustainable trends to persist beyond prudence—and presents possible reasons for these shortcomings.

External Imbalances and Structural Policies

There are several observations to be made on external imbalances which persist over an extended period of time. First, they can reflect efficient economic decision-making. For example, countries with ageing population such as Japan need to save in anticipation of demographic decline and hence run external account surpluses. Likewise, oil producing countries need to smooth consumption over time. This means saving a share of finite oil revenue and running current account surpluses. On the other hand, countries with higher productivity attract capital and hence experience current account deficits. Such external imbalances are the result of efficient decision-making and, in general, can be accommodated without disruptions by the global economy.

A second observation is that external negative imbalances require financing which can come from banks, or investors. Absent that financing there would be a need for correction through a combination of exchange rate adjustment, and changes in public and private consumption and investment. And the imbalance would not persist. In the case of the US, the fact that the dollar is a global currency has provided an important source of financing, thus contributing to the US ability to sustain persistent and even growing current account deficits—see Figure 13.1—without any mechanism forcing an adjustment. In the case of other countries, large and sustained external deficits have more often than not ended up in currency crises, sometimes augmented by a banking crisis.

A third observation is that the imbalances that have developed over the last two decades have challenged intuition. In theory, capital scarce developing countries with low wages have a high potential for catching up. They should have higher rates of return on capital and hence be able to run external account deficits. Rich countries on the other hand, should be exporting capital and run surpluses. Again in this case, this is efficient allocation of resources across countries.

This is not what happened. Whereas some developing countries in East Asia did indeed grow faster and either caught up or are on their way to catching up, this was done with limited access to external savings—and in the case of China, the country has instead exported capital—mostly financial capital. FDI towards China did indeed take place as expected, in relatively large volumes. But in the aggregate, China has been a net exporter of capital.

There have been many debates on the reasons for this counter-intuitive outcome. A common explanation is that China has practiced mercantilism. China's large trade surpluses have given credence to perceptions that China's currency is undervalued and hence that China is maintaining high levels of export growth at the cost of building up large reserves at home, and high deficits and employment losses in other countries.

Figure 13.1

US Current-Account/GDP and Private Flows/GDP Patterns, 1960-2010

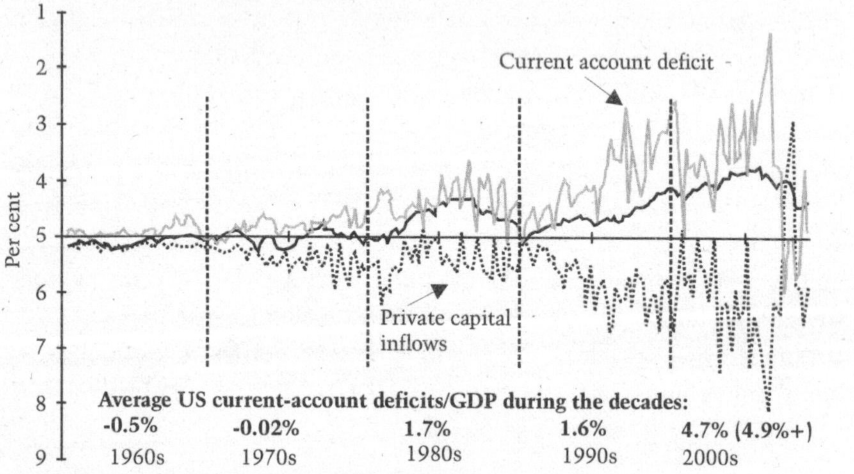

* The current-account deficit/GDP of the US during 2000-2007 (excluding the crisis years).

Note: The decadal averages of the US current account deficit in terms of GDP are reported below the deficit curve.

Source: Aizenman (2011).

It is, however, not in China's interest to run large trade surpluses and accumulate unnecessarily large reserves to prevent its currency from appreciating. The question then is why would China do it?

The answer comes in three parts. The first has to do with the growth dynamics of a rapidly growing economy such as China which consists of three distinct economies: (a) the traditional economy, mainly rural, with labour surplus engaged in agriculture; (b) a more advanced economy, mostly labour-intensive manufacturing, that produces goods competing in international markets and compete with imports and (c) a sophisticated economy producing more capital-intensive goods—from machine tools to spare parts for airplanes. Growth depends on the speed at which labour moves from A to B and B to C. This process is neither easy nor simple. It is in fact extraordinarily complex. It takes two or three generations to complete and in fact very few economies have been able to sustain it over time, and bring it to completion.

When implemented successfully, however, as it was in Japan and Korea and now it is in China and India, it can collapse into few decades what industrialised economies of the West have taken centuries to accomplish. The reason for this faster development is that it is easier to learn than it is to invent, and developing economies can take advantage of technologies already developed in industrialised economies. As labour moves from low to higher productivity activities, powerful dynamics are set in motion. In any developing economy, labour productivity in urban areas is much higher than in rural areas, often by 6 to 8 times as high. The faster an economy can absorb modern technology, the larger this differential is and the faster it can grow. Rapid economic growth of above 7 per cent per year over long periods of time of the kind we see in China and India, or we saw in the past in Japan, Korea and Brazil (before Brazil's stagnation started in the 1980s), is based on labour moving from lower to higher productivity sectors.

The second part of the answer is related to the role of the exchange rate in this process. Since labour productivity varies considerably from A to B to C, the exchange rate appropriate for one of the three sectors is not appropriate to the other. There was a lively discussion in the 1960s among economists in Brazil as to whether the same exchange rate that enabled the (more modern) south of the country to develop during the 20th century had been appropriate for the (more traditional agrarian) northeast. A persuasive case was made that the two economies were structurally not a common currency area. The conclusion was that the northeast's development had been held back because the exchange rate at which the south could develop made production in the northeast uncompetitive. Exchange rate misalignments can destroy the dynamic process of shifting resources from the low-productivity to the higher-productivity parts of the economy. They can simply interrupt the process of transferring resources from low-productivity to higher-productivity uses—which is the way developing economies catch up with advanced ones. Europe is now experiencing similar problems and the effects of a common currency in areas which are structurally not a common currency area.

The third part of the answer is related to the effects of speed. China grew at rates above 10 per cent per year over 2003-2005. The growth rate then rose to 11.6 per cent in 2006 and to 13 per cent in 2007. These are extraordinarily high rates of growth. At 13 per cent growth GDP doubles every six years. An economy growing at such rates is like a car speeding at 200 miles an hour. At such speeds small deviations—small mis-calibrations—cause very large departures from sustainable trajectories. This is how China's trade surpluses can be interpreted—a deviation from a balanced trajectory. Not as a goal of policy, but as the result of some parts of the system not being adjusted to the movement of others. China's current account surplus jumped from 3.6 per cent of GDP in 2004 to twice this amount two years later and an unprecedented 11 per cent of GDP in 2007. Correcting such imbalances requires much more than just an exchange rate adjustment. China's policymakers have been seeking to increase domestic consumption, so that savings-investment imbalances could be reduced. Ensuring consumption growth at faster rates than GDP growth (to rebalance the trade account) requires a large number of structural reforms—related to pensions, housing finance, profits distribution (or lack thereof) of public enterprises, among others. These are difficult reforms, in terms of the complexity of the measures to be put in place, the resistance of vested interests, and the institutions that need to be built—for example, creating a housing mortgage market that would encourage households to reduce the savings needed to purchase a first home.

Summing up, rather than the simple result of a misaligned exchange rate, China's trade surpluses should be seen as the result of deviations from a complex growth path in which many moving parts need to come together to avoid gross imbalances. Appreciation of the exchange rate may help reduce China's trade surpluses, but this could be at the risk of damaging an accomplishment—high and sustained growth in what was one of the poorest countries on earth just 30 years ago—that is of critical importance not only for China but also for the world. It should also be kept in mind that in situations in which productivity is rising rapidly, as it is in China, exchange rate adjustments may disrupt the growth process without necessarily correcting external imbalances. An economic policy dialogue focussed on the (difficult) structural reforms needed to increase private consumption in China could be much more effective.

While this is generally understood in some, *albeit* too few, policy circles, it is also taken as a fact that China's imbalances have reached a size which destabilises the world economy. This proposition is generally accepted without much debate. Since Bernanke's assertion in 2005 that the US economy's rising current account deficits (to around 7 per cent of GDP in the years preceding the crisis) were the result of the world's 'savings glut', and high savings rate in China in particular, there has been general acceptance that the US current account deficits were the mirror image of China's current account surpluses, and that China's high savings rates were the cause of the US low savings rate.

There is another explanation, however, more credible perhaps, that China's high savings rate has been as much the result of China's structural factors raising that country's savings rate, as they were the result of several structural forces operating in the US leading to the decline of the US savings rate.

Figure 13.2 illustrates the decline in the US savings rates starting in the 1980s. Because consumption is a large and an increasing share of GDP, and changes in consumption—and corresponding changes in savings rates—have macroeconomic repercussions. But what are the reasons for the decline in the US savings rate?

Figure 13.2

Personal Consumption Expenditure as a Share of GDP

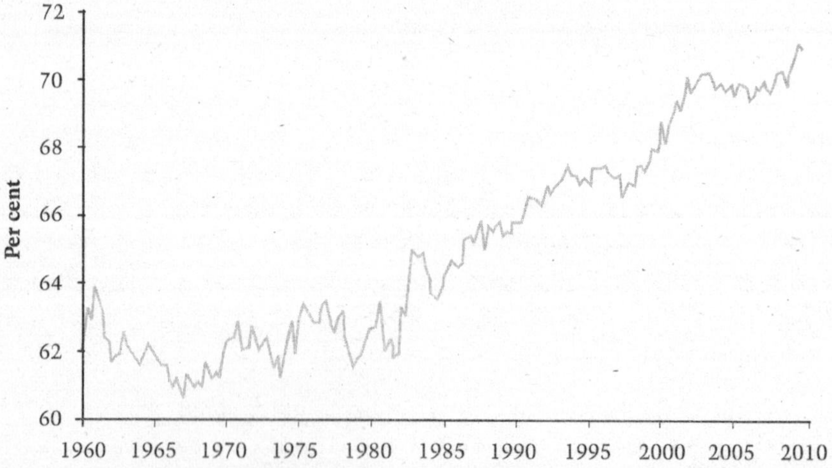

Source: *Report of the President, 2010*. United States Printing Office.

The US 2010 Economic Report of the President presented a set of interesting hypotheses which have not yet received a lot of attention. It started with the observation that some of the reasons suggested by economic theory—changes in demographic structure, GDP growth rate, and real interest rates—do not seem to work. It then observed that swings in the wealth-income ratio, as those illustrated in Figure 13.3, reflect changes in wealth stemming from asset market booms and busts—incomes being more stable than wealth. The oil shock in the early 1970s led to a stock market decline which in turn led to a decline in the wealth-income ratio (and a corresponding increase in the savings rate). The stock market booms in the 1980s and early 1990s, are likewise associated with rises in wealth-income ratios and associated declines in savings rates. The wealth decline in 2008-09 was the most severe of the last 50 years reflecting falling prices of both houses and stocks. In short, as wealth increases, and the need for savings declines, the incentives are to consume a larger proportion of current income and, as a result, the savings rates declines. When wealth declines, it is the opposite. Assuming this is true, the question then becomes what are the reasons behind changes in the valuations of wealth?

More importantly, it may well be that the same reasons that increase valuations of wealth, also lead to declines in saving rates. For example, an increase in optimism about future economic conditions might lead both to a spending boom and to a general rise in asset prices. In that case, the real reason would not be wealth changes since both asset prices and saving rates respond to the increase in optimism. However, while surveys measuring 'consumer sentiment' or 'consumer confidence' have some power in predicting near-term spending growth, they have not been able to explain the secular decline in the US savings rate.

Figure 13.3

Personal Savings Ratio versus Wealth Ratio

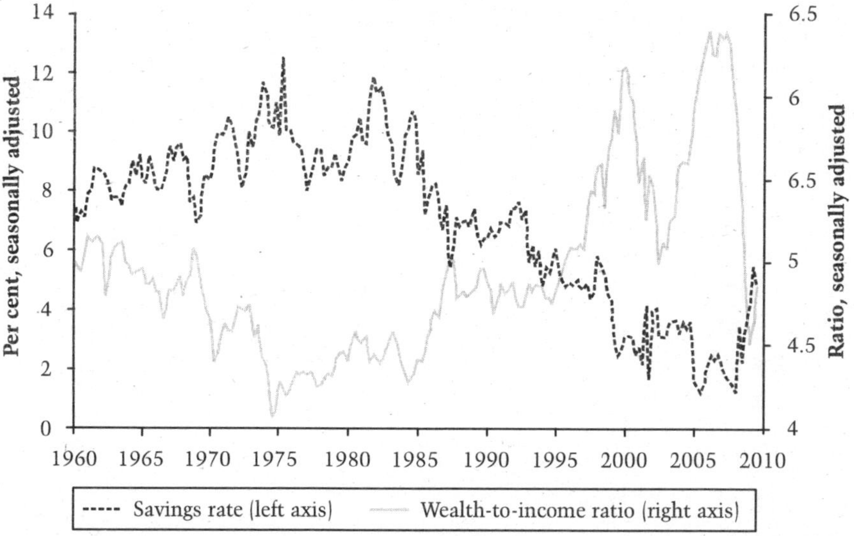

Source: *Report of the President, 2010*. United States Printing Office.

A more promising explanation lies in the availability of credit. The financial liberalisation started in the early 1980s, together with the telecommunications and computer revolutions, permitted creditors to tailor credit offers to the personal characteristics of individual borrowers. As a result, the reach of credit expanded to income and risks groups previously excluded. Expansion of the ability to borrow implies a reduction in saving: 'If there is less need to save for a down payment for a home, for a child's education, for unforeseen emergencies, or for spending of any other kind, then the likelihood is...less saving...Eventually the savings rate should... recover from any dip caused by a one-time increase in the availability of credit, because whatever extra debt was incurred must be paid back over time (and paying back debt is another form of saving). This recovery in saving, however, may take a long time. If, in the meantime, credit availability increases again, the gradual small increase in saving that reflects debt repayment could easily be obscured by the new drop in saving occasioned by the continuing expansion in credit availability.' (Report of the President, 2010).

The same report does not explore, however, two other forces which have been at work in the US: the consequences of worsening income distribution on savings rates and the relaxation of credit standards, erosion of lending norms, and expansion of predatory lending.

It is well known that savings rates tend to be lower, the lower the level of incomes. Rich people save a larger proportion of their incomes than poorer people. All other things equal, a worsening in the distribution of income should lead to a rise in the rate of savings. All indicators of income distribution in the US, and other advanced economies, suggest a significant increase in inequality. Whether measured by the incidence of poverty, Gini coefficients, the median income of the lowest quintile, or wages for unskilled workers, the result is always an increase in inequality. One indicator is the share of GDP accruing to the richest one per cent of the population which has doubled in the US since the early 1980s (Figure 13.4).

The inference is that the other forces at work, access to credit in particular, have been powerful enough to counteract the increase in savings rate that should have accompanied the deterioration in the distribution of income. This is consistent with the theory that access to credit expanded and contributed to declines in household savings rates. This expansion in credit has been accompanied by a relaxation of credit standards, and excessive risk-taking. At the same time, the US economy was investing a declining share of GDP in non-residential capital—an indication that its productive capacity was growing at lower rates.

Figure 13.4

United States: Top one per cent Income Share

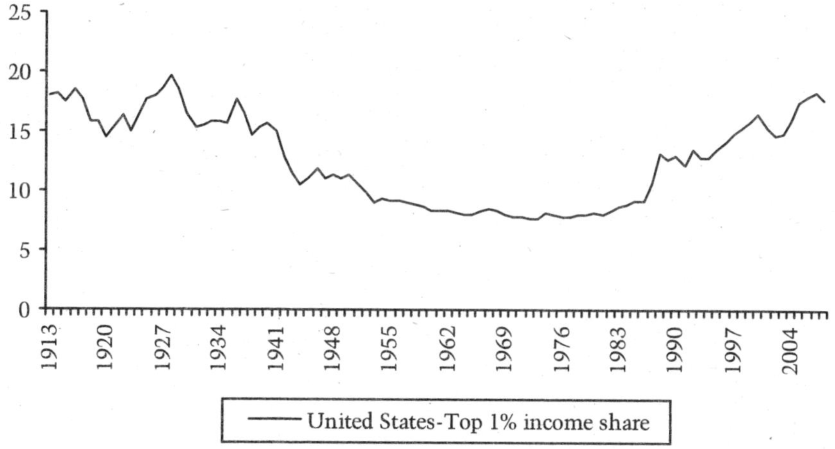

Note: Estimates excluding capital gains. Fractiles defined by total income excluding capital gains.

Source: The World Top Incomes Database, *http://g-mond.parisschoolofeconomics.eu/topincomes/*, accessed November 8, 2011. US fractiles defined by total income excluding capital gains.

Figure 13.5

US Investment Compared to Other Economies, 2000-2005

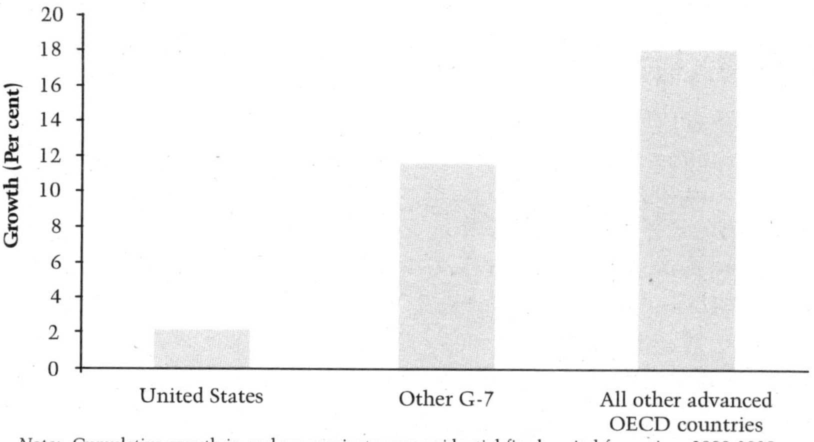

Note: Cumulative growth in real gross private non-residential fixed capital formation, 2000-2005.

Source: *Report of the President, 2011*. United States Printing Office.

Financial Crises: Now and Then

Financial crises are nothing new—they are the inevitable and costly companion of finance (Kindleberger, 1984). The last three decades, not to mention the last 80 decades (as Rogoff and Reinhart (2010) remind us, see Figure 13.6), saw recurrent episodes. They were all based either on sovereign borrowings for unsustainable macro policies, or unsound financing of private investment, or both, which translated into external imbalances.

In the early 1980s, high real interest rates, declining export prices, and a global slowdown combined to raise the costs of debts contracted in the 1970s, when real interest rates were negative and the external environment was more favourable. Rising costs of debt accompanied by declining debt-service capacity and inadequate responses to shocks produced the debt crisis of the 1980s. The common cause was countries' attempt at stabilising inflation through programmes anchored on a preannounced, fixed, or only slowly depreciating nominal exchange rate, lagging behind inflation, while delaying needed fiscal adjustments. Attempts to defend the nominal exchange rate while the real rate was appreciating led to increases in current account deficits and declines in reserves, which ultimately triggered external payments crises, with capital outflows and large and sudden devaluations. In Argentina, Chile and Uruguay, where banks were allowed to hold deposits in foreign currency, currency mismatches on the banks' or borrowers' balance sheets made the banks vulnerable to devaluations. When the devaluations came, balance sheet losses were often larger than the banks' entire capital, and compounded the currency crisis with a banking one. Governments and creditors in Turkey and some countries in Latin America and in East Asia responded with deflationary policies that increased their net exports and wrote-down some of the debt. This, together with an improvement in the external environment, eventually brought the debt crisis to an end. The adjustment was turbulent, however, and the costs were high. The output collapses during the 'lost decade' of the 1980s were comparable to those in the 1929 crisis: GDP declined by 7 per cent in Turkey during 1979–80, 15 per cent in Chile during 1982–83, 20 per cent in Uruguay during 1982–83, 11 per cent in Argentina during 1981–82, and 12 per cent in Bolivia during 1982–1986. By the end of the 1980s, the per capita incomes of most countries in Latin

America and in Turkey were only marginally higher, and in some cases lower, than at the beginning of the decade.

Figure 13.6

A Two Centuries Perspective on Capital Mobility and Banking Crises

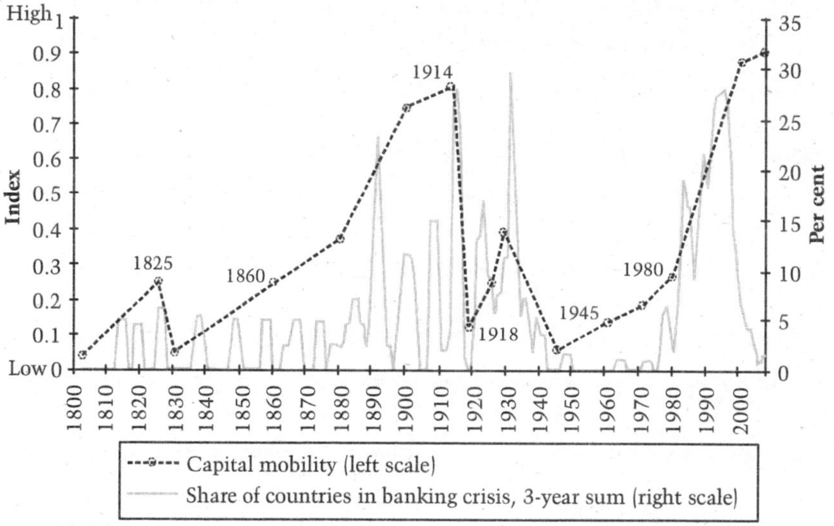

Source: Reinhart and Rogoff (2010).

Governments, banks and economists learned important lessons from the experience of the 1980s. Except in Argentina, governments reduced their recourse to external financing and increased their reliance on domestic capital markets to finance their budgets. Commercial banks in industrialised countries reduced their lending to foreign governments in developing countries. Economists learned that attempts to reduce inflationary expectations through reliance on a nominal exchange rate anchor were not credible if accompanied by adverse balance of payments developments and large external imbalances. They also learned, or relearned, that episodes of real exchange rate appreciation could have devastating effects on the real economy if not driven by sustainable long-term increases in productivity (the Balassa-Samuelson effect). Last but not least, they learned that domestic banks' exposure to exchange rate fluctuations could devastate the banks' balance sheets, and that risk of currency mismatches stemmed not only from their own balance sheets but also from those of their borrowers.

While commercial banks were deeply involved in the crisis of the 1980s, other sources of capital were at the origin of the crisis of the 1990s. Capital flows increased significantly in the 1990s, reflecting the worldwide shift to market-oriented policies, the decline in industrial countries' interest rates, the fall of the Soviet Union, the spread of international standards of banking supervision and accounting, progress in information technology, and regulatory changes in industrialised countries that allowed mutual and pension funds, insurance companies, and banks to invest abroad. The resulting rise in flows to emerging markets was massive (Tirole, 2002). Capital flows to developing countries reached US $265 billion in 1996, six times their volume at the beginning of the 1990s, and four times the peak reached during the 1978–1982 commercial lending boom. Though these amounts were small in relation to the economies of industrialised countries, they were extremely large in relation to those of developing countries: 9.4 per cent of Brazil's GDP (1992–1995), 25.8 per cent of Chile's (1989–1995), 9.3 per cent of Korea's (1991–1995), 45.8 per cent of Malaysia's (1989–1995), 27.1 per cent of Mexico's (1989–1994), and 51.5 per cent of Thailand's (1988–1995). The expectation was that these inflows would help developing countries integrate into the global economy, while diversifying financial risks and reducing economic fluctuations. In the first half of the 1990s, the international Monetary Fund's (IMF) advice to developing countries was not only to remove restrictions on their current accounts (in line with the IMF's Article VIII) but also to remove restrictions on their capital accounts. It was also perceived that these developments would help diversify the risks to investors in industrialised countries, improve developing countries' access to finance, and raise developing countries' investment levels and growth.

The results challenged expectations. Financial crises occurred even more often than in the 1980s— Mexico (1995), Thailand (1997), Indonesia (1997), Korea (1997), Russia (1998), Turkey (2001-02), Brazil (1999, 2002) and Argentina (2001-02)—and the costs were, once again, staggering, with declines in GDP similar to those of the 1980s.The 1990s will be remembered as a decade of macroeconomic crises and turbulence in emerging markets. The average cost of a crisis has been put at about 8 per cent of GDP, and that of a financial crisis accompanied by a banking crisis at 18 per cent (World Bank, 1998). Bank restructuring costs reached 50 per cent of GDP in Indonesia, and one-third of GDP in Korea and Thailand. The output collapses were, for example, 6 per cent of GDP in Mexico in 1994, 11 per cent in Thailand in 1997, 13 per cent in Indonesia in 1997, and 15 per cent in Argentina in 2002. Even though in East Asian countries, Turkey and Russia, per capita incomes have returned to their pre-crisis levels and growth has been relatively rapid, and Argentina has now experienced eight years of rapid growth, the economic and social cost of the crisis have been simply staggering. In some countries, the crises of the 1990s were similar to those of the 1980s in several respects. As in the 1980s, large and unsustainable current account deficits played an important role in Argentina, Brazil, Mexico, Thailand and Turkey, though they were not significant in the other crisis countries. As in the 1980s, these deficits were often the result of stabilisation programmes anchored on a nominal exchange rate. And as in the 1980s, in some countries (Argentina, Indonesia, Korea, Thailand, Turkey) the currency crisis triggered a banking crisis itself, resulting currency and maturity mismatches either on commercial banks' balance sheets, or on their borrowers'.

But the crisis of the 1990s differed from those of the 1980s in three respects. First, indebtedness by the private sector played a central role, both in terms of imbalances between saving and investment and in terms of external debt contracted. Whereas in the 1980s the current account deficits in the balance of payments always reflected negative public sector savings, in the 1990s they often reflected negative private sector savings-investment balances. Second, the 1990s made it clear that not only the stock but the terms of external debt mattered, and especially the maturity structure. In many of the crises of the 1990s, rollover risks stemming from excessive short-term debt played a more important role than did an unsustainable stock of debt or unsustainable current account deficits in the balance of payments. Russia ran surpluses in the current account of the balance of payments both in the year of the crisis and in the years preceding it. Indonesia and Korea's current account balances were negative, but relatively small, and under normal circumstances their financing would not have been a problem (Summers, 2000). Third, twin crises (currency and banking) were much more frequent than in the 1980s, even though banking supervision and bank capitalisation were no worse than in the

1980s, and were much better in some cases (such as Argentina's) and highlighted that it is difficult to sustain healthy banks in a deteriorating economy. The novel features of the crises of the 1990s led to a re-examination of beliefs, regarding among others capital controls, exchange rate regimes, and whether responses to crisis ought to be primarily fiscal or monetary. Though debates will continue, the balance of opinion seems to be that the crisis of the 1990s altered the conventional wisdom that prevailed in these three areas at the beginning of the 1990s (see Feldstein, 2003 and Williamson, 2004b for syntheses and alternative views).

The financial crisis of the last three years originated in advanced economies, not in developing ones. By now its causes have been exhaustively examined, and while research and debate will go on, there seems to be agreement that the fundamental reason is that highly leveraged banks and other financial institutions financed non-creditworthy borrowers—private homeowners in the US and governments in the EU. In that respect, except for its magnitude, the 2008 crisis is not different from those seen in other financial crises in developing and advanced economies alike. The 1989 Savings and Loans crisis for example, that cost about 3 per cent of the US GDP and led to a major restructuring of the industry, was essentially one in which unsound lending practices developed in the aftermath of deregulation and relaxation of credit standards. And the problems of EU banks seem to be a repeat of the crisis of the 1980s in which primarily banks lent to countries with unsustainable macroeconomic conditions.

Some Conclusions

In a recent book, Michael Spence (2011) reminds us that some industries have economy-wide relevance. Energy, transportation, telecommunications and finance have the characteristics that virtually all other sectors in the economy rely on them, and cannot operate without them. The implication is that mismanagement of these sectors has economy-wide consequences.

Ultimately, the reasons for financial crises is related to the ways in which capital is put to use: 'The details of the story are complex, but, broadly speaking, the risk-management systems of the private sector and government oversight of the financial sector in the United States and some other industrial countries failed to ensure that the inrush of capital was prudently invested, a failure that has led to a powerful reversal in investor sentiment and a seizing up of credit markets. In certain respects, our experience parallels that of some emerging-market countries in the 1990s, whose financial sectors and regulatory regimes likewise proved inadequate for efficiently investing large inflows of saving from abroad. When those failures became evident, investors lost confidence and crises ensued. A clear and highly consequential difference, however, is that the crises of the 1990s were regional, whereas the current crisis has become global'. (Bernanke, 2009)

The deregulation of the financial system in the US in the 1990s has contributed to an unprecedented concentration in the banking industry. The 25 largest banks in the world accounted for US $7 trillion in 1990 and US $45 trillion in 2008. In 1990, none of the top 25 banks had total assets larger than the respective national GDP. Today, there are 7. This concentration exacerbates systemic risk, and distorts competition. The economy-wide consequences have also led governments to socialise private losses. In parallel, the growth in these institutions and their increased complexity—in terms of both instruments and inter-relations—have led to a decline in the ability of sovereign governments to supervise them. More importantly, perhaps, their size has created a new political economy in which the influence of financial institutions has become probably too large to represent the collective interest—both nationally and globally. What should be the response to this situation is far from obvious. Some have proposed a return to the partnerships that characterised the banking industry in the 19th century with the view that limited public liability is unsuited to an industry where asymmetry of information and principal-agent problems are pervasive and particularly severe. The current thinking and efforts focus on strengthening balance sheets, increase disclosure, regulate risk-taking, and limit financial institutions' ability to shift risks. The outcome of reforms underway is unclear at present. One can only hope that whatever form they finally take will move us closer towards ensuring that finance is put at the service of the real economy rather than the other way round.

References

Aizenman, Joshua (2011). "On the Causes of Global Imbalances and their Persistence: Myths, Facts and Conjectures", in Stijn Claessens, Simon Evenett and Bernard Hoekman (eds.), *Rebalancing the Global Economy: A Primer for Policy Makers*. A Vox. Eu Publication.

Bernanke, Ben (2009). *Financial Reform to Address Systemic Risk.* Speech to Council on Foreign Relations. March 10.

Council of Economic Advisors. *Report of the President*, several years. United States Printing Office.

Feldstein, Martin (2003). *Financial and Economic Crises in Emerging Market Economies.* Princeton University Press.

Kautilya (1992). *The Arthashastra*. L.N. Rangarajan (ed.), (Rearranger & Translator), Penguin Classics, India.

Kindleberger, Charles P. and Lindert Peter (1978). *International Economics.* Irwin.

Obstfeld, Maurice and Rogoff Kenneth (2009). "Global Imbalances and the Financial Crisis: Products of Common Causes", Proceedings, Federal Reserve Bank of San Francisco.

Reinhart, C.M. and K. Rogoff (2010). *This Time is Different.* Princeton University Press.

Sheng, Andrew (2009). "Global Imbalances and the Financial Crisis". Council on Foreign Relations. Council on Foreign Relations Press.

Spence, Michael (2011). *The Next Convergence: The Future of Economic Growth in a Multispeed World.* New York: Farrar, Straus and Giroux.

Summers, Lawrence H. (1999)."Distinguished Lecture on Economics in Government: Reflections on Managing Global Integration", *Journal of Economic Perspectives* 13(2).

———. (2000). "International Financial Crises: Causes, Prevention, and Cures", in Papers and Proceedings of the One Hundred Twelfth Annual Meeting of the American Economic Association, *The American Economic Review* 90(2): 1–16.

Tirole, J. (2002). *Financial Crises, Liquidity and the International Monetary System.* Princeton University Press.

Williamson, John (2004). "The Years of Emerging Market Crisis: A Review of Feldstein", *Journal of Economic Literature* XLII (September).

World Bank (1998). *Global Economic Prospects.*

14 Currency Wars Again? *Can Global Policies ever be Coordinated?*

RAGHURAM RAJAN

Montek Singh Ahluwalia has a stronger claim than virtually any other Indian to having shaped the reforms that set India on the path of strong sustained growth. My first encounter with Montek took place soon after I got my PhD and joined the University of Chicago as a lowly assistant professor. Wanting to do my bit in India, I wrote to a number of people who seemed to be doing interesting work there, asking to meet them to seek their advice on what I could do to help. With the benefit of experience, I can see why this was not a particularly clever thing to do: the people I had written to probably got three or four unsolicited requests for meetings every day. If they did respond, they would forever be advising the young and inexperienced. But to my surprise, Montek agreed to meet me.

Our meeting was short, but his advice was clear—the best thing you can do to help is to come back and work in India. While I am still trying to put his advice into practice, what struck me then and still strikes me now is Montek's willingness to take the young seriously, to question, debate and persuade, not with the brute weight of his experience and his position but with his arguments. There are many careers that Montek could have been successful at, but it has been patently clear to me for many years that government's gain has been academia's loss. It is for this reason that a festschrift seems entirely appropriate. I congratulate Montek, a great doer and a thinker, and dare I say, a very good friend, on his many years of service to India and to the community of nations.

I

Introduction

Last November, the US Federal Reserve embarked on a second round of monetary stimulus known as quantitative easing. The central bank intended to buy $600 billion in long-term Treasury bonds in an attempt to push down long-term interest rates. These moves led the rest of the world to accuse the United States of trying deliberately to depreciate the dollar. However, Washington was not alone in apparently trying to influence its currency. China also held the renminbi relatively stable against the dollar in the months after the crisis, even though many economists believe the fair value of the Chinese currency should be considerably higher. In September 2010, Japan intervened in exchange markets to prevent the yen from rising too quickly, while many emerging markets have used a mix of capital controls and exchange rate intervention to keep their own currencies from appreciating. Intervention is a zero-sum game: for one country's currency to depreciate, some other countries' currencies must appreciate. Are the senseless beggar-thy-neighbour currency depreciations of the 1930s, where many countries tried to depreciate in a race to the bottom, just around the corner?

Probably not! Today's jockeying over exchange rates has several important differences from that of the Depression years. First, countries today are typically not trying to gain a short-term advantage through currency actions; instead, they are following entrenched domestic economic policy strategies. Taken together, these strategies have led to significant trade imbalances around the world, even before the recent crisis. Second, sustained trade imbalances do seem to lead to financial and political instability, important reasons to shrink them. However, unless the domestic policy strategies change dramatically, these imbalances will likely persist. Global economic stability, therefore, is not dependent on some grand agreement between countries—agreements such as if you allow your currency to appreciate, I will rein in my fiscal deficit—which unfortunately seems to be the focus of recent economic summits. Instead, stability will emerge when governments move to more sustainable domestic policy agendas, which are typically in their long-run interest. Third, the role of multilateral bodies such as the G-20 or the IMF is therefore not to coordinate policies between countries, but to insert the international dimension into each country's domestic policy debate as an additional reason to undertake needed reforms. It is also to set reasonable rules of the game on cross-border capital flows and international bailouts. Neither of these roles is really conducted adequately today. Finally, the silver lining in an otherwise dark cloud is that the rethinking prompted by the Great Recession is altering policy agendas in some, but not all, key countries. Given all this, with more effort and some luck, the global economy will hopefully not repeat the tragic history of the early 20th century.

Why does the Exchange Rate Matter?

The exchange rate affects the international price of a country's goods. By keeping its exchange rate undervalued—and economists constantly debate how easy it is for a country to do this—a country can expand its market share and production by essentially stealing demand from other states. Exchange rate manipulation can be particularly attractive in a recession, when preserving jobs is politically important. Governments often view this sort of direct manipulation as a particularly unfair form of competition, much as they would consider direct subsidies to exporters.

These are the sort of accusations that were levied against the US Federal Reserve in the fall of 2010. Usually when a central bank cuts interest rates, the country's currency weakens as capital leaves for more attractive shores. However, lower rates also tend to increase demand in that country as households and firms spend more, so the net effect of monetary easing is not simply to take demand from others but also to create demand overall. Monetary easing is therefore typically viewed as a perfectly legitimate policy for a country to undertake. But the circumstances under which the Fed embarked on the second round of quantitative easing (the first round was the buying of mortgage-backed securities between December 2008 and March 2010) were different. With short-term US interest rates already near zero, and with large firms able to borrow at very low rates, it was unlikely that corporate investment was being held back because firms thought rates too high. Similarly, households were cautious about spending because their balance sheets were in disarray, not because they thought interest rates were too high. So quantitative easing, other countries alleged, would 'work' primarily by making dollar bonds unattractive—because long bond rates would be pushed too low given the higher expectations of inflation. This would cause capital to flee the United States, lower the dollar, and expand US exports at the expense of other countries.

Although the preliminary effect of Fed chairman Ben Bernanke's announced intent to undertake quantitative easing was to lower long-term interest rates and weaken the dollar, worries about sovereign debt in the Eurozone economies soon led to a strengthening of the dollar. And better news about the US economy, as well as worries about its long-term fiscal health, led to a sharp increase in US interest rates. In the end, quantitative easing may have had neither the effect the Federal Reserve predicted nor the one its external critics feared.

The Deeper Concerns

Nevertheless, the recent debates over currencies revealed deeper concerns. The rest of the world worries that policy in the United States, with its two-year electoral cycle, is excessively focussed on short-term US growth and employment. US politicians neglect the damage these policies do to the rest of the world, and in the long run, to the United States itself. Unlike other countries whose wayward policies are quickly disciplined by financial markets, the United States is given a long rope because investors value its deep and liquid financial markets—what Valéry Giscard d'Estaing, then French Minister of Finance described in the 1960s as an 'exorbitant privilege'. On the other side, the United States worries that too many countries have become dependent on exporting to it, and hold the value of their currency against the dollar by buying US financial assets such as government and corporate bonds. Although these asset purchases provide the United States with the financing to fund its imports, they also prevent the United States from exporting and reducing its trade deficit—in other words, they encourage consumption rather than production. The exorbitant privilege may instead be an extraordinary disadvantage. The United States has become the designated spender for the world and cannot move away from this role easily.

The symbiotic relationship between the United States and the rest of the world creates very real dangers. US monetary policy is imitated around the world, which gives the United States an undesired, yet very real, influence. In the near term, the cutting of interest rates by the Federal Reserve puts downward pressure on rates everywhere, because no one wants their currency to appreciate strongly against the dollar. Although the Federal Reserve does not want to recognise it, it sets monetary policy not just for the United States but also for the world. And what is appropriate for a US economy that is recovering slowly from recession may be overly aggressive for emerging markets that are near full employment, creating inflation and asset bubbles there. Over the medium term, if the United States embraces its role as spender too readily, as it seems to have in the recent past, it risks jeopardising its creditworthiness—not even the United States can borrow forever to fund spending. If the rest of the world suddenly becomes reluctant to fund US spending, the change will be painful, and not just in the United States.

The Triffin Dilemma

Emerging from World War II, the United States had the strongest economy in the world, deep financial markets and immense reserves of gold. As a result, dollar assets were very liquid and the dollar was easily convertible to gold at the then fixed rate of $35 per ounce. Unsurprisingly, these same attributes made the dollar the reserve currency of choice for central banks looking to hold a buffer against bad times. Many countries also used foreign exchange reserves to back their domestic currency issuances. As national economies around the world grew, their need for reserves increased, and so therefore did their demand for dollars. In the early 1960s, the Belgian economist Robert Triffin warned that, eventually, the United States would be forced to supply those dollars by running large current account deficits (loosely speaking, the trade deficit plus aid transfers minus income earned on financial claims) financed by issuing dollar claims. Such a scenario would lead to what would come to be known as the Triffin dilemma: increased holdings of dollars around the world would erode the faith that the United States would be able to repay gold to anyone who cashed in those dollars. In other words, the willingness to supply the demanded liquid asset—in this case, dollars—would eventually erode confidence in its worth.

Triffin was broadly right. The United States initially supplied dollars as it sent grants, loans and foreign direct investment to capital-short Europe and Japan. But as US spending on the war in Vietnam increased, its trade surplus shrank. In the early 1970s, the overhang of dollars outside the United States became so large that the United States had to abandon convertibility and the fixed gold price of $35 an ounce. This triggered the breakdown of the Bretton Woods system of fixed exchange rates.

Much of the language of those criticising the United States (which was directed at the United States' exorbitant privilege and its irresponsible macroeconomic policies), as well as the US response (which pointed right back, suggesting that French, German and Japanese currency undervaluation led to shrinking US trade surpluses) was similar to the heated language of today—Barry Eichengreen's recent book *Exorbitant Privilege* offers a compelling analysis of the debates.

But unlike the current moment, the United States did not run a large trade deficit then—in fact, its trade balance and its current account were in surplus throughout the 1960s, *albeit* shrinking. The world was not dependent on US spending. Also, the fixed nominal exchange rate between the dollar and other currencies was not a choice but required by the Bretton Woods system. And although cross-border private capital flows were already growing at that time, they are dwarfed by the size of such flows today. For all but the poorest countries, the financing for a country's current account deficits now comes not from other governments or multilateral institutions such as the IMF or the World Bank, as it used to, but from private sources. These differences are key to understanding why the problem is different today, and why the solutions have to be different.

Why did the US Run a Large Trade Deficit Pre-Crisis?

To see why the United States has come to run such a large trade deficit, we have to understand why US consumption increased so dramatically. In the years before the Great Recession, household credit, especially for housing, was greatly expanded. Some of this push may have been political; politicians from both parties looked to home ownership as a palliative for people whose incomes had stagnated. Momentum also came from a financial sector running out of control. The precise cause is not critical; however, the important fact is that US consumption increased from about 67 per cent of GDP in the late 1990s to about 70 per cent in 2007, financed largely with debt.

An equally important factor in pushing US spending has been the aggressive stimulus in downturns. Job growth has been tepid in recent recoveries; it took 38 months, for example to regain the jobs that were lost in the 2001 recession. Unfortunately, the United States is singularly unprepared for 'jobless' recoveries. Unemployment benefits generally last only six months. Moreover, because health benefits are often tied to jobs, an unemployed worker also risks losing access to medical care. When recoveries are fast and jobs are plentiful, short-duration benefits provide a strong incentive to look for work. But when there are few jobs being created, a positive incentive becomes a source of great uncertainty and anxiety. The political pressure on successive presidential administrations and the Federal Reserve to do something to bring the jobs back has been enormous. And they have responded by expanding government spending and keeping interest rates ultra low, thus boosting asset prices and encouraging household spending. Not only did expansionary credit policies fuel household spending before the Great Recession, so did aggressive stimulus in response to the 2001 recession.

The Counterpart of US Spending

As the United States increased spending in the years before 2007, many parts of the world reduced spending, becoming more dependent on the United States and other countries such as the United Kingdom or Spain to generate demand. Here again, there were two elements at work: the playing out of long-term strategies and a short-term response to financial turmoil of cutting back on investment.

One of the most successful growth strategies in the second half of the 20th century was that of Germany and Japan, who had been bombed into rubble in World War II. These strategies were later imitated by China and Korea, who were looking to grow out of abject poverty. In all of these cases, governments (and banks) intervened in the economy to create strong firms and competitive exporters, typically at the expense of household consumption. Such an approach made sense because domestic households were too poor to afford much spending.

Over time, these countries created very efficient export-oriented manufacturing sectors. The need to be competitive in foreign markets kept exporters on their toes. But although global competition limited the deleterious effects of government intervention in the export sector, there were no such restraints in the domestic-oriented production sector. In Japan, for example, banks, retailers, restaurants and construction companies, through their influence over government policies, have managed to limit domestic competition in their respective sectors. As a result, these sectors are very inefficient: there are no Japanese banks that rival HSBC in its global reach, no Japanese retailers that approach Walmart in size or cost competitiveness, and no Japanese restaurant chains that rival McDonald's in the number of franchises. Domestic services, such as haircuts, are extraordinarily expensive. Low productivity and limited innovation—and the high prices that follow—dampen demand for domestic-oriented production. As a result, economic growth is dependent on foreign rather than domestic demand.

A slowdown in domestic investment by a number of exporting countries in recent years has only exacerbated this dependence. For Germany and Japan, the slowdown was partly a consequence of growing rich again—after all, there is a limit to how much capital workers can profitably use—and partly a consequence of population ageing. In addition, during the ongoing Japanese two-decade-long crisis, Japanese corporations have cut back on investment in Japan so as to pay down debt.

But perhaps the most dramatic shift in investment took place amongst the Asian emerging markets—such as Korea, Malaysia and Thailand—in the late 1990s. In the earlier part of that decade, these countries expanded investment dramatically, with foreign money pouring in to finance everything from new airports to state-of-the-art semiconductor plants. They did not, however, have transparent financial markets or strong regulation of corporate disclosure and transactions. Foreign investors who did not understand the murky insider relationships, tried to keep their money safe: they offered only short-term loans, denominated payments in foreign currency, and lent through local banks. This last measure gave foreign investors an implicit government guarantee, because governments would likely be drawn into supporting domestic banks to avoid widespread economic damage. As a result, foreign lenders entrusted their money to opaque domestic borrowers—but it also meant that, protected by such measures, foreign investors had little incentive to screen the quality of ventures financed.

When boom turned to bust in the late 1990s, a number of governments had to go to the IMF for emergency loans. Governments bailed out domestic banks as well as foreign creditors. The poor local taxpayer footed the bill, also suffering a wrenching recession and high unemployment. The lesson was well learnt: rather than borrow from abroad to finance investment, East Asian governments and corporations decided to abandon grand investment projects and debt-fuelled expansion. Moreover, a number decided to boost exports by maintaining an undervalued currency. In buying foreign currency to keep their exchange rate down, they also built large foreign exchange reserves, which could serve as a rainy-day fund if foreign lenders ever panicked again. Thus in the late 1990s, developing countries cut back on investment and turned from being net importers to becoming net exporters of both goods and capital, adding to the global supply glut.

Has the Worm Turned?

Today, developed countries, hobbled by high levels of household and government debt, are hoping that emerging markets will shoulder the burden of expanding global consumption and investment. Clearly, consumption in countries such as Brazil, China and India, as well as in the Middle East and Africa, is far lower than average consumption levels in rich ones, and so is the average physical capital—houses, roads, sewerage, and so on, per citizen. There is scope for growth here. Shifting the growth in spending from industrial countries to emerging markets also has a corresponding environmental benefit: knowing that the production of physical goods such as housing and automobiles takes a toll on the environment, better that spending go to move the slum-dweller in Cambodia into a brick house, a process that will eventually have to happen, than to move the empty-nester sub-urban US couple into a house with even bigger bedrooms that they will never use. Such an outcome may be the environmentally sustainable solution to both global trade imbalances and the incipient currency wars. So how to best bring about this necessary shift in global demand?

Some change is already happening. The lesson China seems to have learned in the Great Recession is the need to reduce its dependence on foreign demand: the Chinese know that they cannot continue growing at double-digit rates without encountering protectionist barriers. While much of the world has fixated on China's manipulation of the renminbi exchange rate as its primary means of expanding domestic demand, Beijing knows that it is as important to reduce the pro-producer bias in its domestic policy, so as to boost household incomes and consumption. In practice, this means increased wages, higher interest rates for household bank deposits, and improved delivery of health and education services; at the same time, the government is increasing corporate taxes as well as the subsidised prices that corporations pay for inputs such as energy and land. The Chinese government is also encouraging infrastructure investment to link the interior, poorer Western provinces to the richer, coastal ones.

Of course, various interests in China are opposed to change, including the cash-rich state-owned corporations and banks, as well as foreign firms that set up production facilities in China to benefit from the low exchange rate. They will fight any loss of their relative privilege. China will not reform overnight and begin demanding huge amounts of consumption goods. But this could very well happen over time—indeed, China's 12th Five-Year Plan, to be implemented in early 2011, emphasises the expansion of domestic demand.

Other emerging markets such as Brazil and India, which have historically not repressed consumption as severely as China, are already on a tear, buoyed by growing inflows of foreign capital. Emerging-emerging trade is increasing rapidly. To facilitate the growth in their own demand *vis-à-vis* industrial countries, emerging markets have to allow their real exchange rates to appreciate. A currency war between them at this stage will only delay the inevitable, while making the future much less attractive.

All this, however, raises an important question: can emerging markets manage to increase domestic spending in a more stable way than in the past, or will they experience yet another credit boom followed by a bust?

Will Emerging Markets Provide Stable Growth?

One could hope that emerging market governments have learnt their lessons and will avoid past excesses; history however, does not offer much basis for such optimism. To keep the past from repeating, regulators in both emerging markets and developed economies will have to take on a more assertive role. To ensure that foreign capital inflows do not once again support unviable investment and irresponsible lending, foreign investors need to be exposed to the full risk of losses. At the same time, domestic financial firms should not have the incentive to expand their balance sheets rapidly when money is cheap. Regulators in the country receiving capital inflows should discourage significant amounts of foreign-currency-denominated short-term debt being lent to the domestic banking system. Instead, they should encourage foreign investors to lend directly and long-term to domestic non-financial firms, with loans in domestic currency. Government regulators should increase capital requirements, tighten liquidity requirements, and limit leverage for domestic financial firms when credit expands rapidly. Finally, regulators should also improve the bankruptcy system so that investors will take a quick and relatively predictable hit on unviable projects.

At the same time, regulators in countries from which capital flows emanate should be careful that their major financial institutions are not overly exposed to any one region, country, or sector. Irish taxpayers should not have to bail out their banks' bondholders simply because these bonds are held by German and British banks. Large cross-border banking firms currently operate with impunity, knowing they are virtually impossible to shut down and will therefore be bailed out when in trouble. An international accord on how to close these banks when they get into trouble will be difficult but is very important. Finally, multilateral institutions such as the IMF should force long-term bondholders of a country's debt to take a significant loss if the institutions have to step in to bail a country out—else taxpayers end up having to pay both the IMF and the bondholders. How to best include clear and transparent triggers for write-downs in debt contracts is not an easy question—but not an impossible one, either.

All these measures will raise the direct costs to emerging markets of borrowing and make foreign investors more careful about supplying funds. But the higher direct costs will be more than offset by the benefits of more productive and sensible investment, not to mention the decreased likelihood of future busts.

There are also places we do not need reforms. The recent public debate, I should note, has revived the old discussion of a liquid alternative to the dollar. China, for example, has floated the idea of a world currency modelled along the lines of the IMF's special drawing right (SDR). The notion seems to be that if there was a liquid alternative to the dollar, as well as more automatic access to IMF funding, countries would stop accumulating dollar reserves. Much of this commentary misses the central point that the problem we face today is not the same as the problem the world faced in the 1960s. China has $2.5 trillion in reserves, not because the reserves are a source of liquidity or will help in a crisis, but because of the pattern of Chinese growth. A new reserve currency or more automatic borrowing from the IMF will not change matters so long as the export-led growth strategy is in place.

Will the United States Change?

The slowdown in spending by the industrial world will give emerging markets strong incentives to alter their growth strategy away from exports, stronger than might emanate from any agreement produced by international summitry.

But will the 'great spender', the United States, cooperate and avoid yet again pumping up demand excessively, postponing adjustment by the world? US households have certainly increased their savings rate in response to the downturn and are trying to pay down debt. Worryingly, many of the efforts of the Federal Reserve and the Obama administration—whether keeping interest rates very low or offering new tax benefits and government-supported credit for home purchases—have been meant to encourage household spending. In the meantime, repeated stimulus packages coupled with the usual effects of a recession—reduced government revenues and increased spending—have led to a ballooning of public debt.

Once again, as in past recessions, Washington's central concern is job growth. Unfortunately, many of the jobs that lost in the onset of the latest downturn were tied to construction: not only construction workers themselves but many of the supporting workers such as home improvement contractors or real estate brokers and lenders, not to mention all the jobs generated when these workers spend their income. As my colleague Erik Hurst, a professor of economics at the University of Chicago, has shown, those US states that had the highest run up in housing activity between 2000 and 2006 also tend to have the highest unemployment rates today. Given the extent of overbuilding over the last decade, it is unlikely that government spending or low interest rates will bring these jobs back. Instead, unemployed construction workers will have to gain new skills or to relocate to areas that have jobs. In other word, the jobs recovery will require new ideas, time and patience—all of which are in short supply given the pressure on politicians.

More generally, Washington must focus more on tailoring the skills and the education of its workforce to the jobs that are being created, rather than hankering after the old jobs eliminated by technology or overseas competition. In this light, the Obama administration's focus on improving education standards by measuring student performance, evaluating teachers, and increasing competition, even while providing resources for those who want to reform, is very appropriate; indeed, such reform efforts should be pushed with even greater urgency. The United States also needs a better safety net, not only to reassure workers but also to ensure that slow recoveries do not result in frenetic, and ultimately excessive stimulus.

Finally, more stable and less aggressive US monetary policy will not just lead to more sustainable US growth, it will also reduce the volatility of capital flows coming to and from emerging markets. Given the thin safety net, the political pressure on the Fed to be adventurous with monetary policy when unemployment is high, is enormous. But such pressure can be counterproductive if the Fed's aggressive policies have little direct effect on employment, but generate asset price bubbles and risky lending, which eventually impose high costs and greater unemployment on the economy.

It is debatable whether Congress should allow the Fed to take seriously its *de facto* role as rate setter for the world and unlikely that it will ever expand its mandate to do so. At the very least, though, the Fed's mandate should be extended to take explicit cognisance of financial stability, a responsibility that is left implicit and underemphasised today.

How can Multilateral Bodies Influence Change

In sum, governments know what they need to do—change, however, will not be easy because it involves short-term pain that is likely to be politically difficult. So what role should multilateral bodies such as the G-20 or the IMF have in all this? Thus far, they have been trying to broker grand agreements between countries, guided by the assumption that world growth will be more stable if, for example, the United States coordinates spending cuts with offsetting reforms in countries such as China to expand domestic demand. There are two problems with this assumption. First, even if a grand agreement can be reached and each country carries out its side of the bargain, there is no guarantee that the timing of the reforms and their effects on global demand can be synchronised. Most policy changes have consequences that kick in with variable and uncertain lags, making it a miracle if their effects actually offset one another and smooth growth. Second, it is not clear that policymakers, even heads of state, have the ability to commit their country to any kind of economic agreement. For instance, the president of the United States has no power to promise to adhere to a path of fiscal contraction—he can propose such a course, but Congress is the final arbiter.

Moreover, it can be counterproductive to raise hopes before every international meeting that any agreement can magically bring down trade imbalances quickly. The public is disappointed with the same vague communiqués that end nearly all such summits. Politicians, meanwhile, place blame with other countries, and in trying circumstances, finger-pointing can degenerate into protectionism. It would be better to acknowledge that each country knows what course of action is necessary, because these actions are in its own medium-term interest. The key then is to give those actions the political impetus to overcome those domestic interests that prefer stasis—as well as to offset the short-term pain that inevitably accompanies reform.

Multilateral organisations such as the IMF can help by communicating the international consequences of a country's policies to the elite within a particular country. They have to become more media savvy and should use the internet as well as social networking tools to put a country's international responsibilities on the domestic policy agenda. Although multilateral organisations rightfully have no domestic vote, an agreement between countries to allow these institutions to speak freely within each country on the international ramifications of domestic policies may help nudge these policies in the right direction.

The tension over currencies reflects longstanding country strategies that have resulted in unsustainable trade imbalances. Many economists would place part of the blame for the Great Recession on these imbalances. Interestingly, the consequences of the Great Recession—the slow growth of industrial economies relative to emerging markets—may offer a strong impetus for countries to change strategy. To help this change, international capital flows must become less volatile and more risk-sensitive. The United States can also play an important role in the transition by focussing more on medium-term reforms that will preserve its competitiveness, and less on short-term stimulus that tends to delay change. There is no guarantee that governments will overcome the political pressure to be myopic, but the collective rewards if they do will be considerable.

Index